The Twentieth-Century Lady

*Donna Lou Seymour's
Contribution To Save Our World*

Donald E. Seymour

TALENT DISCOVERY PRESS
MILWAUKEE, WISCONSIN

Copyright © 2002 by Donald E. Seymour

All rights reserved. No part of this book may be reproduced or transmitted in any form or by any means, electronic or mechanical, including photocopying, recording, or by any information storage and retrieval system, without permission in writing from the publisher.

Published by Talent Discovery Press
3900 W. Brown Deer Road, Ste. #110
Milwaukee, WI 53209

Publisher's Cataloging-in-Publication Data
Seymour, Donald E.
  The twentieth-century lady: donna lou seymour's contribution to save our world / Donald E. Seymour —Milwaukee, Wisconsin: Talent Discovery Press, 2002.
    p. ill. cm.
Includes bibliographical references and index.
  ISBN 0-9647532-3-5

  1. Seymour, Donna Lou—Biography. 2. Humanistic psychology.
  3. Ability. I. Title.

153.9/3—dc21   2001135969

06 05 04 03 02 ✦ 5 4 3 2 1

Printed in the United States of America

*To Donna Lou Arneson Seymour
My loving and devoted wife
Who wanted to do something for humanity*

Contents

Preface ix
Acknowledgments xi
Introduction. . . . xiii

SECTION ONE: FAMILY 1

The Jaycee Pageant • Pre-Pageant Affairs
The Beauty Pageant • After The Pageant • Donna Lou
Donna Matures Early • The Dear John Letter
The Beautician • Deep In The Heart Of Texas
The Second Hurt • Donna Moves To Milwaukee
Holy Cow! They Rebuild You? • Don's World
Our Second Meeting • Our First Date • How Was Your Date?
Engaged? • Donna Tells Her Family
God's Little Green Apples • A Man of Few Words
Browns Hotel, Iowa • The Affirmation
Married in Mt. Horeb • Honeymoon
Making Fun of Her Husband • Rhubarb at the Farm
We Settle In • Noodles in Chili? • The Speaker
The Rose • Gregory Arneson Seymour
I Make A Bet • The Bordello • Don Is Fired
The Northwestern Mutual Gamble • I Lose a Bet
In Donna's Eyes • A Scary Year for Greg
The Million-Dollar Round Table • The Princess and Goofy
Jeffrey Don Seymour • The Start of the Research
Flying to Mexico • Mexico City • Our First Home—1960
The Ceiling Comes Down • Donna's Cars
The New Playboy of the Western World
A Thousand Violets Full • The Italian Cook
A Royal Lineage • Martini Massacre At the Farm

Contents

A Daughter is Born • Our Sons • Stick Picking Time
A Cab Driver Flies Our Plane • Donna's Dresses
The Yak • Donna's Friends

SECTION TWO: THE RESEARCH 107

The Tiki • The Stereo Carnage • Smoking
Jeff's Motor Scooter • Greg's Car • We Build A Company
This is Her Man • Greg Goes To College
The Research Continues • Donna And The Snake
The Sheik Has Eyes For Donna • The Ancient Gun
Are We Out Of Business? • The Traveling Salesman
A Better Career Selection Method • The Call Girls
We Build A Home • Neat-nick Donna
Cleaning For The Cleaning Woman
Anniversaries with Warren and Shirley
The Start of Our Business Travels—The Far East
The Geisha House • On to Singapore
Our Man in Singapore • Manila, Philippines—Mrs. Marcos
Bangkok—Donna Up The River With A Strange Man?
Minburi, Malaysia—A Bowl Of Fish?
Her Husband with Native Girls • Take Out the Garbage
But You Have Donna • Donna Entertains and Us Guys Suffer
The Sisters Take A Trip • Donna Loves Paris—Anytime
Director Of Career Guidance • I'm Offered—A Harem?
No Cat in My House • The Egyptian Debacle
The Camel Caper • Midnight on the Nile • Human Activity
Maria Montessori • Donna Says We've Hit the Top
Jeff's Accident—Greg's Quandary • Dead Sea With Greg
The Article • Selling the Companies
Vocational Guidance Institute • In Retirement

SECTION THREE: THE LADY 205

We Lose A Close Friend • Breakthrough in Jackson Hole
Everyone Has A Maximum Talent Capability
Caribbean Cruise with Jane Powell

Contents

1991 Our Fortieth Anniversary
Vancouver—The Beautiful Lady • The Marching Boards
The Writer and The Book
Her Husband Has Excellent Taste • Husband Still In Training
Donna, The Wife • The Meaning and Purpose of Life
A Wonderful Marriage • A Lady Of Few Words
She Takes No Prisoners—In Golf • The Book
Donna Believes • Donna Models For Goodwill
Still A Lovely Woman • Someday They Will Understand
I Am Your Sunshine • The World Tumbles • A Difficult Year
New Year's Eve Party 2000 • Thank You • A Difficult Month
To Make A Contribution • I Lose My Sunshine • Reflections

Afterword. . . . 293
Bibliography 295
Index. . . . 297

Preface

*"Those who bring sunshine to the lives of others…
cannot keep it from themselves."*

—*Unknown*

In my lifetime I have seen things happen that were way beyond normal coincidence; it's almost scary at times. Impossible series of events come together, people come from nowhere when needed and negative things ultimately prove to be positive. It's as though these things were somehow choreographed.

I find this to be true especially when a person is working on things that benefit others. Do loved ones that have died help us when we are in need of things that are right for us to do?

One evening I was very tired and sitting in the family room, looking up at Donna's pictures on the mantel. I felt so very lonely for her presence and was feeling as though I had failed in reaching people to understand the value to every human of their genetic inheritance. I was ready to give up.

Someone else will do it some day, let them do it. The heck with it all, I thought.

For just a short time I felt at peace with myself, my mind a complete blank. Then a gentle voice softly spoke in my mind. "You promised to go on with your work. The results of your research are needed now. You have much yet to do and soon they will listen. You need new inspiration to do this. Remember what you wrote when you were very young.

" 'I have dreams of my ideal girl. To substantiate her possible existence I have to create her in my dreams and then decide if she was just

Preface

a flight of fancy or if she could be real. She must be lovely and have the grace, poise and charm that separately I have seen in other girls. She must be witty, resourceful, contributory and totally devoted to me. If she could be real, who is she, where is she and how could I find her is in this vast world?

" 'But then who am I to be worthy of such a dream girl? I wouldn't qualify. The man she loves must have an abundance of manly qualities, be a success and make worthy contributions, all these things would be necessary to allow the flight of her love to take wing.'

"You wrote that long ago, remember? Donna did exist for you and Donna's life made a wonderful contribution to your life and your research. It was what she meant to do and did it so very well. Her love and contribution to you should not go to waste.

"Write her story in all her humanness. It will give you new life. As Bertram Russell said, 'Every day life starts anew.' Start your life anew now by writing Donna's story. It will be a labor of love and you'll love doing it.

"After you write her story you will have inspiration to go on with your work that is so badly needed by all people and humanity."

I asked myself, "Who is saying all this? Is it my mind summarizing the logical? A guardian angel pulling me out of my lethargy or Donna watching over me?" Whatever it is, if I do it right, Donna's life could be a story to inspire others.

I wonder if I have the inspiration to do it and if there is enough to write about Donna?

Donna always inspired me. The treasure of love she gave to me may give me the inspiration to do it now. The rest you will see as I try to write her story and keep my promise.

Acknowledgments

There were many people who knew Donna and read earlier versions of this memoir. Others came to me with things they remembered about Donna, stories I didn't know.

Unfortunately, I probably don't remember everyone. If I have missed you, please forgive me.

A special thank you to the Arneson clan and the Seymours. All of you contributed to Donna's story.

And, thank you to Sue Armstrong, Jean Barth, Carol Castagnozzi, Betty Collins, Don Desmond, Clarence Harms, Eadie Heins, Art Jurack, Marie Kennison, Betty King, Carol and Gene Krueger, Ione (Inie) Krueger, Carrie and Art Kumm, Barbara Lynch, Al and Lois Malkasian, Shirley Mrotek, Claire Meisenheimer, Sue Miller, Mary Negrate, Kitty and Dewey Nehs, Wally Orlando, Vicki Perdziak, Barbara Schmeling, Carol and Gerry Schmidt, Dee Serron, Bob Senninger, Greg Seymour, Gwen Shannon, Betty Rivard, Ramona Suffern and Mary and Jim Williams.

Introduction

The best of the twentieth century's ladies had natural beauty, style, and grace. They were intelligent, wise, and interesting; they enjoyed life and laughed often; they felt a debt to humanity for their lives; and their honesty and commitment endeared them to many people. They were wonderful friends, wives, and lovers.

This narrative is especially the true story of Donna Lou Arneson Seymour, as I remember her. I was fortunate to have Donna as my friend, wife, and lover for forty-nine years.

Through her life story, I hope you will learn more about yourself and discover your life's purpose. This is what Donna would want.

Over the years, while helping me with my research, Donna found the key to help people realize the meaning and purpose of their lives. Her commitment to talent discovery has opened doors that did not exist before.

Donna's gift to humanity is in this book. Within these pages you will find the tools to discover the talents you were born with--so that you can live a happier, healthier, and more fulfilling life.

Read her story. You'll have fun. You'll laugh. Perhaps, you'll even cry. Donna Lou made an art of being a woman and is indeed worthy of representing a twentieth-century lady.

You were born uniquely different from anyone else in this world, therefore
- ~ there is something you can do better
- ~ than anything else you can do
- ~ only you can do
- ~ and you were meant to do

It is your purpose in life to find it
- ~ to give meaning to your life
- ~ and fulfill your destiny."

DONALD E. SEYMOUR

SECTION ONE
Family

The Jaycee Pageant

I first saw Donna Lou Arneson in 1950. She was a finalist in the Miss Milwaukee pageant sponsored by the Milwaukee Junior Chamber of Commerce (Jaycees). I was the promotion chairman for the pageant and was instructing the ten finalists on pageant procedures and their expected conduct while attending pageant promotional functions. Donna Lou Arneson, unimpressed with me, nudged the girl standing next to her, pointed at me, and said, "Who would ever go out with him?"

Donna worked as a beautician at the Harper Method salon in Milwaukee, Wisconsin. She had recently completed a night modeling course sponsored by one of the salon's patrons. Elsie Manske, who owned the salon, saw the modeling photographs and thought Donna was so attractive that she insisted on showing the photos to her customers. A group of salon patrons also found the pictures attractive and encouraged Donna to enter the Miss Milwaukee Pageant.

Donna thought it was a funny idea and said, "Not me. I'm no beauty. I would feel out of place, and besides, I don't even have the right clothes to wear." The patrons (some owned women's clothing stores) offered to provide Donna with whatever she would need. Not wanting

The Twentieth-Century Lady

to offend the salon's patrons, Donna filled out the pageant application and sent it in. Donna didn't expect to be selected as a finalist and thought this would be the end of it.

A month later Donna received a call from the Miss Milwaukee committee for an interview at the Antler's Hotel. Convinced that she had no chance of becoming a finalist, Donna was completely relaxed and had fun during the interview.

A week later Donna received another call. "Congratulations! You are one of the ten Miss Milwaukee finalists." They asked Donna to return to the hotel on the following Saturday for newspaper pictures and pageant instructions.

After putting the phone down, Donna didn't know what to think. Then it dawned on her. Good Lord, this is getting serious. What am I going to do? Maybe this is just a mistake. She decided not to tell anyone until she knew for sure.

The next Saturday, I was standing in front of Donna and nine other finalists, while she wondered who would date me.

Later that afternoon, Donna's sister Ramona heard a car horn blowing outside of the apartment she shared with Donna. On the street below she saw Donna sitting on the back of a new convertible, and a driver in a wide-brimmed hat at the wheel. Donna waved up at Ramona.

"What's that girl doing now?" Ramona asked herself as she hurried down to the sidewalk, where Donna was waving and smiling to neighbors and other people who came to see what was happening. Ramona burst out laughing. A sign on the side of the new Nash Rambler convertible said: "Donna Lou Arneson—Miss Milwaukee Finalist." Across Donna's chest was a banner that said: "Miss Gimbels."(Her sponsor.)

Up in their apartment, after Donna's driver left, Ramona was still laughing "Why didn't you tell anyone?" she asked.

"Wasn't sure."

Family

Donna and the Nash Rambler.

"They phoned you, didn't they?"

"I didn't believe it. I thought it must be a mistake."

Ramona shook her head. "You're really something else." Standing back, Ramona studied Donna. "Anyway, you do have attractive features. You have a nice complexion and a very nice profile. Your hair is always nice. You walk well and when you smile you are kind of pretty. Huh, never really noticed before."

"I'd better be or I'm going to be the ugly duckling," was Donna's reply.

"No. You're not ugly at all. Holy cow, my sister a beauty queen!"

"Wouldn't go that far," cautioned Donna.

"Wonder what Phillip and Tony are going to think now?"

"I don't want to hear about them. Men are off my list. I'm going to be a stewardess, model, career girl, or something," stated Donna.

"No more men in your life?" Ramona questioned.

"No."

"Anyway, when you start coming back, you come back with a vengeance. What's your talent?"

"I have 4-H blue ribbons for sewing and baking," replied Donna.

"That's a talent?"

The Twentieth-Century Lady

"The judges seemed to think so. It's different, but certainly a talent. I'll pin the ribbons on my dress and find some way to present something on stage," she explained.

"A cooking beauty queen?" Ramona continued.

"Guess so."

"What now?"

"Don't know. I'll worry about that tomorrow."

"Donna Lou, the beauty queen. Holy cow! Anyway, wait till the family and Mt. Horeb hear about this."

"I suppose it will be in the paper," agreed Donna. "I'm going to lose, you know. Then they'll laugh at me."

"Donna! That's a bad attitude. Us Arnesons win. You have to think win!" Ramona encouraged.

When Donna's supporters from the salon heard she was a finalist, they took Donna out for a celebration lunch. They were all enthused. Anything Donna needs, Donna gets.

Shocked at being a finalist, Donna had trouble sleeping, especially as pageant pressures increased. Her boss, Elsie Manske, was worried about Donna looking peakish for the pageant and told Donna to schedule fewer appointments till the pageant was over. "But," Donna argued, "my clients have important things to do, too."

The Jaycees scheduled several events for the companies that sponsored the pageant. The finalists were required to attend for publicity purposes. These affairs helped build up interest for the pageant. Every event that the girls attended brought in advertising revenue and ticket sales, whether it was a parade, a convention, a luncheon, a fashion show, or a manufacturer's promotion.

The pageant was a lot of work and involved the help of over seventy Jaycees. As Director of Public Relations for the Jaycees it was my responsibility to see that the pageant at least broke even and that none of the girls got into trouble. Any bad publicity and the pageant would be in financial trouble.

Pre-Pageant Affairs

I recall one Saturday at the Wisconsin Hotel. The finalists were at a lift truck introduction for manufacturer purchase agents. The lift truck company had provided a cocktail bar and canapés for its customers. I had given the girls strict instructions not to accept drinks from anyone (customers often felt obliged to offer drinks to the girls because they had drinks in their hands). An hour into the five-hour show, I noticed one of the girls losing her balance. What's going on, I wondered. I took the 7-Up bottle from the girl, went into the kitchen, and drew up on the straw. Warm martinis through a straw? I looked out and every girl had a 7-Up in her hands. Although I had never drunk a warm martini through a straw, I had heard what it could do to a person. This was dangerous. We could lose the pageant franchise. I'm was in real trouble.

To avoid creating a scene, I had one of the Jaycees bring out a tray of 7-Up and replace every bottle. I lined up the old bottles so I knew which bottle belonged to which finalist. I found martinis in two bottles and I selected two Jaycee escorts to take each one of the martini-drinking girls home.

Later I noticed finalists Dallace Hart, Bette Francine and Donna Arneson laughing quietly in a corner. They must have known what was going on. I went to investigate and they told me that the customers had obtained extra martinis for the girls to take into the kitchen, where they emptied the 7-Up and replaced it with a martini. The next day one of the two girls said that her drink tasted funny, the other said she drank martinis all the time and it didn't affect her. As gently as I could, I told them we would be required to eliminate them from the pageant if it happened again.

Occasionally a customer with too much to drink, would accidentally or purposely touch one of the girls. Since we were on the alert, we would either quietly remove the girl or take her home if that is what she wanted.

Patricia Kuszewski, Mary Hendrickson, and Donna approached me during a quiet time at an auditorium convention. Mary said, "We now appreciate the instructions you first gave us and we want to thank you for how you and the other Jaycees look out for us." I thanked them for their acknowledgement. Of course my concern was for them, but also to protect the integrity of the pageant.

Donna had lost weight due to the heavy schedule of evening and weekend promotional functions. Plus she was worried about going on stage with her talent.

At home, Ramona asked Donna how she would present her talent.

"Going to sing instead."

"Oh for goodness sakes. You, a singer? The only places I know you sang were in the church choir and at one wedding. Do you think you're good enough?"

"I don't know, but that's all I can do," said Donna.

"What are you going to sing?" Ramona asked.

"You Are My Sunshine."

Ramona laughed. "You're going up against trained opera singers, and you are going to sing "You Are My Sunshine"?

"I sang pretty good in Texas. In Tony's restaurant they had a piano. To add a little entertainment during quiet times I sang or I led off singing," Donna replied.

Ramona shook her head. "You're determined to go on that stage, in front of all those people, and do this?"

"Can't back out now. It's show time."

"Anyway, aren't you nervous about this whole thing?"

"Who me? Not at all. I'm terrified," said Donna.

Donna never talked about it, but I often wondered if "You Are My Sunshine" didn't have a special significance for her. A few words from the song are:

You are my sunshine—my only sunshine—you make me happy when skies are gray

You'll never know dear—how much I love you—please don't take my sunshine away

You told me once dear you really loved me—and no one else could come between

But now you've left me and love another—you have shattered all my dreams

This song would thread its way through Donna's life.

Although most of the finalists were on college break or on leave from their jobs, Donna had to rush back to the beauty salon to take care of her clients. As a finalist she had lost ten of her normal 118 pounds.

Although a little thin, Donna had some things going for her. Her experience as a part-time model at a Neiman Marcus store in Texas, and taking a night modeling course in Milwaukee, gave Donna the poise, grace, and confidence of a professional model. Some of the girls were so impressed with the way Donna carried herself that they asked her to help them with their walk, which Donna was glad to do.

The Beauty Pageant

Donna's parents attended the pageant. When Donna introduced me to them in the lobby of the Antler's Hotel, I told them their daughter was a fine influence and a great help to the other finalists. I could tell her parents were very proud of her. Donna had a bright personality and was very much a lady. The other girls sought her company.

I was impressed when Donna walked across the stage in a shimmering, form-fitting, green formal. I thought to myself, if her talent

Promotion Chairman Donald Seymour with the finalists in the 1950 Miss Milwaukee Pageant (left to right): Dolores Dehler, Mary Hendrickson, Audrey Sherman, Charlotte Shealy, Don Seymour, Patricia Kuszewski, Betty Francine, Donna Lou Arneson, Gloria Lange and Betty Spice.

could hold her in, she could win. My job was to be impartial, but suddenly I was pulling for Donna because the other finalists thought so highly of her.

The pageant was held June 3, 1950 at the Milwaukee Auditorium. The girls were fairly even in appearance; it seemed talent is where the judges would have to decide.

The judges for the Miss Milwaukee and Wisconsin pageants included: Dorothy Waulters from Fashion Mannequin Studio, Jeanne Dixon from the Dixon Dramatics Studio, Gene Norman from the Norman Dance Studio, William Ebert from the Wisconsin College of music, and Dr. A. A. Suppan from the Milwaukee State Teachers College.

During the talent portion of the pageant, Donna followed a baton twirler, an operatic contralto, and a concert pianist. She did very well singing, "You Are My Sunshine." Her dad stood and clapped loudly for his daughter. Mother looked very pleased, as did Ramona.

Donna did not win, nor was she a runner-up. In the 1950s, classical talents gave the pageant prestige. The judges awarded the Miss Milwaukee crown to a classical pianist—Gloria Lange. Donna was, however, unanimously selected by the other contestants as Miss Congeniality—perhaps the best title for Donna. She would be Miss Congeniality all her life.

After The Pageant

The pageant was over and it was getting late. There were an abundance of flowers and gifts for Gloria. I ended up packing a carload of things to take to Gloria's home. I thought I was alone, but suddenly there was Donna, helping me load a dolly.

"Where is your escort?" I asked.

"He had to leave early."

"Oh. Then I would think you would be with your parents," I stated.

"I was, but my parents are dairy farmers and they go to bed early. They were very tired with all the excitement," she explained.

"And you're not?" I questioned.

"Yes, but with all the anxiety and the relief that it's over, I can't sleep."

"Yes, it is quite a strain," I agreed.

"You're taking these things out to Gloria's, aren't you?" Donna asked.

"Guess so."

"Can I come along and help? We both live on the East Side, so you won't have to go out of your way on the way back. Where is Gloria?"

"Guess she took off with friends to celebrate."

I looked at Donna and said, "Thank you. It's late and I'm tired. Your company will be welcome."

As we neared Gloria's house I asked, "Did I congratulate you on winning Miss Congeniality?"

She smiled. "Yes, you did. Backstage."

"Sorry, I forgot."

"With as many things you had going on, I wouldn't be surprised."

"Your award was well deserved. I noticed how the girls leaned on you for help and advice. How did you become so mature at such a young age?" I probed.

"I don't know. I just like helping people. Modeling training and being a beautician helps," explained Donna.

"You seem to emit a friendly confidence that the girls respect," I continued.

"Thank you."

"Many of the past recipients said they learned much being in the pageant. Did you find it so?"

"Well, I'm glad it's over. So much pressure. But a wonderful experience! I guess I learned that all girls are the same, just some are prettier than others. What really amazed me is that I was chosen as a finalist. I thought I would be at the bottom of the entrant list," she answered.

"Why?"

"Some of those girls are beautiful and I'm not."

"The judges must have thought you had a lot going for you."

"That was the biggest shock of all," replied Donna. "I thought I would be eliminated. I even hoped I would be, so that I could go back to my everyday life. I was even close to backing out several times because I felt I was way out of my league and had no business there. But I couldn't disappoint the clients that were supporting me."

"It is not uncommon for a finalist to feel that way," I responded.

We delivered the things to Gloria's parents. Gloria was not home as yet, so we headed back. I didn't know what to say to Donna, but to be polite and show interest, I asked, "You mentioned that you're going back to your everyday life. Where is that life going?"

"Oh, I'm not sure. I guess I just want to help people. There's so much negativity, disappointment, and grief in the world. I like helping people improve themselves, to make them feel good about themselves, to be cheerful and happy. I'd like to make a difference with my life."

"That's a worthy goal." I said. "I think you did that already with some of the girls in the pageant."

"Thank you. I'm glad you think so. That makes it all worth while. It really does."

"For someone so young, you are a very unusual girl."

"I just want to make a difference," Donna said firmly.

"I think you will."

"I hope so."

I commented, "Mostly you appear very cheerful, but at times you seem pensive and quiet."

"Oh, I know. I get like that once in a while. I have to be careful of that."

"Is something bothering you?" I asked.

"Oh please. It's a long story and it's not that interesting. Now that the pageant is over, what are your next projects?" Donna asked, changing the subject.

I wondered what her story was. It was probably interesting—and painful.

"My directorate has responsibility in a number of projects, though none as large as the pageant. For the balance of the year we have the Horace Heidt show at the Riverside Theatre and the First Drama Quartette at the Milwaukee Auditorium with Agnes Moorehead, Charles Laughton, Sir Cedric Hardwick, and Charles Boyer. Then the SoapBox Derby, The Good Government Award, The Youth Voice of Democracy Contest, Thanksgiving for the Needy, and finally, the Christmas Party for Oldsters and the Christmas Basket program for the elderly."

"You do all these things at night and on weekends when you're in town?" Donna asked.

"And on the phone. It gets pretty hectic at times."

"Are you active in all those affairs?"

"I have chairmen for them, but they need training. And sometimes I have to take over if things don't go well. The bigger the budget, the more I'm involved. We put on a number of events to make money, so that we can sponsor activities for the youth, disabled, elderly, and the needy," I explained.

"And you donate your time to all this?"

"The Jaycees put on sixty activities a year. Unless there are people who donate their time, they won't happen."

Donna commented, "We do some things back home, but nothing in comparison to what you people do."

Then it occurred to me, "Incidentally, the Ramblers are now gone and I live close by. I could pick you up for the after-pageant party at the Schroeder Hotel next week. Oh, but you may have other arrangements."

"No, I don't," she answered. "Thank you, that would be very nice of you."

I delivered Donna to her door and we shook hands. "Thank you for everything," she said. "It's been a wonderful experience. It really has. All the girls say, and I agree, you did a wonderful job."

"Thank you. I'll pick you up at 5:30 next Tuesday. Good night."

She smiled. "I'll be ready out front. Good night."

The warmth of her friendly smile lingered with me. I slept peacefully for the first time in weeks. At the next Jaycee board meeting I reported that there were no negative publicity problems and we were just a little in the red, which was acceptable. I had lost ten pounds.

The night of the Hotel Schroeder party, I picked up Donna on my way. As her chaperone, she was seated at the head table next to me. Donna and I danced rather well together. I also danced with the other girls, who wondered why Donna was able to sit at the head table. I explained that Donna lived on the way and was just a friend who had helped me take a load of flowers and gifts to Gloria's house.

That night I delivered Donna to her door and said, "Good luck Miss Congeniality, in case we don't meet again."

She gave me a very bright smile and said, "Thank you for a wonderful experience. Good luck with next year's pageant."

Shaking hands, I said, "Thank you. Good night."

I was relieved to be done with the pageant for the year.

Family

The Arneson farm in 1954.

Donna Lou

Donna Lou was born on May 5, 1927, in Mt. Horeb, Wisconsin to Marvin and Edna Arneson. Donna had two sisters, Marlyn and Ramona, and two brothers, Dale and Hilton. Donna was the middle child.

The Arneson farm, located twelve miles west of Mt. Horeb, was settled in the 1850s. It is still in the family today. Marvin Arneson was a board member of the American Dairy Association, head of the church council, and active in other business and community organizations. Edna was church organist and active in the 4-H and other worthy organizations. They set the stage for the family to be active wherever there was a need or responsibility to be taken.

Donna was a precocious and impish sprite who was forced to grow up quickly. When her mother was hospitalized for a number of months, her father stood Donna (age six) on a chair to knead and make bread for the farm workers.

Edna returned home for Easter and learned that Marvin had purchased a pair of shoes for Donna—which Donna did not like. Mysteriously one shoe was lost. Everyone searched for the missing shoe, but it could not be found. Edna, knowing her daughter, suggested they sift the ashes in the stove. They found a half-burned sole.

15

When Donna felt she was right, she stuck by her belief. When she was twelve, an argument with her sister resulted in Donna climbing up the thirty-foot windmill. No amount of coaxing or reasoning or thrown rocks could bring her down—until she was pacified.

When given the chance to play a musical instrument in school, Donna chose the trombone. That was a mistake! Her family chased her out of the house, so she went around the farm blowing it. How the animals suffered! The pigs gathered in a corner for protection, the chickens jumped two feet in the air at every blast, and the pigeons were finally routed from the barn. Dad, afraid the cows would refuse to give milk, put Donna and "that infernal noisemaker" in the granary—with stern instructions not to open the door until she was through plaguing humanity. Donna was a determined and noisy girl.

One day Donna and her older sister Marlyn were supposed to keep an eye on the young chickens to see that they were forced up on the roost. (When the chicks were young they had to be forced to do this.) Arguing about doing the dishes, Donna and Marlyn forgot about the chickens. Six hundred chicks suffocated in the corner of the coop. Donna and Marlyn ended up in the granary, a small, dry building far enough from the house so people could not hear the howling, to receive dad's come-uppance.

Donna Matures Early

The first view of how Donna was maturing is evidenced in this tribute she wrote to her mother for a Mother and Daughter banquet on April 5, 1940. Donna was thirteen.

> *"Tonight I want to bring a toast to mother that comes from my heart and the heart of every daughter who thanks God for a Christian mother.*
>
> *It was your name, mother, that we first learned to say; it was your presence we first sought; it was your open arms that brought gurgles of joy when we had no other way of expressing ourselves. It was you also that we hurt most by our disobedience and selfishness. You*

gave up so many things for us and we accepted them with never a thought of what it cost you.

You put up with our snobbishness and conceit and let us never know that you wept bitterly in the night as you prayed to our Father to accomplish in us what you were helpless to do. You understood us when we sat daydreaming, rose to heights of ecstasy and fell to the depths of gloom. You knew that this would pass away and with a sigh, you let it go and didn't even scold. We hope we may have that same understanding of our daughters as they grow to womanhood—if we ever have any.

You travailed in soul for us until we found peace with God and gave our lives to Him. You weren't surprised, for you had prayed believing that He would bring it to pass. Most of all we thank you for that.

You took interest in our schoolwork, and wanted us to excel but not at the expense of being a well-balanced girl. You smiled at our "crushes" and gave counsel when we quarreled with teachers and friends. We are thankful that you didn't lead us to believe that we were always right.

We are thankful that you have lived long enough so that we have come to our senses and can appreciate your wisdom and love all through these years. We are thankful that we still have the opportunity to make your life happy by doing for you some of the things you have done for us.

God bless you, Mother, for blessing us."

Prior to high school Donna was a plain farm girl. She was heavier and somewhat of a tomboy. In early high school she outdid some boys in baseball—which they didn't like.

Because the school bus took several hours each way to get back and forth to the farm, Donna stayed in Mt. Horeb during the week to help care for her disabled grandmother, who had two teachers as boarders.

Donna was active in school activities. Her teachers noticed Donna's maturity and concern for others, so Donna was asked to be a student counselor to girls with serious problems, including pregnancy. With this experience, she matured even more.

Donna was very close to her grandmother. Watching her grandmother waste away with rheumatism (which in those days could have been emphysema or cancer) left an indelible mark on Donna. In regard to her condition, her grandmother said, "What must be, must be." On top of all her other activities, Donna was also a waitress at Olsen's Bakery and Restaurant. Her grandmother was concerned that Donna was doing far too much.

The Dear John Letter

While a senior in high school, Donna dated Phillip Lukken. When he graduated and went into the service, they corresponded faithfully for two years.

They were tense and worrisome years. Donna lived for the day Phillip would return and they could be married. Just before his return, however, Donna received a Dear John letter. Phillip had met and married another girl.

After all the love, kisses, letters, and promises, Donna was now heartbroken, devastated, and embarrassed. The future she had planned for no longer existed. She cried herself to sleep and couldn't talk to anyone about it. Her family felt sorry for her, but there was nothing they could do.

The only course Donna could see was to leave Mt. Horeb and start anew in a far away place. Having seen a picture of Phillip's bride, Donna looked at herself in the mirror and said, "I can't blame him. She's beautiful and I'm not. Look at me. I'm frumpy, I walk like a farmer, and I'm not feminine. I'm competitive at sports with the guys, and they don't like that. I'm so sorry Phillip. I didn't pay attention to myself. I wasn't worthy of your love, and now I've lost it all." The tears never seemed to stop.

The Beautician

With the help of her sister Marlyn, Donna enrolled in the Harper Method beautician training program in Madison, Wisconsin. The

Harper hairdressing method, which caters to professional and wealthy women, includes a head and shoulder massage to increase the circulation for healthier hair.

Madison was still not far enough away from Phillip, the sad stares, and the embarrassment. After completing the Harper training, Donna read the *Harper Method Newsletter* to look for openings for Harper Method jobs around the country. Noticing an opening in San Antonio, Texas, she decided that was far enough away and that it would be an interesting place to live. Donna's parents were unhappy that she had chosen to move so far away.

As a going away present, Grandmother Arneson gave Donna a ring that was given to her by her husband (Donna's grandfather). Donna treasured it.

Donna rode the train to Texas. Although to her family she appeared joyful and enthusiastic, after she boarded the train, it was different. During the long train ride Donna shed tears for the life she was leaving behind and for Phillip and the dreams they had once shared.

Deep In The Heart Of Texas

Her new boss in San Antonio found a room near the beauty shop, and a roommate, for Donna. A week later the roommate ran away with the ring Donna's grandmother had given her, her little bit of hard-earned money, her jewelry, and the best clothes Donna had. Now stuck with the full cost of the room, alone in a far-away city, broke, her best clothes gone, and too proud to ask for funds from her boss or parents, Donna cried with frustration. She had $500 in war bonds back home but her father said she could not cash them until she was married or twenty-one. All Donna had left was the Arneson inner strength and her faith.

One night, looking in the mirror, with tears streaming down her face, Donna said, "Okay, that's it. I've had it. This picture is going to change. Dear Lord, you must help me. I must change my life. I will change my life. I will. And then . . . look out world, here I come."

Not making much money, paying full rental on the room, needing clothes and having to eat, Donna took a waitress job on nights and weekends at a restaurant-bar near the sports stadium. It was owned by Tony X.

At five feet, four inches, Donna's weight dropped to 115 pounds, revealing a lovely shape and facial features never before seen. One of Donna's customers noticed her changed appearance and offered her some part-time modeling for the Neiman Marcus store. At Neiman Marcus Donna received her first tips on poise.

Tony X watched Donna change into an attractive young woman. Her new appearance, sunny disposition, and new popularity resulted in her being made the hostess. Even worldly Tony became attracted to her.

On quiet weekends, when there were no sports events at the stadium, Tony and Donna spent time with friends who had places on the Gulf coast. Riding in Tony's new convertible they sang "Deep in the Heart of Texas," "You Are My Sunshine," and "San Antonio Rose," all the way to the Gulf. This was the life.

The Second Hurt

Donna loved these trips and she and Tony became very close. So close that Donna wrote to her brother Hilton and asked him to send the $500 of war bonds down, presumably to purchase a wedding dress. Donna, very expense conscious, would not have invested in a wedding dress unless a wedding was going to take place.

Donna sent a picture of her husband-to-be (signed Tony X) to the farm. When Donna's father saw the picture he exasperatingly asked, "What kind of a name is that?" Tony X was Catholic and the family wouldn't be able to go to church together. Marrying outside of her religion was quite a serious move for Donna, because her father made it clear that one should not to marry outside one's religion. He believed the family that went to church together stayed together. And with Donna living in Texas, they would seldom see her. This did not set well with her parents.

Donna was not a daughter to make things difficult for her family.

But Donna was a very independent young woman and she took her commitment of marriage to Tony seriously. So as not to embarrass her family by marrying an Italian Catholic restaurant-bar owner in Norwegian/German Mt. Horeb, Donna and Tony decided to be married in New Orleans.

Before they were married, however, something happened between Donna and Tony—something Donna could not forgive. Deeply hurt, she immediately quit both jobs and accepted a Harper Method position in Milwaukee, Wisconsin.

Living with Donna in Milwaukee, Ramona recalls that Tony X telephoned Milwaukee once. The conversation was curt and short. Donna never talked about Tony to anyone, not even Ramona. The hurt lasted a long time. Like "You Are My Sunshine" says, Tony had somehow shattered all her dreams.

Donna Moves To Milwaukee

In Elsie Manske's beauty salon in Milwaukee, Donna again became popular with the patrons. Elsie could tell that Donna was friendly and proficient. Almost from the beginning, Elsie treated Donna like the daughter she never had.

When she first moved to Milwaukee, Donna did not date. She was still hurt and her self-confidence had taken a serious blow. At night she and Ramona played gin in their small apartment. On the weekends they did not go to the farm, they went across Prospect Avenue and down the hill to the Lake Michigan beach. When the weather was inclement they went shopping downtown.

A patron that owned a modeling school suggested that Donna take a night modeling course, which Donna completed. When Donna saw photos taken of her taken as a part of the course she could not believe it was herself she was looking at! The photos made such an impression on Donna, that in time, modeling posture became natural to her. Rather than give up her regular income for undependable modeling fees, Donna retained her beautician job and accepted a few modeling jobs at night and on weekends.

The Twentieth-Century Lady

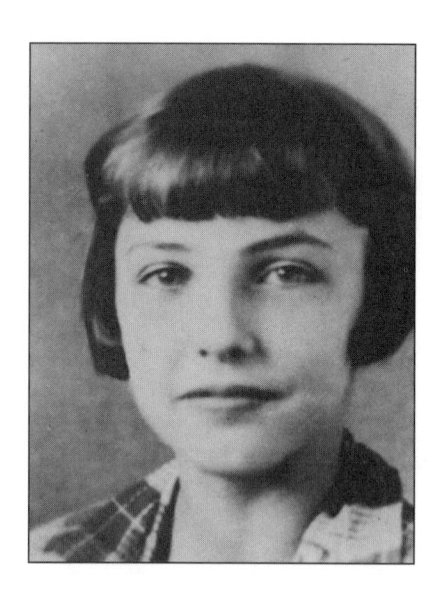

Clockwise, from top left-hand corner: Donna, age thirteen; Donna, age sixteen; Donna, age eighteen and Donna, at 20 after graduating from the modeling course.

Family

Holy Cow! They Rebuild You?

On weekends, Donna and Ramona would often take the bus home to Mt. Horeb to visit their family. Still cringing from the embarrassment of Phillip's Dear John letter, Donna avoided public functions. She couldn't face Phillip or other people who knew what had happened between them.

One weekend at the farm, the family was going to attend a wedding reception. Donna, encouraged to go, decided to chance it. She put on high heels and dressed in her finest. When she came down the stairs her brother Hilton scrutinized her.

She looked down at her dress. "Is something wrong?" Donna asked.

Hilton motioned for her to turn around. She did. "What happened to you? You've changed. Your face, your shape. The way you walk, everything. Holy cow. My sister is beautiful. If Phillip could see you now, he would eat his heart out."

"Oh, Hilton," she started to cry, then contained herself and said with a sniff, " I'm not beautiful."

"The heck you're not. You're gorgeous, and I mean it."

"Thank you, brother." Coming from Hilton, it meant a lot.

Hilton called to the kitchen. "Mom, come here." When Mother came Hilton motioned for Donna to turn around. Donna did her best model turn and smiled. "Mom, what do you think?"

Mom's eyes turned a little glassy. "I think our Donna has turned into a beautiful young woman."

At the wedding reception a female classmate who had moved away during their sophomore year came up and squinted at Donna. "Donna? Donna Lou Arneson?"

Donna smiled at the woman and nodded.

"Holy cow! Have you been in an accident or something? They rebuild you?"

"Of course not."

"Then how the heck did you get to look like that?"

Donna laughed again. "Like what?"

"Like you look."

"Well, how do I look?"

"You're gorgeous, and we were the ugly ducklings."

"No we weren't. We weren't that bad," Donna argued.

"The heck we weren't. And look at you now. You look like a fashion model on the cover of *Harper's*."

"Oh, now com'on."

"It's true. You must have one heck of a fairy godmother or a secret you could make millions on."

Donna laughed again.

Later, while Donna was talking to some friends, she overheard a conversation behind her.

"Did you notice the change in Donna Arneson? She's become a beautiful young woman. What a dramatic change."

Others complimented Donna on her appearance.

In bed later that night, Donna sobbed with relief. She was now convinced that she was on her way. A little late for Phillip, but she had accomplished what she had set out to do. She could hold her head up with confidence in Mt. Horeb.

In the first few years of her adult life, Donna had two bitter disappointments with men and a ruinous theft. These events did not make her bitter, but rather matured her character and increased her caring and compassion for people. Through her experiences and responsibilities Donna developed a quiet confidence.

Don's World

On September 15, 1922, I was born in Minneapolis, Minnesota. I was the only child of Doris and Clarence Seymour. We moved to Milwaukee in 1927, where my father was transferred to a job managing a tire store. Soon after my father left for Cleveland and never returned. Later my mother was granted a divorce.

My father died in Cleveland in 1933 at the age of thirty-five. Mother married Herman (Happy) Will in 1929. He was a friendly, hard working truck driver, and a caring stepfather. He treated me as his own. He died in 1941.

Between the ages of twelve and twenty I held many part-time jobs, often three at a time. This was not so unusual, as many people did this during the Depression of the 1930s. I recall standing in a long line of men and boys at five-thirty one morning, hoping to get a job for a few hours weeding a carrot farm for ten cents an hour. At twelve I sold *Liberty Magazine, The Saturday Evening Post* and Christmas cards door to door. When I attended school, I had a *Milwaukee Journal* route, a *Milwaukee Sentinel* corner and sold Christmas trees.

In the ninth grade I spent my spare time composing stories, poems, and essays; which was strange considering my dislike of English. My grammar and punctuation were so poor that I was ashamed to let anyone read what I had written.

I did not take well to formal education. I found most of it boring and it took me an extra semester to graduate from both grade school and high school. Occasionally I failed English and arithmetic.

In 1940, at the age of eighteen, the morning after our graduation, they bused the West Division high school male graduates to the Army induction center. I was one of six out of ninety inductees labeled 4-f because I had a punctured eardrum and wore glasses. I was dejected and felt terrible. On the street, people thought I looked young and healthy. Why was I here and their young men gone?

After high school I had twelve full-time jobs in construction, heavy manufacturing, electrical maintenance, auto parts sales, motor rebuilding, shoe sales, and FM-radio engineering. I didn't remain at any one of these positions for long because they paid very little, were temporary, were eliminated, the business closed, or I was unsuited for the work. I did, however, gain valuable experience from this wide variety of occupations.

In 1943, at twenty-one, I married Clara (Claire) Strife. Our son, Scott, was born a year later. Although Claire was a very attractive woman, she was not a homemaker or a cook. Nor did she want children. Her grandmother came to stay with us to take care of Scott, and to help with the housework and cooking. Claire worked in the office at A. O. Smith in north Milwaukee.

My partner and I had just started a business re-building motors for the Navy. As a war effort, we worked long hours. Clara played softball on the A. O Smith team. After the games the team would go to a tavern. Work prevented me from being there with Claire. Eventually she and the coach, who was a fireman at A. O. Smith, became rather close. (The coach's home was someplace up north, where his wife and two children lived.)

Donald and his mother in 1970.

I came home early on the day of our fifth anniversary with candy and flowers. I had made reservations at Claire's favorite restaurant. Claire should have been home by then but she was not. I asked her grandmother where she was. Her grandmother didn't know.

A few hours later the doorbell rang. A police officer handed me divorce papers that indicated I had to leave the premises. Claire had run off with the coach. I had not the slightest indication this was going to happen.

At the divorce hearing, I tried to be idealistic and noble. I instructed my attorney not to blemish the reputation of my son's mother, by not mentioning that she had run off with another man.

I was devastated by the loss of my family. My mother had been divorced when I was five and I had sworn that it would never happen to me—and it had.

My concern for humanity started when I was very young. I found the following note in my "things to save" file. It was dated 1939.

"At one time there occurs to every man a thought of his existence. In what way can he contribute to humanity and compensate for his life? How can he accomplish something that he is not lost in oblivion without having left some small token of his existence in the traverse of humanity? How can he find peace and happiness in his every-day world and leave it, content that all his debts are paid? How can he ever know he has accomplished being a man to himself? For we do not find peace in what others think of us but rather in what we think of ourselves."

My concern became noticeable again immediately after my divorce. I tried to get over the devastation of the loss of my family by throwing myself into civic work. I joined the all-volunteer, 600-man Milwaukee Junior Chamber of Commerce. I devoted all of my spare time to the Jaycees and was ultimately appointed director of public relations.

I dated a few girls during the next five years but did not have a special feeling for any of them. My regular income-producing work was as a northern Wisconsin salesman for a Chrysler Mopar Parts distributor. Like Donna, I too had bitter disappointments that probably strengthened my character and helped me prepare for a more meaningful life.

Our Second Meeting

One Saturday I happened to meet Donna and Ramona on the street in downtown Milwaukee. I remembered that Donna was from Mt. Horeb, Wisconsin, where Little Norway, Blue Mounds and the Cave of the Mounds were located. These could be good publicity locations to bring in more pageant contestants from western Wisconsin. I asked Donna and Ramona to lunch to discuss this.

At lunch I was so impressed with Donna that I almost forgot why I wanted to talk with her. No longer tired, she was relaxed and warm. Her smile and laughter were very attractive; she was so different from the tense contestant I had first met. Ramona had the same down-to-earth sincerity. (It must run in the family.) As we parted, I asked Donna out for dinner a week from this coming Saturday. She smiled and accepted.

Our First Date

Donna and Ramona lived in a large, old mansion on Prospect Avenue that was divided into several small efficiency apartments. The night of our date, I entered through an old stained glass door, walked up the stairs and down a dimly lit hall to the apartment number Donna had provided. I rapped on the door. A slight, young girl—she looked about sixteen or seventeen—answered the door. Evidently dressed for cleaning, she wore flat-heeled loafers, tired slacks, a working shirt, and a headband held her hair back in a ponytail. In her arms she held a small stack of magazines. She wore no makeup—she didn't need it. She had a lovely, fresh glow about her that no amount of makeup could enhance. I thought this might be another sister. I politely said, "I'm here to see Donna."

She looked down at her clothes and up at me, smiled a little and said demurely but sweetly, "I'm Donna Lou. Don . . . our date is next Saturday."

I was so taken back I didn't know what to say. This pretty young girl looking up at me was the sophisticated Miss Congeniality? I was tongue-tied. She laughed slightly at my discomfort. Under the circumstances another girl might have capitalized on the situation and said, "I have a date later tonight, but I look forward to seeing you next week. Good night."

Not Donna Lou. No guile or pretense in this girl. She smiled and said, "If you come back in an hour I can get dressed and we can go out if you like." Did I ever? She handled it beautifully, left me off the hook gracefully and honestly.

When I picked her up an hour later Donna was warm and slightly sophisticated. Wearing high heels and a mid-length fitted dress, she had bright clear eyes and her hair was neatly done. It looked like Donna had just come from a makeup artist, but her good looks were natural.

I took Donna to Frenchy's, one of Milwaukee's well known restaurants at the time. She was easy to talk with. We talked the night away, as if we had been friends for years. Donna had a natural, friendly magnetism. She asked how this year's pageant was coming.

"After re-analyzing this year's budget, on Tuesday last I recommended to our Board of Directors that we not renew the pageant contract," I said. "We did a better job than Jaycees in most other states that have a pageant, but we always seem to end up in the red, and our other civic activities suffer. The Board agreed, so we will no longer sponsor the pageant."

After that night Donna and I simply drifted into a friendly dating routine. Weekends when she did not go to the farm, we went to the American Club on Friday nights for their shrimp salad and on Saturdays we went to Frenchy's or the Italian Village on East Michigan, where we could dance. Donna was a soft armful and easy to dance with. We danced well together.

We went out together for six months and I never so much as tried to kiss her. For some reason I didn't dare.

How Was Your Date?

Later Donna related to me a conversation she had with Ramona about a date with me one evening. (Donna had a cute way of answering questions when she was impatient or wanted to be evasive. Her short clipped answers were often amusing.)

"Anyway, how was your date?" asked Ramona.

"Fine."

"Only fine?"

"I enjoy being with him. He's fun. A good dancer. An interesting guy."

"Geez, you're going out with him for six months and all you can say is that he's interesting? Is it serious?"

"Stop questioning me. I don't know. Never kissed me. Probably shy."

"Shy?" Ramona laughed. "A man who was married five years and has a child? Shy?"

"Don't know. Stop questioning me."

"Is he Catholic? I guess you know what Dad always told us. We shouldn't bring any Catholics into the family."

"He's Lutheran and Danish."

"That's good. What's so interesting about him?" Ramona pursued.

"Oh, I don't know. Christmas is coming and he said something interesting. He always looks till he finds a church at Christmas with a manger on the altar. He doesn't think it's right to have Christmas in a church without a manger."

"Sounds thoughtful. Hey, anyway. He's got that going for him. Do you like him?"

"Yes, I like him very much," Donna answered.

Ramona laughed. "Then why don't you kiss the shy divorced man to see if he's alive?"

"Oh, Ramona!"

"Anyway, do you want it to be serious?"

"He's a very special person. He cares about people and about his life having a meaning and purpose and making a contribution. And it isn't just talk, like most men. He does things. I never met anyone like him before."

"Uh, oh. It's serious."

"Well." Donna thought a minute, then said, "Maybe it is."

Ramona rolled her eyes back. "Oh geez? Wait until Mt. Horeb and the family hear that Donna Lou Arneson, beauty queen, is going to marry a divorced man with a child."

"Don't say it like that." Ramona had hit a sore spot.

"But it's true."

Donna asked, "What can I do? I like him more than anyone I've gone out with. He's been so nice and considerate of me from the pageant on. I couldn't just drop him."

"Well, no, not if you really like the guy. Won't it be strange, married to a divorced guy?"

"I suppose, but for some reason, with him it doesn't seem to make any difference. It doesn't taint him in any way. I'm very comfortable with Don. Ramona, do you like him?"

"Yes, he seems nice and a real gentleman. I agree, he's one of the better men you've gone out with," said Ramona.

"How do you think Dad will react?"

"They met him at the hotel during the pageant and seemed to be favorably impressed."

"But they didn't know about Don being divorced," stated Donna.

"Why was he?"

"The little I know is that his wife was very good looking but did not like homemaking. Her grandmother took care of the boy, the housework, and the cooking. She was on the A. O. Smith women's baseball team, and went to a tavern after the games, where she got thick with one of the coaches while Don was working. Don came home on their fifth anniversary with candy and flowers, ready to take her out to dinner. An hour later a policeman came to the door with divorce papers. She had run off with the coach, who was recently divorced. It hit Don pretty hard for two years. Then he threw himself into civic work and the Jaycees."

"Oh geez. Poor guy, did he tell you all this?"

"A few of the girls at the pageant heard some of it from his friend Tony Edtmiller, who did our stage directing"

"Those girls sure are nosy about Jaycees. How long ago was the divorce?"

"They say five years."

"Anyway, so she was to blame?"

Donna paused. "He doesn't say, but Tony Edtmiller said so."

"What about the boy?"

"He picks him up and does things with him."

"How do you feel about that?"

"I don't know, but I like kids and get along well with them. And if he's like Don, I wouldn't mind that at all."

"Well then, that should be no problem."

"So, what do you think the folks will say?" Donna repeated.

"Mom will probably feel sorry for the guy. Dad, I don't know. Anyway, first you tried to bring a Norwegian soldier-farmer home, which was okay. Then an Italian-Catholic Texan tavern owner, which wasn't; and now, a divorced father, Danish visionary. Geez, you sure know how to pick them! At least you're graduating up," teased Ramona.

"I know, it's awful, isn't it?"

"So, what are you going to do?"

"I don't know, Ramona. But I am not going to stop seeing Don. I like him and I respect him."

"I think you love him."

Donna didn't respond.

I grew to like Donna more and more. She was intelligent, had natural poise and charm, she was fun to be with and nothing she did or said rubbed against me. The only thing different about Donna was her musical, bell-clear laugh. It was spontaneous, unrestricted, and joyful. Her laugh had a magical affect on people—it brought joy to them.

Engaged?

About this time, Donna made a spaghetti dinner for the three of us. She served it on a little table in their apartment. It seemed to me that Ramona was taking special notice of me and I didn't know what to make of it. Perhaps she wondered why I had been divorced and how I would fit into their family.

When Donna and went out to dinner, I usually parked on a quiet street overlooking Lake Michigan. One night when we were talking about the things she wanted to do for people, and the things I wanted to accomplish, we somehow simply drifted into a mutual understanding that we could best do these things together. Holy cow! We were going to be married.

Family

That night, inside her front door, I thought it was only proper to seal our engagement with a kiss. I leaned over and gently kissed her . . . Donna looked a little shocked. She smiled a good-night and ran up the stairs. I presume Ramona was told that I was alive.

My mother worked at Gimbels department store in downtown Milwaukee for forty years, as a waitress, cashier and hostess. After I had told my mother about our engagement, inquisitive Donna went to Gimbels' dining room to see what my mother was like. When my mother saw this lovely, young lady who introduced herself as her son's wife-to-be, my mother didn't know what to say. So she blurted out that I didn't have any money. Donna knew my finances were nil and had a good laugh at that.

My mother always said, "Marry a girl who laughs a lot." That was good advice.

After our engagement, I was always on my best behavior. One night several weeks later, Donna was having second thoughts about our marriage. She did not tell me why. It could been because I was divorced and paying child support for a son. Or could it have been that she had been accepted for a stewardess position and was having second thoughts about marriage in general. Or could it have been that eyes would be raised in Mt. Horeb once she told her family that she was going to marry a divorced man with a child.

All these things were going against me. That night I had an uneasy sleep and I suspect Donna did too.

The next morning I saw Donna walking to work. As usual, I stopped to pick her up, as I often did when I was in town. She stood on the sidewalk for a moment, hesitant, considering, then smiled and got into the car. That bright morning seemed to make everything all right again. Donna began to make serious wedding plans.

33

I didn't have much money for a ring. My mother suggested that I consider the jewelry estate sale going on at Gimbels. I could take advantage of her employee discount. I wanted a nice sized diamond to present to Donna. I found a diamond with a slight flaw in the back, which could be reset so that the flaw was not visible. The jewelry manager said he would hold the diamond for a week while I agonized over the cost of it. I bought it. When Donna saw it she was so pleased that tears came to her eyes. She loved that ring.

Donna Tells Her Family

One weekend Donna wore her ring to the farm and announced that she would bring her future husband home the following weekend. She explained that I was the man they were introduced to at the hotel during the pageant and that I had been divorced five years earlier and had one son that lived with my remarried ex-wife.

I don't know what Donna's family thought of that announcement. I heard later that no open objections were raised. Thank goodness I was Lutheran, for mixed marriages were hardly in vogue with her father. And as Miss Congeniality in the Miss Milwaukee pageant, Donna had created some excitement in Mt. Horeb. The fact that I was director of the pageant may have given me a little prestige. Thank heavens I had that going for me!

When I arrived at the farm, Mother Arneson was smiling and seemed to enjoy the thought of her daughter getting married. Donna's brothers treated me politely and Ramona was supportive. (Marlyn then lived out-of-state.) Father came from the barn, cautiously shook hands and said, "Nice to see you again." Then he asked, "Ever do any farm work?" Before I could think of a good answer, I was tossing heavy, sticky bales of hay with Donna's two brothers. He had just recruited another farm hand.

On Sunday the family and I went to church. I sat between Father (who sternly looked straight ahead) and Donna. Mother was playing the church organ. Heads were straining to see who Donna Arneson had dragged in. As word traveled, people up in the front pews turned to look at me. I began to blush. Donna and Ramona had to cover their mouths to keep from laughing.

I whispered to Donna, "Didn't you ever bring a man to church before?"

She smiled, covered her mouth, shrugged and said, "No."

On the way out, I was introduced to the pastor. Soon everyone would know I was a city slicker from Milwaukee. It would be all over Mt. Horeb in thirty minutes, that is if the phone system could handle that many calls. I was introduced to nice, but inquisitive, people. Donna seemed to enjoy the attention—and my discomfort. But then, as she continued introducing me, I also realized she was proud of me.

After the service I was taken to the house next to the church and introduced to Donna's three great uncles and an aunt. The great aunt was very pleasant but Uncle John and Uncle August were very stiff and grim—the audacity of their great niece marrying a divorced man!

Back at the farm, just before dinner, Donna came to me with her bright-eyed mischievous smirk. She couldn't contain her mirth as she offered me a thimble-sized glass of wine. I thought, What is this, a nunnery? Are these people monks? The look of awe on my face made Donna burst out laughing. I'm a red-blooded, American, normal, two-martini man, and this was the twentieth century, "This is positively medieval," I whispered to Donna. "Is this all they have?"

She nodded, then said, "Sometimes a little beer."

Okay, I get it. This girl is going to play her cards right. First impressions, you know. She could have told me I would have to go martini-less, but no, she wants to create a good impression and at the same time laugh at my reaction. There is a limit as to how far a martini man will go to get married! Us martini guys are a positive influence on the world.

God's Little Green Apples

One weekend when I was at the farm Donna's brother Dale cautioned me to be careful whenever I walked behind the cows while I helped carry the milk pails. "If their tails go up, back off," he warned.

There are many apple trees on the farm (some planted by Johnny Appleseed himself) and when the cows eat the green apples they get a little gassy. A little! If it hadn't been for a stone wall and me the stuff from that cow would still be flying! Before I could react to the cow's tail moving upward, I was covered! I couldn't see out of my glasses. Dale and Hilton almost fell down laughing. Father covered his face with his hand and went quickly into the milk house. When Dale finally got himself under control, he guided me up to the windmill. Turning on the water he hosed me down as good as possible.

Soon the girls and Mother came running from the house. They thought I had been in a serious accident. When they saw what it was, they put their aprons to their mouths and politely went into hysterics.

I showered, changed clothes, and brushed my teeth. Donna gave me some mouthwash, but I could still taste that stuff on my lips.

Later, at dinner, when I was trying to put the incident behind me, Hilton burst out laughing. Everyone looked at him. When he could finally talk he said, "I wonder what would have happened if he . . ." pointing at me, ". . . if he had had his mouth open?" Ramona almost fell over backwards. Donna went into the living room holding her stomach. Mother put her apron to her mouth and went into the kitchen. Father and Dale had their heads down in their hands, laughing.

Finally, wiping tears from their eyes, they returned to the table, where I calmly sat wishing the ordeal would end. But Hilton wasn't finished yet. Looking at me, he said, "If Don had had his mouth open he wouldn't be very hungry."

The hysterics started all over again. The embarrassed, silly looking grin on my face just made the whole thing worse.

Dad finally thought it had gone far enough. "All right, that's enough. We better eat while the food is hot." But I noticed he was having trouble keeping a straight face.

Hilton couldn't stop. He looked at me and said, "Now you know why the Good Lord made little green apples." Dinner got very cold.

Later Hilton said to Donna, "Sorry, I guess I overdid it, but he looked so funny. I like Don, he pitches in and he's a good sport."

I heard later that the story of my green apple experience traveled through Mt. Horeb, the surrounding counties—and was still going. For a few months, every time I came out to the farm they had to cover their mouths when they saw me.

Whenever I was at the farm I helped carry milk to the barn, throw bales of hay up or down the hayloft, shovel feed, or whatever else was required. I kept up with Donna's father and brothers cheerfully and without complaint. Dale and Hilton could see I was no tenderfoot and that I held up my end. I think I passed their muster. I wonder if Donna planned it this way, because she knew I was used to hard work and would qualify with the family.

A Man of Few Words

Father Arneson was a strong, silent, stern man. He was short and had a dairyman's generous girth. Rather imposing, he was typically quiet. I figured I was being measured and when he was ready to voice his opinion about me he would let someone know.

Donna told me her mother broached the subject of their daughter marrying a divorced man to her husband. The rest of the family held their breath about what he would say. He surprised everyone when he said to Mother, "Donna's a smart girl. We don't have to worry about Donna. She knows what she's doing." Evidently I had passed.

When I asked Father for his daughter's hand in marriage, mother and daughters were straining to listen from the kitchen.

"Sir, I would like to ask for your daughter's hand in marriage."

I heard a "whoop" from the kitchen; they must've thought I sounded funny, like I was asking for the hand of a royal princess. Father, ignored the commotion from the kitchen, hesitated, then looked up from his desk. He smiled a little and then said," I understand that arrangements are already being made." And that was it.

Laughing later, Hilton said of his father, "I knew there would be no problem. He wasn't going to take any chances of losing a good, free, working farm hand."

The Arneson women were special and equally responsible for the respect the Arneson name carries. I only met Grandmother Arneson once, just before our wedding. She lay in the sunroom, barely able to raise her hand. She said, "Thank you for coming. I wanted to meet the man Donna Lou thought so highly of that she would want to marry."

When we left, Donna asked me to wait a minute and went back into the house. When she returned, Donna said, "Grandma likes you. You have honest and sincere eyes."

Browns Hotel, Iowa

We enjoyed the months before our marriage. Donna was a very lovely and desirable woman, but if I had ideas about any extra curricular activities before marriage, I learned to limit my interests to rather formal activities.

A few weeks before our wedding, the distributorship I worked for announced it was closing. The only Chrysler parts sales position available in the Midwest was in Des Moines, Iowa. I was to visit the area over the weekend, so I made a reservation for one night at the Browns Hotel. Donna surprised me by saying she wanted to go with me. Spending the night together, in a hotel? I couldn't imagine what she was thinking. She laughed at the look on my face. "I can go. It's no problem."

I'm not so sure, I thought, this is one attractive lady.

Fortunately the Browns Hotel had a two-bedroom suite. After dinner and a long conversation about the area Donna kissed me, said good night, and then we went to our separate bedrooms.

In the morning as I was still asleep, this lovely nymph in a nightgown came into my room, threw back the covers and jumped full length on top of me. The softness of her body against mine and the perfume of her sent my head reeling.

Before I could decide if I should put my arms around her, Donna sat up, reached over and splashed a glass of cold water in my face. Laughing all the way back to her room, she quickly dressed and was waiting for me in the lobby with her overnight case. Her bright-eyed mirth was obvious.

At breakfast in the hotel dining room, I hesitantly asked, "What was er . . . ah . . . that all about upstairs?"

She beamed a nonchalant smile, shrugged, and said. "Just letting you know what you're in for after we're married. Wasn't it fun?"

Was it ever . . . I needed cold water. "Well, yes. But I could have taken advantage of you."

"Not you, you wouldn't. You're a Boy Scout. You're too idealistic and honorable. You know it's proper for me to wear honest white when I become your wife. That is the best gift I can ever give you. Our marriage must start with complete honesty in the eyes of God, so He will bless it. There may come a time when we need that commitment to protect our marriage, in trying times."

I fumbled around for words to answer this solemn declaration. Failing, I finally said, "I know, but you're still a tease."

She laughed and said, "You loved it, didn't you?"

Did I ever.

Donna was attractive, graceful, warm, and friendly. She came from a hard working, religious family. What more could a man want for a wife?

The Affirmation

On our way back to Milwaukee, I thought it was time to tell Donna about my first marriage in more detail. I told her of the distressing two years that followed the divorce, when I read the Bible twice.

"That's a lot of reading. Why did you read the Bible twice, all the way through?" she asked.

"I'm not sure. It was kind of a long prayer. I was looking for answers."

"Did you find your answers?"

Looking at her lovely profile, I replied, "I may have."

She put her arm through mine and rested her head on my shoulder. This action affirmed that her decision to marry me was right.

Back in Milwaukee, in the foyer of her building, Donna looked up at me and said, "I'm glad I went along."

"You kind of surprised me when you said you wanted to go," I admitted.

She muffled a little laugh. "I could tell you were a little shocked, but I wasn't worried that anything would happen." Then quite serious, "I know you more now. After all the hours we've spent talking, I know for sure the kind of man you are, where you're going, the vision you have for helping other people and making a difference. You aren't just talking—like most men. I know you're going to do it, because I know how hard you worked as a Jaycee to help less fortunate people and your community. You are a kind, honest, and thoughtful man, and I want to help you do those things. I was never more sure of anything, than wanting to be your wife."

I didn't know what to say, but Donna prevented me from saying anything by putting her arms around me and ever so softly and sweetly kissing me. Then she started up the stairs, looked back at me a little glassy eyed, smiled, came back, and kissed me again, then hurried up the stairs.

I don't think I touched the ground all the way to my car.

Donna and I spent the weekends together; either in the city or at the farm. Aside from exchanging Valentine's Day and birthday cards, I don't think the word love was ever mentioned before marriage. Looking back, I don't think either of us was infatuated or head-over-heels in love. We were very attracted to each other, comfortable with and respected each other, shared a common purpose, and felt we could build a strong marriage.

Married in Mt. Horeb

May 26, 1951, our wedding day, started out cool and blustery. I dressed in the upstairs bedroom at Donna's parents. When I tried to get out, the door was stuck and wouldn't open. I had to climb out the window and down the porch roof to the ground. Everyone seemed genuinely concerned and there were no snickers I could see. No one ever fessed up to it, but the door never stuck again that I knew of.

During the ceremony dark clouds spilled rain. As Donna came down the aisle; she was natural and graceful; a lovely vision in white. She showed a gentle confidence for all to see. Yes, she was marrying the right man . . . in case anyone was questioning.

The happy couple.

Emil Ewald, my best man, and Tony Edtmiller, my groom, made a handsome pair. Donna's sisters, as bridesmaids, were beautiful.

I don't remember much about the ceremony, but I do remember that when we signed the marriage certificate the pastor remarked that Donna was a special lady. I tried to say something to agree. Wanting to say that Donna was a blue-ribbon lady, instead it came out that she was blue ribbon, like a prized Holstein. Donna overheard and looked at me in utter amazement. "You're comparing me to a cow?"

Shaking hands with my best man, Emil Ewald.

I could have sunk into the ground and thought my marriage would be annulled right there. My attempted complimentary remark had turned out all wrong. I tried to explain, but Donna only laughed at my crestfallen face and discomfort. The comment was forgotten.

After signing the marriage certificate I thought I had become Donna Lou's husband. Well, I had that wrong. I had just qualified for training to become Donna Lou's husband . . . and that training was to continue into the next millennium. Donna's husband in training was not allowed to act, say, or do stupid things.

The wedding dinner was held upstairs in the church. It was hosted by the churchwomen. Donna and I, tired from all the wedding commotion, were glad there was no dancing and drinking, like most Milwaukee weddings.

While taking pictures in front of the church, the rain stopped, the wind quieted down, and the sun shined through the clouds. It became a lovely day, as God blessed our marriage.

Family

Honeymoon

Donna and I left the church and drove north. The sun was still up in the west and we were each quiet with our own thoughts. In future years we talked about what we had been thinking.

(Donna) *There, it's done. Thank you, dear Lord, he's mine. I will always love him and make him happy, like the song says. I will never fail him or hurt him. I will help him in his vision to help others and to make a difference with our lives. He's not perfect, no one is, but he's wonderful and I will help to make him more so. Dear Phillip, I can never forget you, as Don cannot forget his former wife, Claire. You were a part of my life and will always occupy a small corner of my heart. Goodbye, Phillip. My love belongs to another, who I love more than I did you. And, goodbye, Tony. It was fun. We were almost married, and then you hurt me. I'm glad I didn't marry you. Don is so much more than you could ever be.*

I looked over at Donna; she had a tissue to her eyes.

"Something wrong?"

She smiled at me, put her arm through mine, and lay her head on my shoulder. "No."

"But you're crying." She nodded on my shoulder. "I don't understand," I said.

"I'm . . . I'm . . . I guess I'm crying because I'm joyful." *(I didn't think I would ever be happy again. What a fool I was to think that. What mistakes I could have made.)* "It's just that the most wonderful thing just happened in my life. I have you." *(And now I have the man I dreamed of.)*

I put my hand on her hand. "And I have you, and to me that is the start of everything."

My mind went back to the terrible years after my divorce. Burying myself in the Bible, I thought my life had ended and I'd never be happy again. *And now, look at the precious one here beside me. Maybe I didn't understand. Maybe it was all for a reason. Thank you for this precious gift Lord. I will always cherish her. I will never profane her love or her trust.* I sighed.

"You sighed. Why did you sigh?" she asked.
"Oh, I guess in a way I was just thanking the good Lord for you."
"Oh, that's a nice thing to do. So, you love your brand-new wife?"
"Yes. I love her very much."

You better, my husband. And, you just wait. You'll forget your ex-wife, because I'm going to love you like you've never been loved before.

I wonder what she's thinking.

We spent our first night at the Dartford Lodge in Green Lake, Wisconsin, where we discovered we were gently and wonderfully compatible. The next day we continued on to St. Ignace, Michigan. From our motel in St. Ignace we could see Mackinaw Island across the bay. We had wanted to stay at The Grand Hotel on the island, but it did not open until the May 31st, so we stayed in St. Ignace.

In the morning we took the ferry over to the island. A ticket agent gave me the boat's time schedule that indicated the last boat left the island at five o'clock sharp. There was no other transportation across the rough water. We enjoyed wandering over the historic island, where to this day no automobiles are allowed.

※

It was on Mackinaw Island that I first became aware of a glaring fault in my new wife—her love of shopping! (I learned later that it runs in the family, must be a genetic thing.)

※

The last boat was leaving. I pleaded with Donna that we had to go, but this shopping thing had a hold of her. We missed the ferry back to St. Ignace. With my binoculars I could see our car and motel room across the bay—and no way to get there.

At The Grand Hotel, people were scurrying to prepare for the opening. I pleaded our case with a manager: we were on our honeymoon,

Family

stranded on the island, and needed a place to stay. He said they did not bend the rules. Two young people without luggage?

He directed us to the smaller Blackhawk Hotel down the street, where I again stated our problem. The kind manager looked at us, smiled and said, "Don't worry. We'll take care of you. Please wait in the lobby until we can get a room ready."

We were taken up to a room surrounded by windows that overlooked the bay. Fresh flowers were on a table. We were told to come down for dinner in an hour. We were the only people in the large dining room, and on the table were more fresh flowers. No menu was available yet, so they asked if steak, baked potatoes and salad would suffice. It sure would.

Later, back in our room, we found an assortment of things, including toothbrushes, toothpaste, scented water, shaving equipment, and pajamas. We were treated like royalty, including a full breakfast the next morning.

Before we left I asked the manager for the bill. I didn't have much money and worried about the cost. He smiled. "There will be no charge, we aren't open yet." He wished us his best. (Years later Donna and I returned to the Blackhawk Hotel to thank this wonderful man for a lovely memory, but we could not find anyone who remembered him.)

Life can be like that, a tragedy in the making so often turns into a beautiful memory.

After a week-long honeymoon, we both had to return to work to earn money to start furnishing our apartment. We returned to Milwaukee from Michigan via the *Milwaukee Clipper* ferry that was running then.

Standing by the rail, we were quiet as we

Donna riding the ferry home from our honeymoon.

45

watched the Allen Bradley clock loom like a second moon in the distance. I looked at Donna. "You are very quiet. Was your honeymoon not what you thought it would be?"

She put her head against my chest. "Oh no . . . oh no, sweetheart. I was just trying to decide how I would describe our honeymoon in our wedding book. No, never a disappointment . . . nor was it a crescendo like some say . . . it was . . . sweetly, ever so wonderful, like I always hoped and dreamed. I think I may have even heard the bells people talk about. It's just that I'm so sorry it's coming to an end." She softly kissed me.

Making Fun of Her Husband

The weekend after our honeymoon we drove to the farm. As we drove through Mt. Horeb I pulled over in front of the church that we were married in—only a week ago. It was a pile of rubble.

"Donna, they tore down our church."

"Looks like they did. Oh well, Mt. Horeb is kind of stuffy and suspicious of good looking city slickers," she said with a straight face.

"I thought Emil, Tony, and I were perfect gentlemen. I don't think we created such a bad impression or contaminated the church so badly that they had to tear it down. I'm surprised your sheriff didn't stop me from entering town."

She shrugged her shoulders. "Well, you know these small town people. They don't forgive easily. Being very protective, they don't take to city slickers coming in and taking their girls away."

"So they tore down the church?" I exclaimed. She covered her mouth with her hands and nodded. But her mischievous bright eyes told me something was amiss. "Oh I get it, the church was old and they are building a new one, right?"

With that, she nodded, and burst out laughing.

This was a new side of Donna that I had not seen before . . . making fun of her husband. Of course I knew they wouldn't tear the church down just because of us, but by making an issue of it I had asked for it.

This set the pattern for many a discourse during our marriage. Any time either of us could make fun of the other, one of us was fair game.

Rhubarb at the Farm

Upon our arrival at the farm I detected some apprehension in Donna's father, perhaps about my taking liberties with his daughter. He soon (I suspect gleefully) rushed off in his truck.

An hour later Father came blazing down the road in a cloud of dust, with a trail of huge rhubarb leaves following behind him. He dumped the whole load of rhubarb on the lawn in front of the farmhouse—it must have been six feet high.

He gave me a knife and showed me how (I knew, but didn't let on) to cut off the leaves, and trim and strip the rhubarb. I watched, nodded, looked at the pile and asked, "All of it?" He nodded solemnly and walked away. I think he had this planned in advance because how and where could he get all that rhubarb so fast?

I wanted to ask if I was going to get help, but I didn't dare. Perhaps Donna or Ramona would come from the kitchen and help once he left? I could hear Donna, her mother, and Ramona in the kitchen laughing. My guess is they were watching this contest.

No one came near me or offered to help all afternoon, except Donna, who came out once to be sure I was doing it right. With a mischievous smile she disappeared back into the house. I surmised this was another test I had to pass by myself.

I spent the entire afternoon on the stone garden wall with a paring knife in my hand. When Father came from the barn at five o'clock, all the rhubarb was cut, stripped, and neatly stacked on the wall, ready for rendering or freezing. No rhubarb leaf in sight—they had all been gathered up and taken to the pigpen (as Donna suggested).

He looked over the stack of rhubarb, grunted, but didn't say a word, nor did I. I think he had gotten even with me for taking his daughter away.

We Settle In

After we were married, Donna continued to work full-time at the beauty salon. I had not been impressed with the sales potential in rural Iowa; so I continued with my sales territory servicing Chrysler, Plymouth and Dodge dealers in northeastern Wisconsin until they closed. Since my route consisted of central Wisconsin, above Madison, and as far north as Tomahawk, I typically would be gone from Monday morning until Friday night.

Fortunately, Robert W. Baird eventually accepted me as a stockbroker trainee, and I no longer had to travel so extensively.

Our first apartment in Milwaukee was on East Kane Place. We could see Lake Michigan—if we pressed our faces against the window hard enough.

Donna's had purchased a bedroom set with her savings. Other than that, the only furniture we had was a small metal folding table to eat on and two orange crates to sit on. And, there was a beautiful silver service set on a large tray (given to us by her parents) that sat in the middle of the empty living room.

I knew Donna was well liked by the other tenants in the apartment building; so I was surprised when one of the Jewish ladies who lived on the same floor as we did accosted me in the basement. "You know, that wife of yours is a sweetheart, but she has one really bad habit."

Taken back I said, "I'm sorry?"

"She cooks!"

I was puzzled. "She *cooks*?"

"Yes, she cooks and bakes. Ei yi yi, every morning she bakes. Up bright and early, the aroma of rolls, coffeecake, cookies and stolen comes rolling down the hall to greet our husbands when they open the door for the paper. It makes them madder than hell at us wives who don't like to do so much cooking. Ei yi yi she works every day and every morning and night she cooks."

I must have gained forty pounds during the first six months of marriage. Donna was smart, loving, capable, responsible, a penny pincher, a wonderful homemaker, and a gourmet cook. I don't know what she saw in me—but I sure was smart to marry her.

Noodles in Chili?

Our first disagreement took place while we were sitting on the orange crates eating dinner in our tiny kitchenette. Donna had made chili and I was eating it quietly

"Don, how do you like my chili?"

"Oh, it's very good." I must not have said this with the right amount of enthusiasm. Donna is an excellent cook and when she only receives a "very good" she knows something is up.

"You don't like it, huh?" she asks.

"Oh yes, very good."

She knows me, and senses I think something is wrong with the chili.

"Don't you like my chili?"

"I love it. I do."

Now very disappointed, Donna looks at me seriously. "What's wrong with it?" She will not be placated.

"Nothing."

"Don, you're not telling me what's wrong with my chili. Everyone else likes it."

"It's very good, really," I say as convincingly as possible. *Oh, no. She's not going to let it go. I'm going to have to tell her.* "It's just that my mother always made chili with elbow macaroni in it."

"Your mother puts *noodles* in *chili?* No one puts *noodles* in *chili*," she says exasperated.

Oh, boy. Now I'm in real trouble. Yet I open my big mouth again.

"My mother does, and I kind of like it that way," I say.

Donna looks perturbed. "Your mother puts *noodles* in *chili?* That's disgusting."

"I can't help it if I like it that way," I argue.

"That's not chili. It's soup."

She's irritated with me, I can tell. "It wouldn't hurt to put a few noodles in the chili," I say carefully.

"I take it your mother's a better cook and you don't like how I cook," she states.

"Oh, Donna, please. I love the way you cook," I plead.

There are tears in her eyes. She doesn't know whether to cry or get mad at me. So I make it worse by adding, "My mother's a good cook." I'm an idiot. That was the worst thing to say.

"And I'm not?" she asks dejectedly.

That was more like an accusation. I'm getting myself in deeper and deeper. Will I ever learn?

"Hon, it's just a difference of noodles. I can get to like your chili, too." I say kindly.

"You don't like my cooking." She looks like she's going to cry.

"I love your cooking," I say firmly.

"No, you don't."

"I do too." I think she's getting angry.

"You want noodles, huh?" Donna gets up, goes into the cupboard, rummages around and comes back with a box of macaroni. She pours a pile of uncooked elbow macaroni on top of my chili. "There, now you got your noodles, just like your mother's." With that Donna trounces into the bedroom.

I go into the bedroom to console Donna. She is crying softly. When I put my arm around her, she shakes it off. I don't know what to do or say. Me and my big mouth. This lovely woman tries so hard to please me. I return to the table and eat every bit of my chili, except for the uncooked noodles. I put those in the wastebasket, out of sight.

A little later Donna comes out dressed for bed. She cleans up the dishes and gently puts a piece of cake and a cup of coffee on my desk, where I am working. She does not appear angry, as she disappears back into the bedroom.

When I go to bed, Donna is turned away from me. What can I say?

Suddenly I hear a muffled noise coming from Donna. She's crying and laughing at the same time. Turning to me, she puts my arm around her. "Oh, Don. Our first argument is over noodles. Isn't that ridiculous?"

Donna always made delicious chili—with elbow macaroni. Every time she served chili, we recalled our first argument and smiled at each other.

The Speaker

At our monthly Jaycee meetings we had outside speakers. The meeting chairman called and asked if Donna (Miss Congeniality) could be the celebrity speaker at our October 1951 Milwaukee Yacht Club meeting. I had my doubts. I didn't want these guys making a fuss over my wife, but I didn't want to admit to Donna how I felt either. I would let Donna decide if she wanted to accept the invitation or not.

"Don, I don't feel like a celebrity. They are your friends and I don't want to be unappreciative for all the work they did on the pageant. What do you think?"

"It's up to you."

"Well, I don't suppose it will hurt."

That was a mistake. Donna looked gorgeous at the meeting. She spoke about Mt. Horeb, Cave of the Mounds, and the Song of Norway show presented annually at Little Norway, where her brother Dale's wife, Eleanor, was a soloist.

After the short meetings there was always socializing and drinking. The guys were drawn to Donna like bees to honey. I couldn't get near her. When we left, a few of the men followed Donna out to the car and wouldn't let us leave. Back at our apartment, I was slightly upset (jealous).

"Donna, you didn't have to encourage those guys like that."

Hunching her shoulders in a shrug. "I didn't do anything."

"Well, you must have done something. They were drooling like a bunch of mutts. They should have had kids with towels, like they do on a basketball court, wiping up the floor."

"I was cheerful and polite," she said.

"They were hanging from the car when we left, especially Tony Edtmiller."

She laughed. "That was funny."

"I didn't think so."

"Don," she said, as she pointed at me and laughed, "you're jealous."

(Probably beet red with it.) "Well, you didn't have to look so gorgeous."

"Me? Gorgeous? How did you want me to look?"

Well, she could have worn an old dress, like the elderly woman on the Dutch Cleanser can, and had her hair up in curlers.

The Rose

One cold and blustery night, after twelve hours of work, I came home to our apartment. Donna was still up and sitting in a love seat just beyond the entryway to our small living room. I hung up my hat and coat in the closet and as I turned towards Donna, she stood up. She let the sheet that was covering her slowly slide off one shoulder at a time to the floor. There she stood, with her head slightly turned, a demure smile on her face, and only a rose to cover her lovely self.

I remembered she had warned me back in Iowa that things like this might happen. (No, this never happened again. Donna never repeated a great performance. There were other surprises, but this one was so beautiful it is etched in my mind.)

Gregory Arneson Seymour

Hardly anyone knew Donna was pregnant until she started to show in her sixth month.

Gregory Arneson Seymour was born on July 31, 1952. He was a wonderful child and loved by all. Since he was the first male Arneson grandchild (and because of his middle name) he was a joy to Mother and Father Arneson.

Six months later Donna returned to the salon as her clients were very anxious to get her back.

I Make A Bet

One Saturday I wake up to the sound of music coming from the living room, which is very unusual. I come out of the bedroom and see

Family

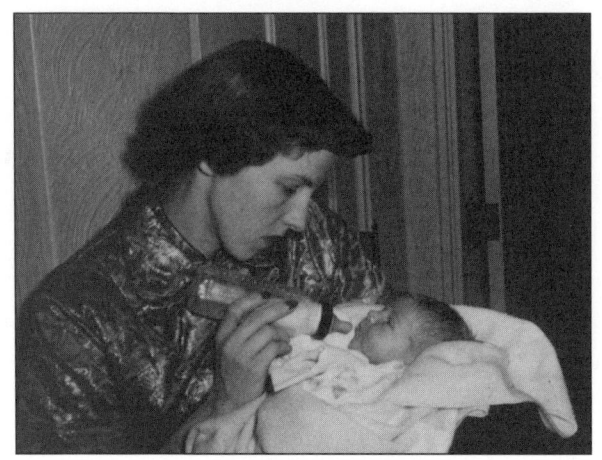

A proud mother with her firstborn.

Donna, looking awfully cute in shorts and a halter top, exercising and dancing to the radio. Greg is in his bassinet, laughing and clapping his hands at his mother's antics.

"Hey, what are you doing?" I ask.

"Getting my shape back," she puffs.

"But, as a beautician working on your feet most of the day, you get lots of exercise."

Puff, puff. "Not all the right kind." Puff.

"You look fine," I argue. "You can't expect to have the same shape after having a baby."

"Wanna bet?" Puff puff.

"Sure." I thought it was a safe bet, since what's ours was ours. And I always observed that after other women had had babies, they never looked quite the same, plus I had seen Donna's stretch marks.

"How much?" Donna wheezes.

What do I have to lose? "A thousand dollars," I offer.

"You have a bet. You better start to save your money," she warns.

The Bordello

One evening I came home and Donna says, "Follow me." She leads me to the apartment next to ours.

She unlocks the door with a key and steps inside the empty apartment. "What do you think?" she asks.

The only difference I notice is that this apartment does not have windows on the east side. "Looks nice. How many bedrooms?"

"It has two bedrooms and it would be so easy for us to move."

"Hey, that's great."

"Come, I'll show you." She takes me into the largest bedroom. One wall is orange, one is brown, one is yellow, and the fourth is purple. The ceiling is green.

"Cripes," I say. "It looks like a bordello. You think this garish room has some unique effect on people, like a bordello?"

Donna laughs. "Could be. Well, if we move in here, it would be limited to a one-woman bordello—me—and only one customer—you."

"You mean you'd leave the room like this? Don't you think the colors are a little disconcerting?"

Donna points at two paint cans on the floor. "You can fix that."

I lift one of the cans. "Off-white over these harsh colors? I wonder how many coats it will take?"

"I don't know, but the apartment is ours if we want it."

"You think it's safe for Greg to have his own bedroom?"

"No, but this bedroom is bigger than what we have now, and there is second bedroom." She pauses, waiting for my reaction. "Since we married, Ramona is alone in her apartment. I know she would like to come and live with us. When we go out, she would be right here to baby-sit."

"That's a good idea," I respond. "I wouldn't mind. I like Ramona."

Donna puts her hand to her chest and lets out a sigh of relief. "I'm so glad you agree because I sort of already told Ramona she could."

"You were pretty confident, already getting the paint."

"If we paint it, we get a month's free rent. How's that for negotiating?"

"Pretty good."

"Then, you agree?"

"Of course."

She puts her arms around me and kisses me. Then with that mischievous look of hers Donna looks me in the eyes and says, "Before it's painted, wouldn't you like to try sleeping in this bordello, just to see what happens for one night?"

This woman is outrageous!

That is how Ramona, who worked at Northwestern Mutual Life, came to live with us. She took care of Greg at night when we attended Jaycee functions.

Ramona was pleasant to have around. We were the Milwaukee branch of the Arnesons, a close threesome that took care of each other.

In addition to having a lovely wife, I received a bonus. I grew to love and respect Donna's parents and brothers and sisters as my own. In all the years we spent together I never heard a single word of anger spoken between them. Usually with five sibling marriages you will find someone who doesn't get along, but not in this family. When we visited the farm we had fun and everyone was considerate of everyone else.

Don Is Fired

It was Christmas Eve 1952. We had a baby and a new apartment. I knew Robert W. Baird gave Christmas bonuses, and I was looking forward to buying Donna a gift with it. Mr. Haack, Vice President of the company, called me into his office and abruptly said, "Here's your paycheck. You're through as of now. I don't think you'll ever make a salesman."

I never felt so low or worthless as I did that Christmas Eve. I didn't tell Donna until after Christmas. She was obviously disappointed and very quiet the night I told her. She had gone to bed and I dreaded crawling in next to her. It was late when I did. She came over and put her head on my shoulder. "Don't worry Don. Maybe it's for the best. I have faith in you. There's something special out there for you to do and now you'll find it."

Without consulting Donna I had recently purchased a TV for twelve payments of $17.59 a month. I was out of a job and we were just getting by. Donna was understandably angry. She hated obligations.

The Northwestern Mutual Gamble

My friends said I should apply at Northwestern Mutual for a sales position, since their home office was in Milwaukee and they were one of the premier life insurance companies in the country. The Momsen Agency, the local Northwestern Mutual office, was located in a stone mansion overlooking Lake Michigan. It was an impressive office.

One of the premier agencies, not only for Northwestern Mutual but in the life insurance industry as a whole, Momsen did more business than many small life insurance companies. There were many successful and degreed sales agents in this office.

When I approached the Momsen Agency I was told that they required their new hires to have a college education, so that a new agent would have a built-in source of young, quality sales leads.

Fortunately, one of Donna's salon customers, Olive Stiemke, who served on a civic board with Bill Momsen (owner of the Northwestern Mutual Momsen Agency), encouraged Bill to give me a try, even though I had not attended college. She told him that we were an exceptional young couple. After interviewing Donna and me, Mr. Momsen gave me some tests. (This was my first introduction to occupation and interest tests, which ultimately guided my thinking toward human capability research.)

The results were positive. He agreed to give me a six-month try, but there would be no salary or draw—just commission on the sales, which take time to process.

Momsen had a quality sales-training program, but at the end of six months I was a classic failure and an embarrassment to the agency. When Bill called me into his office I knew what was going to happen.

Family

The gentleman he was, he tried to let me down easily. He said that although the tests were positive, I apparently did not have what it took or the personal connections to become a successful life insurance salesman.

Wanting to help us, Bill Momsen sent me to Dr. Paul Mundie, a prominent occupational psychologist whose firm was influential in selecting and confirming presidents for many large Milwaukee companies. Mundie's challenge was to help me find another job—quickly. During the six-month trial period I had borrowed money to support my family. I needed immediate income.

After a week of meetings with Dr. Mundie, taking a battery of tests and hours of counseling, Dr. Mundie suggested I should probably have my own business. He suggested the new home drywall construction industry; where after some training in drywall installation I could go out on my own with very little capital. My previous sales experience and training would help.

"What other occupations do the tests show?" I asked.

"There are some other interest areas, such as engineering and the ministry, but they require a college education. With your educational background and immediate financial need, these do not appear to be an alternative," Dr. Mundie replied.

"Anything else?" I asked.

"The life insurance profession is fairly high on the test," he admitted, "but you failed at that, so we can rule it out."

"What can there be about life insurance that the tests recommend? Calling on strangers to buy life insurance, in case they die, does not appeal to me."

"Maybe that is why life insurance sales is not for you," Dr. Mundie responded. "The insurance interest may indicate you are entrepreneurial and want to be your own boss—like you are when you sell life insurance." Then he added, "Tests tell us more of what we think we like to do rather than what natural abilities we have." He showed me the results of several tests I had taken. He selected the results from my Strong Interest test and explained how to interpret them. I found it fascinating. "This is an interest test," he explained. "A comparative test to other successful people in certain occupations. If your test is close to the test answers of successful people in a particular profession then you too are supposed to be successful in it. It seldom works that way."

He went on, "Some highly motivated people can bull themselves to be a success in a business where they do not belong, but the stress of doing what they are not designed to do will probably hurt their health and family in the long run." (I was to remember this statement many times in the future.)

Dr. Mundie's test results continued to trouble me. If the tests showed that I could succeed at life insurance sales, maybe I could. Every job has its difficult parts, maybe I could overcome my distaste for calling on strangers and being turned down. I ignored Dr. Mundie's comments about the stress of doing what I was not designed to do. But, I didn't know if my self-confidence could survive another job change and failure. Donna would be embarrassed and could lose respect for me, which would hurt our marriage.

I went to Bill Momsen and told him how I felt about the company, the agents in the office, and that I believed this is where I needed to make a stand. He shook his head and said, "Don, people who fail as you did just don't make it. It takes a certain kind of person to succeed in life insurance, and evidently you're not it."

"I've already invested six months—and I have many sales proposals out," I argued. "I made a start and the tests say I can succeed. I need to try again.

"Don, you're making a mistake. You're going deeper into debt and your self-confidence is low. It's a bad combination."

I kept at him for a few days. Finally Bill agreed to talk about it. He set up an appointment with Donna and me to be sure we both understood the gamble. Bill took a liking to Donna and said, "You know, you two are quite a combination. If anyone in your situation can do it, you two can. All right, six more months. If you are not making it by then you have to agree, no more argument, and that will be the end. You will have no financial help. Don, you are completely on your own." And then turning to Donna, he added, "It's not going to be easy. He could fail. Is this what you want Don to do Donna?"

Donna hated debt and Bill made it clear that this was a gamble. She thought for a moment, looked at me, and said, "I have faith in my husband and his ability."

I used my own style of selling. I didn't sell policies. I sold the future. I questioned potential clients thoroughly and used my writing to develop the story of their future on paper. My proposals were so complete that I wrote future letters from their father (if deceased) to their children upon entering college. Most people appreciated my detailed work and, if they could afford it, they bought some insurance. I could not use pressure tactics to sell. It was not in my nature. As people could afford it, more started to buy the necessary life insurance.

One of Northwestern Mutual's best agents, Ben McGivern, personally paid for what he called "Minute Steak" training luncheons held at the prestigious Milwaukee Club, where he was a member. Ben introduced a small group of new agents (including me) from the local Momsen and Craig Agencies to unusual sales ideas. Many of Ben's ideas about life and business were way ahead of his time. Not all the Minute Steak agents survived in the business, but Ben was a great help to me.

I Lose a Bet

One evening Donna and I were getting dressed to go out for dinner (Greg was at the sitter's). I was sitting on the bed putting on my socks when Donna came in from the bathroom with only a towel wrapped around her. She stood in front of the mirror and began to take the curlers out of her hair. Her towel fell to the floor—and she made no attempt to pick it up.

I was surprised and sat there with my mouth open. I hadn't seen Donna in the nude since before Greg was born (she was probably a little modest at the changes in her body).

The Twentieth-Century Lady

I continued to sit and stare at my gorgeous wife.

She saw me in the mirror and a mischievous grin appeared on her face as she combed her hair. I was entranced. Donna was not only just as firm and beautiful as she was when we were married, but somehow she seemed even more beautiful.

"Are you enjoying yourself?" she asked.

"I . . . er . . . well, heck, can't I look at my wife?"

"You weren't looking, you were ogling." she corrected.

"What the heck's the difference?" I ask, not wanting to admit the truth.

"It means leer and gape with roguish intention," she replies, still smiling and fluttering her eyes.

"Well, I think I was looking at you nicely," I object.

"Leered very nicely," she corrects me again.

"Well, Donna, I can't help it. You looked so beautiful that I was mesmerized."

With that she comes over, bends down until she is face to face with me, looks into my eyes, and says, "Ah, ha. So, my shape is back to where it was, huh?"

"Well . . . er . . . ah . . . yes. It seems even nicer," I mumble.

She holds out her hand. "One thousand dollars, please."

Uh, oh. Now I remember. And now I know what this is all about. Donna knows that I don't have the money, so what do I do now?

"Don't have the money, huh?" she states.

I spread my hands and shake my head.

"Yes, I see you don't." Then, as she walks away with that mischievous smirk of a smile, she says, "Oh, well. Since you don't have the money, I guess I'll just have to take it out in trade. Like doing the dishes for a month, and the laundry."

"So, now you're going to make me suffer, huh?" I ask.

Donna throws up her hands and gives me a lovely smile. "Who knows?" Then with a fluttering of her eyes, "Maybe I'll allow you an occasional extra-curricular activity."

Family

In Donna's Eyes

I was making a success of selling life insurance. At a service award banquet in May 1954, the Senior Service League of America presented The Distinguished Service to Youth Award to such prominent people as former governor Walter J. Kohler, William J. Grede of Grede Foundries, Frederick C. Miller of Miller Brewery, and Donald E. Seymour. Donna was very proud of her husband.

By November 1954 I was in line to receive third place in the Momsen Agency's coveted Composite Award, which recognized a combination of sales factors. This was quite an accomplishment, because the Momsen Agency was one of the top life insurance agencies in the country.

I was desperate to hold onto my third place position. Only the top three Composite Award winners were in the winner circle and publicized. I would gain respect in the industry and with my clients, plus this recognition would rebuild Donna's respect for me.

Bill Momsen worked very closely with me during those first two years. He took a few others and me duck hunting (which I had not done before). We discussed sales philosophy and my potential sales while waiting for ducks to fly over the duck blind. Bill went an extra mile for me in a crucial time of my life.

The yearly Award Banquet was held in January at the University Club. Over one hundred Momsen Agency people and their wives would attend. Also invited were the officers of Northwestern Mutual and the Northwestern Mutual Board of Directors, many from major Milwaukee banks and companies. Also, some of the directors' wives were patrons of the salon where Donna worked.

Trying to maintain the third position, I worked long and stressful hours seven days a week from October through December 15th. Life insurance policies usually took two weeks to issue and by the middle of December I had all the sales that I could get processed for the year. The last policy numbers were posted in the Northwestern home office the 31st of December.

Usually our big producers submitted large policies at the end of the year, which could throw the figures off. I knew what I had accomplished—but not what anyone else had.

At the banquet, after all of the minor awards had been called off, they finally began to announce the Composite Award winners. I heard the third-place winner called off. It wasn't me. I was crestfallen. I had failed Donna. I almost cried. Under the table Donna placed her hand in mine, smiled, and shook her head. Maybe, just by chance, I had moved up to second? The second-place winner was announced. No. It wasn't me. How could I have lost it all? I had tried so hard, but I just wasn't good enough. Donna touched me again and I looked at her. She was smiling and shaking her head and nodding. Why? Then I heard in the background, "And the winner of the 1954 Composite Award is Don Seymour."

Everyone stood and applauded. Dazed, I don't recall what I said when I went up to accept the silver pitcher that was inscribed to me. I'm sure it was something about the support of a caring general agent, a great staff of people, and a wonderfully supportive wife. I do remember looking down and seeing Donna standing there, clapping and dabbing her eyes at the same time.

Northwestern agents are class people. They don't like to lose, but if someone else wins they are very congratulatory and gracious. Bill Momsen taught us that. Bill introduced me to a new way of thinking about business, our responsibility to people, and life. The things he and Ben McGivern taught me prepared me for the responsibilities I would have one day. (Bill Momsen, long gone, is one of two non-family members I mention in my nightly prayers.)

On our way home, I said to Donna, "That was quite a surprise. You knew, didn't you?"

"Of course, wives know everything."

"C'mon, how did you know?"

"Bill Momsen called me a week ago. He told me that nothing should prevent you from being at the banquet. I had to promise not to tell you that he had called."

"I see. So, you knew all the time."

"Yup. I knew you had won an important award."

As I was driving Donna gaily, but carefully, bounced the engraved pitcher on her knees. "We're going to have to make a pedestal for this. Perhaps find a Roman wreath to suspend over it."

"I'm no gladiator."

"You're much better . . ." Continuing to carefully bounce it. " . . . and I'll put my African violets around both sides and . . . maybe a blue spotlight."

"Isn't that overdoing it?"

She turned the pitcher and her head happily back and forth. "Oh, I don't think so. This is very special."

"You going to take it to work during the day?"

"Too obvious. Not to worry though. If our patrons don't already know about it or haven't read about it in the paper, they'll hear the gossip about how well I trained my husband for business success."

"I've been in training?"

"Of course."

"I didn't know that."

"Well, you know, that's women talk. We wives have to have some small part in our husbands' success."

"More than a small part, my dear wife." (Much more than you know my love. I would trade it all, just to see the renewed respect in your eyes.)

I had the feeling that things were happening for a reason and that this was just one more step toward a more important purpose.

A Scary Year for Greg

Since our apartment was on the second floor, Greg would drag his scooter down the stairs before riding it around the block. Everyone on the block knew him and would get out of his way.

One time he escaped just before we were to take him to Ruth, his babysitter. He was out of sight before I could turn around. While I was

A bedtime story for Greg (age 3).

chasing Greg around the block, an older gentleman out for a walk stopped me with his hand.

"Hey, aren't you the blur's father?"

"The blur?"

"Yeah, you know, that kid with the scooter, whose feet go faster than the eye."

"Well, I suppose."

"Well, you're going the wrong way."

"He just went by here, didn't he?"

"Sure, but you'll never catch up with the blur. The only way you'll catch that kid is head on."

On weekends Greg would drive Donna frantic as he had developed the courage to leave our block and head down the hill to Lake Drive. There were no street crossings, and away he went. I usually worked on Saturdays and would get a call at the office. "Honey, you better get on

Family

Donna admires Greg.

your horse." I knew what that meant. I jumped in my car and cruised busy Lake Drive until I rounded up the culprit.

Occasionally I would take four-year-old Greg into my office on Saturdays. The office was in and old mansion. One of my office doors opened onto a walk-down fire escape to the roof of the stone entryway below. Greg would sometimes play with his cars on this roof. I should have realized Greg would eventually try to find a way to get down to the ground—but it was a twelve-foot drop to the driveway—surely he could see that.

When Greg played on the roof I watched him closely. One time when I looked I saw him hanging outside the porch, trying to touch the ground with his feet. Terrified, I ran down the inside stairs, out the door, and stood underneath him. As I turned up to him he fell into my arms. I was shaking so badly I had to sit down with him in my arms. He would have hit his head on the cement stairs. The Lord must have been watching out for us. I thanked Him all the way home. I was still shaking when I placed Greg in his mother's arms. A matter of seconds and we could have lost Greg. I shake every time I think of that. Imagine, just a fraction of a second.

That winter polio was going around. One weekend Greg was listless with a very high fever. We took him to Dr. Polachek who said we must take Greg directly to the polio hospital on the south side of town and that we must burn everything of Greg's, including his favorite "moc" (blanket) and "ug" (teddy bear).

It tore at our hearts to visit Greg every night, to see him behind glass in a strange bed, holding out his arms and crying for us to hold him. This awful ritual went on for several months. Finally, we could bring Greg home. He had a little limp that eventually he outgrew. We were lucky. Many kids were maimed for life and some did not come home from that hospital.

Donna and Greg (age 6) at her parent's farm in Mt. Horeb.

The Million-Dollar Round Table

Seven years later I had earned all the life insurance industry awards, including the prestigious Million-Dollar Round Table Award and the National Quality Award. And. after taking six years of night courses I had earned the Certified Life Insurance Underwriters (C.L.U.) and associate degrees.

As a member of the Million-Dollar Round Table (MDRT) I attended the annual meetings. During these week-long business meetings, I met powerful and capable salespeople who worked for life insurance companies from all over the world. They appeared to be individualists, much like me. They were people that needed freedom to use their abilities in their own way and wanted control of their destiny.

These highly talented MDRT members came from all walks of life; many were former doctors, lawyers, accountants, and bankers. They were the most unlikely looking group of successful people I had ever seen. There was nothing exceptional about these people, except that they had found the means, freedom, and environment to become exceptional.

It occurred to me that if this most unusual and diversified group of Million-Dollar Round Table salespeople could be successful, then perhaps anyone given a free environment to find and use his or her talents could become successful. (This was the beginning of my belief that most people have undiscovered natural abilities or talents that don't surface because they are repressed by education or business conformity.)

In 1955, my last year as a Jaycee, I was elected Vice President. At the age of thirty-six I retired as an active Jaycee and joined the ranks of exhausted roosters. I had learned more from my Jaycee responsibilities than I could have ever learned in college. (Of course, I would have liked to have gone to college, but my grades were not good enough.)

The Princess and Goofy

One evening Donna was placing photographs in an album. I happened to see some large photos and picked one up. "What is this?"

"It's me, silly," Donna replied.

"Well, yes, I can see that. But you look gorgeous. If I had seen these before we were married I would have been scared off."

"You're goofy. I guess it's lucky for me that you didn't see them."

"Donna, I've meant to ask you. Why do you sometimes call me goofy?"

She laughed. "Because you remind me of Mickey Mouse's dog, Goofy."

"I remind you of a dog!"

"Sure. Goofy was sweet, playful, funny, he never hurt anyone, he was a perfect gentleman, and awfully, awfully nice to have around."

"Woof."

I picked up more photos. "I guess I never really noticed. You have a very beautiful profile, features, and shape. Wow! Good grief! I married a beautiful princess."

Donna burst out laughing. "Don't make so much of it. They're flattering; a professional photographer took them at the end of a modeling class. They always make you look better than you are."

"Not so. It's you and you are very beautiful, like a princess."

"Silly man. I'm just a farm girl who is a practiced beautician and works hard to look a little attractive for my husband."

"Cinderella didn't come from a better background."

I pulled her up out of the chair and held her to me. She was still muffling a laugh. "Holy cow! I married a princess."

She wrinkled up her nose and with a pretty, mischievous grin said, "Aren't you lucky?"

Was I ever!

Jeffrey Don Seymour

On December 17, 1958 Jeffrey Don Seymour was born. He was a fun boy, even though he was always getting into things. Donna would have to follow him around, putting things back that he threw down. Finally, in desperation, she put everything out of his reach.

We were very fortunate to have Ruth Pokrzyinski for a babysitter. She lived only a few blocks from our apartment. Over the years Greg and Jeff blended in with Ruth, her husband, Joe, and their daughter. We used no other full-time sitter in all those years.

Family

In 1957 we moved into a Swiss-style lower flat a few miles north along the lake in Shorewood, Wisconsin. It had a large master bedroom and a smaller bedroom for Greg. Donna loved to cook and entertain, and now she had a lovely dining room with windows that reached to the floor, and a step-down living room with a natural Swiss fireplace.

The Start of the Research

Developing life insurance plans for a great variety of people and listening to their career problems had given me insight into how poorly most people actually selected their careers. When my insurance clients had career trouble I tried to help by giving them a Strong Blank Interest Test. Eventually I became very good at interpreting the results and counseling my customers—but in a different way than most career and job counselors. Rather than using the positive test recommendations I used the negative answers to the questions to propose low-stress lateral career moves or new occupation possibilities. To my amazement, a number of people found that my suggestions were more on the mark than the complete batteries of tests the might have taken at colleges and universities. My interest in finding an effective way to help people select more agreeable, low-stress occupations prompted me to spend any extra time I had researching the history of career, interest, and psychological tests.

It was through my studies and my giving people occupational tests that I began to wonder if there wasn't a better way to find low stress occupations that fit each individual's unique capabilities.

Flying to Mexico

Donna and I had been very busy with our family, church functions, and school events. I was retired from the Jaycees and had earned my insurance CLU degree—so we decided to take a vacation.

In the spring of 1961 our friend Hugo Cherubini organized a group trip to Acapulco, Mexico. We were asked if we wanted to go and

Donna said yes. We had not been out of the country and Hugo knew his way around Acapulco.

The long flight to Mexico City gave Donna and me time to rest and to talk leisurely about things we didn't have a chance to talk about at home—at least not in any detail.

"Don, I want to tell you how much I admire you for earning your CLU degree. Bill Momsen said that with your educational background, he didn't give you much of a chance of passing the exam since college graduates sometimes failed. Having appointments throughout the day and into the night, sometimes coming home at ten or eleven, and then studying that boring actuary stuff for a few hours took a super human effort. I'm very proud of you."

"Boring is right. I often fell asleep at my desk."

"I know. Sometimes I had to come out and get you into bed at two in the morning."

"At least it's done now. And, Donna, thank you for all your patience during that time."

"That's what I want to talk about. When you're at work I sometimes glance through the books you're reading. Aristotle. Plato. St. Francis. Gracian. Newton. Montessori. John Dewey. You are reading some very dusty stuff, like that book you're reading now."

"I know. Listen to what Einstein says: 'I have no special talents, I am only passionately curious.' Isn't that interesting?"

"Yes," Donna agrees. "He says 'no special talents'? Most people think he's the most talented person of all time."

"He also says, 'I am not any more intelligent than anyone else, just fortunate to have found an area that matches my interests and abilities.' Is he trying to put himself down for some reason?" I ask Donna.

"He didn't like notoriety. But there are two interesting words he uses, which seem to match your research: interests and abilities," responds Donna.

"Yes, but I don't know what he's driving at," I admit, "even though everyone has interests and abilities."

"Don, you haven't talked to me about where you're going with all this research. You seem kind of secretive. Do you want to talk about it?"

"I'm sorry. I may be ignoring you, spending so much time working and researching a subject that I am not qualified to delve into. I want to discuss it, but I'm so uncertain of my direction. I seem to be looking for answers that may not even exist."

"Like the vision you had for helping people you told me about before we were married?" she questions.

"Yes, something like that. And I am not even close to discovering a way to help people find the right career."

"I was wondering when you were going to get around to it. What brought it on now?" she asks.

"As you know, I hadn't had much spare time, but then giving my clients the Strong Blank Test sparked my interest again. And there are other things that seem to impel me."

"Care to tell me?"

"Education is in so much trouble," I begin. "Youth suicide is on the rise. Bad and stressful career selections are being made, which results in people living purposeless and unfulfilled lives. Terrorism is growing. They now use disease, viruses, bacteria, chemicals and other ways to threaten humanity. Humanity and our planet suddenly have so many problems that we are in a biospheric crisis. There are so many things going wrong with us, and I don't think it's supposed to. We are either doing something terribly wrong or not doing something right. I sense the answer has to be found before it's too late. And the answer is more than just wrong careers."

"Don, I know your vision was always to help people with their careers, but now you are taking a different route. You think you can solve all these problems—when today's great minds can't? Oh, I see. That's why you're evading talking about it."

"I know it's preposterous—ludicrous—to think I could, but I can't deny this urge. Something is desperately pushing me to try. There could be a simple answer that no one can see."

"I hear you say 'purposeless and unfulfilled lives'. You're not only looking for right careers, you're looking for something no one has ever found—the meaning and purpose of life. And in doing so you believe these desperate problems could be solved. Wouldn't that be wonderful?"

"So, you figured that out? But it's probably pointless for me to try."

"Pointless?" She put her hands together against her chin in prayer fashion, a habit Donna has when she's deep in thought. "Hon. Go back to your reading. Let me think about this."

A few minutes later she gently puts her hand on my arm. "I've been thinking. My husband is a very unusual man, with strong abilities and deep dedications. It wouldn't surprise me at all if you succeed where no one else has. And I agree that someone has to do it. Your concern for humanity was there when you were in your teens. How many teenagers had a concern for humanity like you did at that age? You seem to have a mission in life. I believe in you. Go for it. I'm with you and will help in any way I can."

"You actually think I could do such a thing?"

"If anyone can, you can. And evidently you do, or you wouldn't be so dedicated. It takes super dedication and motivation for a man of limited education to do what you are doing. Who knows, maybe God gave you a wife who believes in you to help."

That almost brought tears to my eyes, for I have often felt I was blessed with Donna.

She went on. "God doesn't give out responsibilities lightly, and you may have one."

"That is very lofty."

"I don't think so. We all may have been given a responsibility in life, it's just that somehow your interest and concern for humanity has surfaced at a time when it's needed. Remember, 'you've built a world we can't forget. We will build it greater yet.' And, 'In what way can he contribute to humanity and compensate for his life?' "

"That sounds familiar. Where is it from?" I ask.

"It is the last two lines of a poem and a statement written by a young man in his teens."

"Who?"

"*You* silly. Don't you remember your own poems?" she teases.

"You're reading those terrible old poems?"

"Got to know every thing about my husband—and they are not terrible."

I took Donna's hand in mine and looked at her. "You find ways to give me confidence. You are a remarkable woman."

She laughed a little, put her hand on my cheek and kissed me. "I have to be to keep up with my remarkable husband. Go back to your reading."

Mexico City

Donna and I checked into the Hilton on the main avenue. We were tired from the long trip and went to bed early. In the middle of the night a storm came up and our fifteenth-floor room started to shake. There were several loud cracks of thunder. I mean very loud. Donna wrapped her arms around me as the room was shaking and swaying. Finally everything was still and quiet.

Donna said, "It's very breezy in here."

I thought so too, got up, and looked around. There was a five-inch crack down the middle of the wall. I could see the city lights through it.

"Donna, that was more than a storm. It was an earthquake."

They moved us to the El Presidente Hotel that had a beautiful thirty-foot waterfall in the lobby.

Four days later we board a Mexican plane to fly us to Acapulco where we will meet the others in the group. As we pass over the Sierra Madre Mountains, the Acapulco airport below us looks like a postage stamp. Suddenly the pilot banks the big commuter plane and dives at

The Twentieth-Century Lady

the postage stamp, like he is going to strafe it. Above the noise I holler to Donna. "What's he doing? He can't possibly land at this angle and speed."

I didn't trust the age of the plane and feared the wings would come off. We hung onto each other, with the wind roaring in our ears. At the last second the pilot pulls up and heads out to sea. I don't know how the wings stayed on. My stomach is in my throat and I am wringing wet. Donna, still clinging to me, won't open her eyes. Everyone on the plane looks like they had put their finger in a light socket. Coming in off the ocean and landing, we get off the plane and feel the worst heat and humidity I had ever experienced.

This trip is starting out to be a disaster, I thought.

After going through customs, a cab driver collected our luggage, and we were on our way to the hotel.

On the outskirts of Acapulco the police stopped us to let a motorcade pass. President Dwight Eisenhower, with a big grin, waved at us as he went by.

The cabby asked the name of our hotel again. I said, "Bahia."

He shrugged. As we drove around Acapulco the cabby asked several people where the Bahia hotel was. No one knew. We went around for an hour. Finally I asked him to stop the cab and I got out. I approached the first person who looked like they could speak English.

"Pardon me, do you know where the Bahia Hotel is?"

He pointed. "Sure, right up there on top of that hill overlooking the bay." We had passed it a half dozen times.

I went back and pointed it out to the cabby. "Ah," he said, "you mean the Ba-eea. You got to say Ba-eea." He added the extra hour to our bill.

<hr />

We arrived at the hotel the same time as Hugo. He suggested that we go to the local liquor store to stock up for the eighteen people in our group. The storeowner told us that for such a large group plus guests for a week, it was much cheaper to buy liquor in bulk. Hugo thought that was a good idea. By what he ordered I thought his other friends must be pretty heavy drinkers. Back at the motel a truck drove up to the entrance and a guy carried five two-and-a-half-gallon jugs up to the balcony overlooking the pool where our rooms were. There was a gallon each of tequila, gin, brandy, vodka, and bourbon.

I scratched my head. "Hugo, that's an awful lot of liquor."

Hugo smiled. "We have a lot of friends that will come and visit us."

The night before we left the jugs were still half full. Since you can't take bulk liquor back to the states, Hugo suggested that we dump the leftover liquor into the pool and go swimming. We all joyfully jumped in the pool. I don't know that you could call splashing each other with open mouths swimming though. The mixture of liquor with a chlorine chaser was like a strange Zombie. The whole group seemed to tire very fast and went to bed early. When we checked out in the morning we were told that during the night three of the porters tried to drown themselves in the pool.

Because we were finally enjoying some success in life, Donna relaxed a little. These were the years that Donna's dreams were starting to come true—the joy of building a family and having fun with friends. There were few tears during these years, God had protected those she loved from disaster several times.

Donna's natural warmth and friendliness enhanced her beauty. Donna was grateful for her life and felt she owed humanity a debt for the life she loved.

Our First Home—1960

The first home we bought was at 2608 East Newton Avenue in Shorewood. It was only two blocks from our flat and Lake Michigan. The house was built in October 1929, the month the Wall Street crash occurred.

The house looked outdated and had been on the market for some time, but the price was right. At first glimpse Donna said, "Looks old and unkempt."

I opened the door. "The reddish carpeting is a little dar . . ."

"Victorian," she said. *Victorian* meant *bad* to Donna.

We were in the dining room. "The wallpaper is . . ."

"Garish."

"We could take out those radiators and . . ."

"Ugly."

"We could knock out that wall in the kitchen and open it . . ."

"Atrocious."

"We could replace the appliances with . . ."

"Hideous."

In the master bedroom, which consisted of two connecting rooms, I tried again. "We could knock out that wall and have a nice big . . ."

"Abominable."

The bathrooms had black and white checkered tile, a standing tub and sink. "We could have a tile man and plumber replace . . ."

"Intolerable."

"Donna, it's only two blocks away from where live now. It's closer to the schools, stores, and the bus line."

"This place is insufferable."

"You want a baby girl. She will need a bedroom and we need a second garage," I reasoned. "You are going to have to get a car. I know you like your work but with another baby you are going to have to give up your job. The price is right and we can't go on paying rent the rest of our lives."

"It's upscale."

"Our family needs a nice home. I've worked it out and I can make it. I know the carpeting is . . ."

"Celery green downstairs and light blue in our bedroom," she finished.

Oh, oh. What's happening here? I tried again. "The kitchen appliances could be . . ."

"General Electric stove for cooking and baking."

"The bathroom fixtures?" I asked.

"Kohler would be very nice."

"I thought you hated this house."

"Humph. A lot my husband knows about women," she said.

Our first home on Newton Avenue in Shorewood, Wisconsin.

It took a lot of work and Donna's excellent taste to turn this house into a beautiful home.

We had just moved in and most of the unpacked boxes were in the basement when we received a telephone call. Marlyn's husband, Brooks, had died at age thirty-six from a heart condition. We dropped everything and headed out to the farm where Marlyn and her five daughters were.

When we returned home after the funeral we discovered that water was backed up to the basement ceiling. There had been a heavy rain and a rag was blocking the drain. After being under water for a few days, our clothes, wedding gifts, photographs, records, nice linens, and other things were destroyed. It took a few months to get everything cleaned up and to start life in our new home.

The Ceiling Comes Down

The only time Donna got really, really angry with me was when she had assigned me the task of removing the alcove, built-in table, benches, and drop ceiling in the kitchen. Before she left to go shopping she warned that I was to keep the swinging door to the dining room closed and that there had better not be any dust outside the kitchen, even

Donna, Jeff, and Greg enjoyed many laughs at our new home.

though she had covered the dining room table with a drop cloth as a precaution.

Our plan was to have the three narrow windows in the alcove replaced with a large bay window. The plastering we were having done by professionals, but Donna decided we could save money by me taking out the wall, table, benches, and drop ceiling.

I easily removed the table and benches and put them in the basement. I then hit the false ceiling with a hammer and pulled a section of the ceiling down. This was a mistake. The whole ceiling gave way and an awful cloud of debris came down from the tile bathroom above. Covered with all this gook, I couldn't see much but I heard heavy objects hitting the floor. I jumped away and escaped into the dining room—with a great cloud of dust following me. The cloud rolled through all the rooms, both downstairs and upstairs, before settling over everything.

Plaster and sawdust were everywhere. It covered the drapes, furniture, carpeting, dishes in the dining room cupboards, bathrooms, and upstairs bedrooms. It took me an hour to shovel two wheel barrels of debris that some lazy worker had dumped into the false ceiling when the house was built.

I knew I was in trouble. More than that; I was in ter-r-r-r-ible trouble. It would not be good for me when neat-nick Donna came home. When I returned from emptying the last load of debris I saw Donna standing in the dining room doorway with her hands on her hips, lips pursed, brow furrowed, and a look that would scare a grizzly bear. This was one of the few times that a bad word came from those lovely lips, plus a string of expletives that ended with, "So, you made a mess anyway."

I tried to explain that it wasn't my fault, but to no avail, the damage was much worse than the excuse.

We never hurled harsh, stinging, or hurtful words at each other. The few times Donna got angry with me, there was always an "I love you" softness in the tone of her voice.

We started cleaning immediately. I did the vacuuming and Donna washed and dusted. Every time she opened another cupboard or drawer I heard another moan. By three o'clock in the morning I had finished the first round of vacuuming the entire house and basement. The curtains were in the washer and the drapes were ready for the cleaners. I was drooping. Shaking her head at me in mild disgust Donna said, "Go to bed." I thought my love life was over forever.

The next day I came home and Donna was happily singing, scraping away at the wallpaper in the dining room, which she had never liked anyway. Because of the mess I had caused, I was indentured. I was now the source of much volunteer labor. I must have lost twenty pounds stripping three layers of wallpaper in the dining room, stairway, hallway, and bedrooms.

A family vacation.

It took Donna a week to get the drapes back, the curtains and bedding washed, and all the rooms back together, lamenting all the while that the house would never be the same.

After all of the rooms were freshly papered or painted and the new kitchen was finished, Donna was very proud of her home.

Let me explain Donna's hands-on-the-hips stance. When a lovely, warm, and friendly, woman feels she needs to be serious with her family—to straighten them out— she uses a different pose so that they know she is serious. Of course, it doesn't always work, because to us Donna looked funny and we would laugh. Also, after stating her case in a very serious tone, we could make one funny remark and Donna would lose her composure and break into laughter.

Occasionally Donna could stir up enough anger to maintain her position, which might include a hard stomping of her foot. When this happened, we bowed to her will, because we loved her.

Taking on the obligation of a maximum mortgage on our house, which needed remodeling, was a challenge, but I also took on the expense of joining the Tripoli Golf Club. This didn't set well with careful spending Donna.

A good athlete in school, Donna would welcome the challenge of learning golf, I rationalized. I bought her a set of golf clubs for her birthday, which she seemed to like. Greg told me later that I almost got one of the clubs wrapped around my neck! But Donna could not stay angry with me for very long. We belonged to the Tripoli Golf Club for eons—and guess who played the most golf and has a flock of golf trophies? Donna Lou.

Donna's Cars

Although we lived only one house away from Prospect Avenue and the bus stop, I didn't like Donna riding the bus to work or walking the three blocks to the drugstore or grocery store (of course Donna could use my car when it was available). Always trying to save money Donna continued to ignore my offer to buy her a car. We had a two-car garage so I finally bought Donna a used car from a fellow agent. I was able to sell Donna on it because it was very cheap. Yellow, however, was not one of Donna's favorite colors and on occasion the car was noisy. She drove it, but she didn't like it.

At this time Emil (the best man at my wedding) was parts manager at a car dealership. He also sold cars part-time. Now that Donna was used to having a car, I knew she would prefer to replace the yellow noisemaker. I asked Emil if he had a good deal on a new car. There was a grass green Plymouth coupe he was having trouble selling because of its color. By trading in the yellow car Emil gave me a good deal on the green Plymouth. I did not like the color, but it was inexpensive and I knew Donna would appreciate that. As her first new car I assumed she would not mind the color.

It was to be her Christmas present. Emil found a wide red ribbon and with a big bow, wrapped it around the car. The green and red (Christmas colors) car was parked in front of our house late Christmas Eve, after Donna had gone to bed. The disliked yellow car was taken away.

Christmas morning Donna looked out the front window and saw the green coupe with the huge red ribbon. She joined the neighbors that were standing outside looking at it, trying to figure out to whom it belonged. Since parking was only allowed on our side of the street it could've belonged to a number of people. Donna called to me, "Don, come look at this strange car with a big ribbon that's in front of our house."

Just about that time one of the onlookers turned a large tag upright so that Donna could see it. "To Donna with love. Don." I gave the keys to a teary-eyed lovely woman underneath the mistletoe.

I was pleased that Donna told everyone how much she loved her new car. Several weeks later, however, I was telling someone over the telephone about her car when Greg overheard me. When I hung up, Greg carefully let me know that Donna detested the green color. "She called it a 'green perversion'," he said.

The New Playboy of the Western World

After having lunch with Emil one day he motioned for me to follow him back into the showroom. There was a deep blue Plymouth convertible, with a white top and white sidewall tires. It was beautiful. It was gorgeous. Emil knew I had always wanted a convertible but driving a fancy car wasn't appropriate for a life insurance agent. Life insurance agents should park a rickety old jalopy in front of their clients' houses, so that they looked like they were starving to death.

Family

Ramona helps us celebrate our 25th-wedding anniversary.

But—my name had been in the newspaper and people knew I was a successful life insurance agent. I was selling more business and corporate insurance now, so . . . maybe?

Oh Lord, I wanted that convertible! I agonized over that car for a month. Emil's employees must have thought I was a statue standing there, looking at it so many times. I could see myself driving it with a big grin on my face and the wind blowing my hair. I knew eyebrows would be raised if I parked the convertible in the agency lot. There were a few Lincolns and Cadillacs—but a classy convertible? With great consternation and hesitation I decided to buy it—but how would I get it approved by Donna? "Why don't you let Greg pick out your new car? He'll get a kick out of it—and he can't help but choose the convertible," suggested Emil.

Every three years, once the depreciation ran out, I bought a new car. I told Donna that when I bought a new car, I would trade in her "green perversion" and she would get my three-year-old. She liked that idea. Greg asked if he could pick out my next new car. "Okay, why not?" I said.

Donna shrugged, perhaps a little too quickly, but at least she would be rid of the green perversion.

It was fun for Emil and me to watch Greg, at age fifteen, wander through the new car lot trying to pick out my next automobile. Once he was in the showroom, he stopped at the convertible and pointed. "That one?"

Emil and I looked at each other in amusement.

"But Greg, Mother will have a fit if I come home with a convertible."

"You said in front of Mom that I could pick out the car—and she didn't object. A promise is a promise," my son said. Well what can a father do? A father must be honor bound and must set an example for his son. Obviously I was cornered and the decision was made for me.

Plus, I had another thing going for me. This coming Saturday was the third year since I had won the Composite Award. Once you win the award, they raise the pole higher, so you have to work much harder and so that it's easier for others to win. I had done quite well this year, and suspected I could hold onto third place. I deserved something I always wanted. Maybe Donna would buy that argument, I thought.

Greg and I drove into the driveway with the convertible top down.

I held my breath when Donna came out. Immediately I could tell it wasn't good because she stood with her hands on her hips.

I'm in trouble.

She looked at me. "What is this? Are you the new playboy of the western world?"

Oh, yes. I'm in real trouble.

"Oh, Mom. Look, isn't it beautiful?" injects Greg.

Family

She is looking at me—like I concocted this whole deal. Keep talking, Greg.

"And Mom, like we said before we left, I got to pick it out all by myself, from all the cars," Greg argued.

Donna is nodding her head like something's rotten in Denmark, and I'm Danish, which is all the worse. Say more, please, Greg. She's not buying the story. She's thinking that I'm in my second childhood. Oh boy, I'm in trouble.

"And, when you drive it, all your friends will be envious of you," Greg added as an afterthought.

Don't overdo it Greg. Donna does not like envious talk.

"And Mom, will you ever look beautiful driving in this gorgeous convertible."

That's better.

"And, Dad deserves something he's always wanted. He works so hard for us."

Much better. How did Greg know that? I'll bet Emil told him.

She looked back at the car and dropped her hands. She's giving in awful easy, I think.

"Well, it is kind of pretty," she said, as I handed her the keys. As she drove around the corner I could see that Donna was accelerating and had a big smile on her face.

It's the Saturday of the agency party. Donna looks beautiful sitting in our shiny new convertible. She wore a thin scarf to protect her hair, but I still drive slowly so as not to disturb her hair, which I knew could be a problem for her in the convertible.

"I know you're doing well, but how will you do in the agency standings?" Donna asks.

"Well, you know it's hard to repeat. But some of my handicap has fallen away. Even though some of the guys submitted a record number of sales last month, I think I have a chance at third place," I answer.

"That's nice. I'm pulling for you."

The busy parking attendants wave us through. It is a beautiful, quiet night, so when I park the car in the University Club parking lot I leave the top down.

Although the Momsen agency and our sub-agencies continue to grow, the number of awards is still the same. Third place is called, and it isn't me. Donna pats me on the leg and smiles that it's okay. Second place is called. Not me. Now I know I'm out. Oh well, I did pretty well and made it to the top in 1954. Donna pats me on the leg again and smiles.

"And the 1957 Composite Award goes to Don Seymour. And how about this, we have a repeat winner."

How the heck did I do that? Everybody is standing and clapping. Donna has her hands to her mouth and her eyes are glassy.

Again everyone is sincere and generous with their praise.

※

After the banquet I get the car while Donna waits for me in the lobby. It has rained and water pours out when I open the car door. Oh, boy. I'm in trouble again. I had towels in the trunk and wipe as much water as I can from Donna's side. I'm going to get an "I told you so." for this.

When Donna sees the car she puts her hands to her face and closes her eyes. "I should have wore my swimming suit underneath my new dress. Oh well," she flops into the still partially wet seat, throws up her hands, and laughs. "Oh well."

I know she's very uncomfortable because she is moving around in the seat. She's wet all the way through, as am I.

"I'm awfully sorry, Donna, to put you through all this," I apologize.

She sighs. "I have to give you, Greg, and Emil credit. You maneuvered this wet car into the family very well."

"You knew?"

"I know everything about my family."

"I thought you gave in awfully easy. How come? Oh, I know." I looked at the silver pitcher she was holding.

"Silly, that's not the reason. My husband deserves something he's always wanted."

"But I have you."

"You deserve something more."

What more does a man deserve?

"You knew about the award again," I say. "They had to have my pitcher to add the second award inscription."

Donna shifts her position on the wet seat. I hear a mucky water sound. "Yes dear," she sighs. "That's how I knew."

Perhaps because of the publicity I received for this award, I am asked to teach insurance at the Milwaukee Vocational and Adult School three nights a week. I found it fun and my course became so popular that they had to give me a large lecture hall. Imagine me, who barely got through high school, teaching a class! I taught there for three years.

A Thousand Violets Full

As I passed by, I noticed Donna was looking at a magazine.

"Look Hon, a recipe for violet jelly. Ever heard of such a thing?"

"Sounds interesting," I said, "I wonder what it tastes like."

Our home was just a few blocks from Lake Michigan and the morning dew must have been perfect, because violets grew profusely in our backyard.

A few weeks later one of Donna's friends stopped over when Donna was in the backyard picking violets.

"Donna, what on earth are you doing? Going into the flower business?"

Donna laughed. "No. I saw a recipe for violet jelly and when I mentioned it to Don, he wondered what it would taste like."

"You must love the guy a lot. It's going to take at least a thousand of those small violets to make a little jelly."

"I guess you might say, I love him a thousand violets full," Donna chuckled.

The Italian Cook

My friend and golfing companion Wally Orlando invited Donna and me to his home to enjoy his mother's Italian cooking. When we first met his mother in the kitchen, we had to duck. There were lines strung back and forth across the kitchen with pasta hanging to dry.

Consiglia Orlando was a superb Italian cook. Her husband, Agabito (Mike), grew the herbs and tomatoes in their garden and made an excellent Port wine. Consiglia took to Donna right off and told Wally, "That is the kind of girl you should marry." From that time on Donna and Consiglia were close friends. Donna learned the rudiments of Southern Italian cooking and Consiglia enjoyed teaching her.

Wally and I (martini drinkers) were served olives and cheese snacks in the living room while Mike was drawing wine from the keg in the basement, and Donna and Consiglia were in the kitchen.

Dinner started with an excellent light spinach and trout soup. Then Mike poured his superb white wine. After the martinis the light-tasting wine was potent. I learned I had to watch it. Italian bread and a green vegetable accompanied a large bowl of spaghetti and delicious meatballs. A lemon-lime pie was served for dessert, and lastly, a delicious crisp salad. Salad last? This surprised Donna but made sense when it was explained that the oil and vinegar aided digestion. We were invited there many times. Not just by Wally but by his mother. Donna had them over at our home a few times, too.

One day I walked into our kitchen and almost had my head removed as a line caught my neck and splashed wet spaghetti up my face and across my glasses. Donna laughed and thought I looked rather funny.

With Consiglia's instruction Donna became an excellent Italian cook, preparing everything from scratch. The Seymour family, and guests too, always looked forward to dinner when the aroma of Donna's

Family

Donna's parents, Marvin and Edna Arneson, celebrate their 40th wedding anniversary in Mt. Horeb (left to right): Donna, Hilton, father Marvin, Dale, Marlyn, mother Edna, and Ramona.

spaghetti sauce came from the kitchen. Donna loved to cook for her family. The least look of disappointment on any one of our faces hurt her; needless to say it seldom happened.

A Royal Lineage

Since I was the only surviving male Seymour I took an interest in my family name. Seymour seemed English, so I had a top heraldic firm in London do a family search. They came back for more information. Scouring the branches of the family in Minneapolis, I answered as many questions as possible.

A month later a letter arrived in the mail from London. "Congratulations," it said, "we have traced your family to English Prime Minister Lord Seymour and Henry VIII's wife Ann Seymour (whom Henry had beheaded). Therefore you have a right to the Seymour coat of arms, royal crown above, and sepulchre alongside."

I ordered and received the plastic heraldic shield, royal crown and

89

sepulchre; which I then hung above our fireplace. At our Christmas party, as each couple came in, I led them to the fireplace and explained how I was from royal blood. Donna heard me in passing, poked me in the ribs, and whispered, "Aren't you overdoing it a little? These people don't want to hear all your grandiose." She was right of course, so I toned it down—a little. I still led all the newcomers to the fireplace, where of course, they would ask about the grand heraldic things. I then explained they were in a house of royalty.

A few weeks later I received a call from a great aunt in Cleveland, whom I didn't know existed. She was a baby when our family emigrated from Denmark. She wanted to talk to the last male Seymour. I told her all about my family and also about the Seymour's heraldic background. I even described the coat of arms hanging above the fireplace. Surprisingly, my aunt made no comment.

She asked about my wife. I told her of the Arnesons, and again brought the conversation back to our royal lineage. She still did not comment.

She asked about my children. I told her—but I finally asked why she wasn't interested in our coat of arms. There was long silence on the phone, then quietly she said, "Donnie, when we came to America, your grandfather changed our name from Thorup to the more English name of Seymour." We had a good laugh at that (at least I think I did). I thanked her for the information and the enjoyable conversation.

Oh boy, I'm in trouble again.

When I told Donna she burst out laughing. "Now, aren't you glad I suggested you tone it down?"

"I don't think I overdid it," I replied.

"Overdid it!" she said. "I'm surprised you didn't buy an ermine cape and have people kiss your ring finger."

Am I ever glad she didn't give me that idea before!

"So," she laughed, "how are you going to tell all your loyal subjects that you're only a Thorup?"

"Well, can't I just let this whole thing fade away?"

"Fine by me." By now Donna was laughing so hard she had tears in her eyes. "But what if your royal subjects decide to have a royal crowning ceremony for you at Westminster Abbey?"

Did she really have to go into hysterics about this whole thing?

A nice picture was placed over the fireplace and my objects of royalty were deeply hidden in the basement. (Just in case.)

Martini Massacre At the Farm

As we were packing the car to visit her parents for the weekend I told Donna, "I'm bringing martini makings along."

"Don't you dare," she warned.

"What's the problem? Did they have some drunks back in the family?"

"I don't know," Donna replied. "It's just a no-no passed down from my grandparents."

I hid martini makings in the car to take out to the farm.

At the farm, the kitchen was a warm, wonderful smelling and fun place. Although crowded, the women allowed the men in the kitchen while they prepared the food. Usually we sat on the long window seat, watching, talking, and nibbling Norwegian-German snacks and cheese made from the farm milk.

It was time. I went out to the car and brought in a bag containing a bottle of gin, vermouth, and olives. I pushed aside a few plates of goodies on the kitchen table The women watched in amazement as I opened the door of the refrigerator, took out an ice cube tray, put ice in a glass, and proceeded to make myself a martini—right there in front of God and everyone.

There was silence. The clinking of pans and dishes was no longer heard. The only sound was ice tinkling in my glass. Donna came over, looked at the martini things, and then at me. She shook her head, threw up her hands, rolled her eyes back, and backed off. She had to let everyone know that she had had no part in this desecration, so that she and her descendants (except me) would still be welcome to Arneson clan gatherings. Everyone watched as I put the ingredients together carefully, so as not to bruise them. I had crossed over the line. Like the

The Martini Gang: (couples l to r): Bill and Ramona (Arneson) Suffern, Rick and Marlyn (Arneson) Grinde, Don and Donna Seymour, Dale and Eleanor Arneson, Hilton Arneson.

signers of the Declaration of Independence, I may be sacrificing all for a martini. Either the revolution had begun or I would forever be banished from the Arneson kingdom.

I looked to the men for a fellow revolutionary. Bill, Ramona's husband, shrugged his shoulders, smiled, and said, "What the heck? I'll have one."

That done, Rick, Marlyn's husband, looked down, turned his head from side to side and said, "Might as well."

Dale said, "Well, why not? Count me in."

Hilton laughed and said, "Well, if everyone else is having one, I'll have one, too."

The revolution begun, we raised our glasses in a silent toast. I sighed, sat down and looked around. The house didn't shake, the windows didn't rattle and the sun didn't go out. Everything seemed perfectly normal—except for Dad—who was standing in the doorway. Oh, oh. No turning back now. I had to face the music. I was going to be banished anyway, so I might as well be polite. "Would you like a martini, Dad?" I asked.

"Well, maybe just a small one," he answered.

I almost fell off my seat.

Watching Dad with his martini, I scratched my head. Now what the heck was that all about?

Then, the girls wanted one. These tea-totaling rummies are going to run me out of gin.

A Daughter is Born

On May 3, 1961, Jean Ann Seymour was born. I was happy to have a daughter. I had another Donna. But—our joy was not to last. Jean Ann's lungs were filled with fibrosis and her breathing was impaired. An hour later Jean Ann was gone. I let out a moan. In her hospital bed Donna turned to her pillow and started to cry.

※

Back home from the hospital, Donna was very quiet, not her normal, cheerful self. A few nights later the boys and I sat at the kitchen table. Donna brought over a hot casserole, set it down hard on the table and said, "I can't stand this any more. I want to get out of here." She was crying and waving her arms hysterically. I didn't know what was happening. I stood up and tried to hold her, to comfort her. She flayed her arms. She was screaming and hit the wall with her hand. I couldn't hold her any tighter without hurting her. Donna became more hysterical. I let go of her arm and slapped her—I wanted her to stop so that she didn't hurt herself. She did stop. Deathly still, she glared at me for a minute, turned and walked upstairs. The boys had quietly watched all this.

I sat down at the table and put my head in my hands. I had never felt so low. I had never hit or abused Donna in any way. Even though

I thought the slap was necessary, I was overcome by tremendous guilt. I had hit the most precious wife a man ever had. Oh Lord, what have I done? The kids picked at their food. Later Greg went into the basement and Jeff went to play with his toys.

As I was cleaning up the dishes Donna appeared in the dining room doorway. She had a small suitcase hanging from her hand.

"I'm leaving," she said quietly.

I felt a terrible sinking feeling in my stomach. Oh God, I felt awful. Gently I asked, "Where are you going?"

"I don't know. Just away."

Quietly I asked, "When will you be back?"

"I don't know . . . if I will."

Tears came to my eyes. "Oh Donna, please. I'm so very sorry I hit you. I love you so much. Please don't do this."

She ignored my plea and coldly said, "I have to go."

As she walked past me I wanted to reach out and restrain her, but I didn't dare lay a hand on her. I felt immobile. A cold chill had come up my back and enveloped my head. Donna went out the back door, got into her car and quietly drove off. Greg came up from the basement and saw her leave.

Our wonderful world had come to an end. I didn't know what to do. I sat there with my head in my hands, tears streaming down my face. Jeff came over and questioningly ran his finger down the tears on my face. Greg put his head on my shoulder and said, "Mom will be okay Dad. You'll see."

In a daze I cleaned up the kitchen and then sat quietly in a living room chair. The words "I hit my wife" rang through my head again and again. I tried to console myself by believing I had to do it before she hurt herself, but it didn't help.

Finally, I saw Greg take Jeff's hand and lead him up to bed. I went up to help.

I wandered around the house all night, thinking of all the things that could happen to Donna. I lay down in my clothes a number of

Family

times, but couldn't sleep. Wandering the house, I looked out the windows, praying car lights would appear in our driveway. They didn't.

In the morning I made breakfast for the boys. I called my secretary and told her to cancel whatever insurance appointments were scheduled for that day and evening.

It was nine o'clock in the morning—still no Donna. Should I call the police? No, I can't do that. If they picked up Donna and forced her to come home, it would just make matters worse. What should I do? Maybe she has just gone to the farm. She had to come back on her own; She would, especially for the boys. She would never abandon them.

I fixed the kids lunch and they quietly moved away again.

I sat and put my head in my hands. What had I done to their mother? Please Lord, let her forgive me.

More hours of watching. The lack of sleep was dragging me down. Unable to keep my head up, I went to lay on our bed and fell into a deep sleep. A few hours later I awoke with a start. I had to make dinner for the kids.

I went downstairs and was about to enter the kitchen when I saw Donna at the sink scraping carrots. She didn't look up. I don't know if she knew I was there. I backed away into the dining room to get a hold of myself. I was ready to bawl my head off with relief. Oh Lord, what do I do? What do I say? Having gotten control, I walked into the kitchen. I said, "Hi."

"Hi," Donna replied quietly, without looking up.

I set the table. She automatically moved aside when I needed to get the knives and forks, but still Donna would not look at me. Dinner was small talk with the kids, but to Donna it was as if I wasn't there.

She stood and said, "I'm tired. I'm going up to bed."

The kids went back to their things and I cleaned up. Then it occurred to me, she had seen an attorney and is going to divorce me. *Oh God what a fool I am. What have I done?*

I sat in the living room, staring straight-ahead and wondering how I could ever take that slap back. How could I bring our marriage back to the way it was? Even if she forgave me, that slap would always stand between us. Our marriage could never be the same. I had ruined a beautiful marriage.

I helped the kids to bed and went back to the same chair in the living room. I went over and over in my mind how I could make things right again. It was late. Should I get a pillow and blanket and sleep down here? Should I sleep in the guest bedroom or go upstairs to our bed? Would she object if I was in bed with her? Maybe she will wake and talk to me and I can say something.

I went up, took my shower, and quietly crawled into my side of our side-by-side twin beds with common covers. I lay facing away from her, listening for some sound. Suddenly a hand gently tugged at my arm and I rolled onto my back. She came over, lifted my arm around her, and lay her head on my chest.

With a great intake of breath, she sobbed, "Oh Don, can you ever forgive me? I've failed you and Jean Ann, too. There can never be a daughter. Oh Don, I'm so sorry. Please forgive me. Please, Don. Don't stop loving me."

Oh, for heaven's sake! Tears filled my eyes. How could I ever stop loving her?

I would have loved to watch Donna raise a daughter; and we often wondered how Jean Ann would have changed our lives. Imagine the joy of another Donna.

I discovered later that cystic fibrosis is inherited. The chance of both the man and woman in a Caucasian couple being carriers is 500 to one. Each of their children has a one in four chance of being born with cystic fibrosis. Our daughter, Jean Ann, was one in three. Statistics also said that if one daughter was born with cystic fibrosis, chances were good that other daughters would, too.

I also learned that carriers have a tendency to lung infections and emphysema, and that carriers have trouble absorbing fats, as I do.

Family

To Donna

Darling, for your birthday
    Let me send my treasure
        Though it lacks in value
            It's oh so great in measure.
For things like this are priceless
    And grow more through the years,
        They find each day a newness
            Withstanding time and tears.
It's not tied up in ribbons
    Of every lace and hue
        It's wrapped up in my heart
            It's just my love for you.
                — Don

Our Sons

When Jeff was five a drunk driver hit Donna's car broadside. We almost lost Jeff when his head hit the cigarette lighter in Donna's car. The only thing that probably saved him was the fact it was a spring-out lighter. Sporting a golf ball sized bump on his head and a black eye, Jeff garnered all the attention Christmas 1961.

❦

Donna finally agreed to give up her job at the beauty salon. Now she could take the kids out to the club for swimming meets, play women's golf, and plan more parties and dinners for our friends and my clients. She could also do the crafts she enjoyed.

Donna mothered some of Greg's friends, through Sunday school, Cub Scouts, Grey Y, Boy Scouts, and Shorewood's football and basketball teams. Our surrogate family members were: Cam Byrnes, Larry Cotter, Steve Curro, Dallas Lillich, Mike Malone, Kevin McDermott, and George Murphy—to name those I remember. Donna and I also helped organize and were the first chairpersons of Shorewood High's Greyhound Backers.

I once said to Donna, "I don't recall all these guys being born here, but they must be family because they live, eat, and sometimes sleep here." Our home became a rallying ground. The boys liked Donna, as she was always baking for them, driving them around, or listening to their problems. She was a surrogate mother of sorts. On the other hand, they knew if they messed up Donna's house they were in trouble. They used to say behind her back that Donna was either the witch of the east or west, depending on their deportment. For a number of years the nickname "witch" stuck, but in a very affectionate way.

I too was involved with the boys. I was in scouting for forty years, as a cub master, scoutmaster, Northeast Scout Commissioner and a leader in the Scouters of Missouri Synod.

Stick Picking Time

Donna did not tolerate either one of her sons not toeing the line for very long. When she grew up on the farm, she was made to toe the line by having a stick applied to her up in the granary. When our sons strayed too far from their expected performance, Donna insisted that I apply a stick to them in the basement.

When I came upstairs, Donna would give me that "See you can do it" look. I never let on that once I let Jeff put a comic book in his pants or that once he wore his heavy snow pants.

I tried to put off the physical discipline as long as possible because I wasn't good at it. But, when I came home and found Donna standing with her hands on her hips and staring at me without saying a word, I knew I'd run out of time with one of the kids.

I would send the culprit down to the woodworking bin to select a stick. He was to call me when ready and I would go down and do the terrible deed. I let him stay in the basement for an hour suffering his stick decision and then I'd go down to see what the selection problem was. Sometimes they tried to get away with a small twig, so I would let them work on their decision for another hour. Even with the right stick, I could not hit them very hard. They usually howled a great deal louder than the application justified. Stick picking for one of the kids bothered both kids, so we got a two for one effect.

This is how the scenario usually went, with the culprit bent over my knees in the basement.

Swish-switch.

Upstairs Donna smirks to herself (he finally got to do it—meaning me).

Swish-switch. The noise was more from the swish of the air passing by the wimpy stick than the force of my swing.

"Ouell," Greg squeals.

Mrs. hands-on-hips upstairs in the kitchen thinks to herself, Greg had it coming.

Swish-switch.

"Ouell."

Hope he doesn't have to do this too often, she says to herself.

Now Greg starts his song, "Yowell-yow—youell."

Not too fast now, I think. He must work this song up slowly to be convincing.

Swish-switch.

"Yow—youell."

Greg will remember next time, she is thinking.

Swish-switch.

"Yow—youell."

Don, don't you overdo it, she thinks.

Swish-switch.

"Yow—youell."

Now Don, don't you hurt him. Donna is getting angry.

Swish-switch.

"Yow—youell—yowell." Greg is building up to a crescendo.

This has to be timed just right, I think.

Don, stop hurting my boy. Donna is starting to seethe.

"Yow—youell-yowell-yow—youell."

Don! Donna screams to herself.

Swish-switch.

"Yowel-yow."

Now Donna's fists are clenched and her eyes are blazing. Don, you just wait. I'll fix you for hitting my son.

Swish-switch.

Greg finishes his operetta in a sympathetic whimper. A very nice performance.

I admit there were a few times when there was the need to apply a little harder. But Greg is a good kid, a straight arrow. Just having to pick out the stick and having his father going through the motions of spanking him was usually enough discipline to keep him in line.

I come upstairs to the kitchen.

Peeling potatoes with angry thrusts, Donna won't even look at me. I hurt her child and now I'm going to suffer for it. Conversation at dinner is polite, but she is seething at me underneath.

Of course, at the dinner table, Greg is moving his fanny around on the chair to assure the powers-that-be that the punishment was adequate. He can tell how good it appeared by how much Donna's eyes are seething at me.

Everything is washed and put away (I always dry the dishes) and I hear Donna at the sewing machine upstairs. She roughly tears out seams and sews when she seethes.

Later she comes down to check on her domain. Mrs. Hands-on-hips turns off every light but mine. Still not looking at me, she goes up to bed without giving me my good-night kiss. I'm in the doghouse. I watch TV or read. (I'm a night person and stay up late. She is a morning person and gets up early.)

In bed, hands clasped under my head, I can't sleep. Donna has her back to me. Is she sleeping? She doesn't move. After awhile, she turns halfway, considering her next move. Having decided, she comes over, lifts my arm up and down around her, places her arm across my chest and her lovely self against me. She pulls my head to her, kisses me, snuggles down, and then says softly, "You didn't have to hit him so hard or so often."

Family

Donna, Greg and Jeff. 1967

If she believes her son's performance, that woman could be sold the Brooklyn Bridge.

A Cab Driver Flies Our Plane

It's April 1965. Four couples: Emil and Betty Ewald, Joe and Dedee Austrup, Dr. John Becker and his wife, and Donna and me decide to vacation in Puerto Rico. Our reservations are at the Americana Hotel on the beach. While there, we decide to take a small airplane ride around the islands. The plane only holds two couples When we board the plane with Betty and Emil, the pilot is reading something. Emil jokingly says, "He's probably reading the flying instructions."

Joking in return, the middle-aged pilot with a slightly gray beard says, "Got to find out how to fly this thing." (He was joking, of course.)

Just before he receives his take-off instructions, the pilot again looks at the booklet. Donna asks, "Is this thing hard to fly?"

"Nah," the pilot responds. "I'm a former New York cab driver. If you can drive a cab in New York, you can drive anything."

Emil and I look at each other and frown. That was not reassuring.

He gets the plane off the ground with a little stray and wing wiggle. "See," he says, with what seems to me a sigh of relief, "nothing to it." As he flies us around the island and points out the sights, we relax a little. When he starts to head back to the airfield the pilot takes the booklet out of the glove compartment, looks at it, nods and with a shrug puts it back. A few minutes later he takes it out again, reads something, frowns and puts it back. He's starting to land the plane and our hands are now tightening on the armrests. He hits the runway so hard we think the wheels are going to come off. The plane is hopping down the runway with a fence looming in the distance. We stop just short of the fence. The pilot lets out a deep sigh. He turns and smiles at us, "See, nothing to it."

On the ground we stagger away from the worst experience of our lives.

In the airline office, after we get our breath back, Emil is very upset.

He asks the guy who scheduled us on the flight, "Does that pilot know how to fly?"

"Oh sure," he assures us. "He's just having a little fun with you." He does not say this very convincingly.

"But he almost took the undercarriage off that plane," says Emil exasperatingly.

He turns a little white and says, "Yeah, but that plane is pretty sturdy."

"But he's not allowed to do that."

He falters, "Well, I know. But pilots are hard to get." That made us feel good.

Emil asks, "Are you sure that guy has a pilot's license?"

He pales a little. "Oh sure, he has to have," he replies. Then he adds brightly, "Besides, he was a New York cabby . . ."

And we all repeat along with him, ". . . if you can drive a cab in New York, you can drive anything."

We shake our heads and walk away.

Betty asks, "Do you think that really could have been a put-on?"

Looking back at the office Donna says, "I don't think so. That guy looked a little white and his smile faded a little too fast. Plus when we left, he rushed away to some place pretty fast too."

Donna's Dresses

Donna and I disagreed about the length of her skirts and dresses. As a rule, I don't like short dresses or skirts and Donna didn't need to wear short things to look feminine, but I always felt her hems were too long. Modest Donna, however, stuck to her guns.

Whenever Donna showed me a new dress and I didn't think it was right for her, I would naturally say, "It's beautiful." If I said it was "very nice" she knew what I meant and, in a huff, back it went.

Even if Donna came home with a dress that was down to her ankles and I didn't think it did justice to her lovely legs, I had better say, "It's beautiful," and with the proper amount of enthusiasm. If I didn't she would roll her eyes back and throw up her hands in a huff, like I didn't know anything.

Why did she ask me? I was never able to figure that one out.

Donna made many of her clothes and if she did buy clothing, she often altered it. It had to be exactly right (I suspect something of Donna's handiwork had to be in everything). Her cousin Betty Collins said of Donna, "She always dressed simple but elegant."

The Yak

I came home one day and Donna has her hands on her hips.

What did I do now?

"I thought you were going to see to it that your son (meaning Greg) was going to get a haircut. He looks like a yak." *Whatever that is.*

I responded, "I gave him the money and told him to."

"Well, he still looks like a yak," she says.

"Greg," I call down to the rec room. "I want to talk to you." He comes up.

"Yeah, Dad?"

"I thought you were going to get a haircut."

"Well," he stammers, "it's not quite long enough yet. Thought I'd save you some money."

From the genes of his penny-pinching mother.

"Tomorrow you get a haircut."

"Dad, we should wait a few more days. It's not long enough to trip over and hurt myself."

Now he's going to save us medical bills.

The next day Donna has had enough and off they go to the barber.

I come home and it looks like the barber used the wrong bowl to trim. Now Greg looks like a pruned bush. "That's a haircut!"

"Looks kinda cute, don't you think?" says Mrs. hands-on the-hips.

"You like that haircut?" I ask incredulously.

"Well dear, it isn't what I like. But as Greg said, we don't want him looking different from the rest of the gang."

Family

I hadn't seen the gang for a few days so I didn't know what they looked like. Greg got to her. And I'll bet we're going to be blamed for setting another crazy hairstyle.

Donna's Friends

Donna took on her friends' problems as sincerely as she did her own. Her friends felt Donna would feel slighted if they didn't call her if they needed help or advice. They said it was always a pleasure talking to Donna. She made them feel good because she made them laugh and be joyful.

When they felt down, blue, or bored they called Donna.

When bad things happened, they called Donna.

Donna always wanted to help make a friend's day better.

Betty Collins said of Donna, "She wasn't just my cousin, she was my joyful friend."

These were joyful years when Donna knew she was winning the game of life. Warmth and friendliness were natural to Donna and she was becoming a lovelier woman. She needed to share and help others feel joy in their lives, too. It was a way Donna could show gratitude for her life, which had become ever more precious to her. It was all so wonderful; she prayed that it would continue.

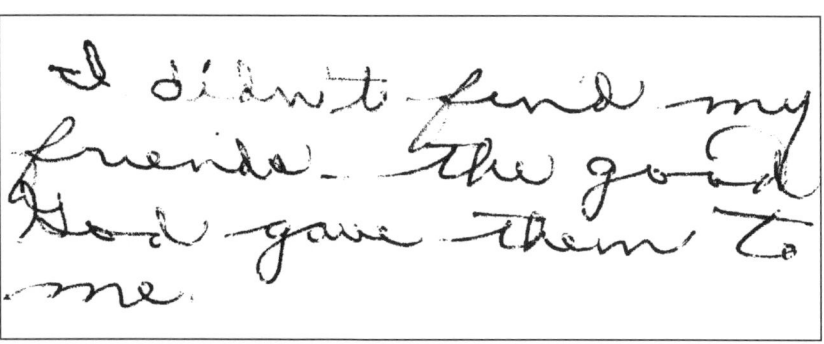

I found this note in Donna's papers. It reads:
"I didn't find my friends—the good God gave them to me."

That Christmas we bought Jeff a Kidalac (riding pedal car). Greg and I decided to build him a four-by-six-foot garage for the car. It took us three weeks of nights to design and build it. We told Jeff the garage was for garden things.

It was cold outside on Christmas but when that kid saw his new car, he wanted to go outside immediately. Realizing the new building was for him, he pedaled his car into the new garage and slammed the doors behind him. Didn't even say thank you. Greg and I looked at each other and shrugged. Jeffy strikes again.

SECTION TWO
The Research

The Tiki

The same four couples we went to Puerto Rico with decided to vacation together in Maui, Hawaii. We stayed at the Kaanapali Beach Hotel.

We have returned from an outrigger trip in the ocean and are sitting in the picturesque Shipwreck bar having cocktails. As Donna looks at the man-sized Tikis (woodcarvings) around the hotel she laughingly suggests that the men in our group could make Tikis that look just as good as the natives'. Joe says, "Sure, we could have a Tiki carving contest when we get back home."

Personally I thought he had had a little too much to drink, but rather than spoil their fun, I say nothing. They'll forget it before we return home, I think.

After we return home, Donna insists that I phone Joe. *Nothing gets by this lady.*

"Joe, Donna wants to know about the Tiki contest."

"Oh yeah, why don't you be chairman?"

Sure. Why did I know this would happen when Donna got involved?

"Okay, I'll call a lumber company and have a block of wood dropped off at each of our homes," I say.

"Good idea, looking forward to it." Click. *Wait until he sees.*

I call a lumber company and ask if they have a log about five feet long and a foot around. They do have a twenty-foot piece of redwood. I ask them to cut it into four five-foot pieces and drop one section on the front lawn of our homes.

A day later my block arrives. It is so heavy it creates a hole six inches deep in the lawn where it is dropped. It must weigh four hundred pounds.

Donna looks at it and gives it a nudge. It doesn't move. "What are you going to do with it?"

"Tiki."

"Oh." She brightens up. "I forgot. Looks kind of heavy."

I try to lift one end. No way. It takes a dolly, Greg, and four of the football gang to get the wood on my workbench in the basement. I wonder how the other Tiki guys are making out.

Using a small black Tiki I brought back as a souvenir as model, I draw some lines and start chopping. The axe doesn't make a dent. Donna stands there with a smirk on her face. "Kinda tough, huh?"

"Out of here while I create my artistic design," I say.

"You're going to ruin your axe."

"Out. Out." She leaves, shaking her head. Why is she shaking her head at me for, this wasn't my idea.

I go out and buy a big, sharp one-sided axe and a sledge. The house shakes at every smash of the sledge on the back of the axe. I am finally making a dent. Seymour is going to make this thing if it kills him.

Donna comes down. "What's going on down here? All the dishes are shaking in the cabinets."

"Artist at work."

"How long will this go on?"

"Art takes time."

"Will the house survive?" She has a point. The chopping is loosening my teeth.

I purchase a blade that cuts metal for my overhead saw and start cutting away at the wood. The saw binds time and again and the smoke from the resistance rises in the house. She comes down. "Should I call the fire department?"

This wasn't my idea and now she's a smarty-pants about it.

It took several blades but I reduce the weight considerably—and the wood was drying out. I still had a lot of chopping to do. It went on for months, much to the consternation of the lady upstairs who jumped at every hit.

I'll bet she rues the day she got involved.

Donna is watching me, again. "Sweetheart," she says with concern. "I know you mean well, but why don't you give it up? You're going to ruin your back."

I already have. I was hobbling and my love life was suffering, but I was undaunted. When a Seymour says he is going to do something, he does it.

I was almost finished when a deep two-inch wide crack formed down the center of the wood, through the Tiki's right eye from top to bottom. It looked awful.

Don's Tiki creation.

Donna inquires, "What are you going to do with that thing when it is done?"

"Put it out in the garden."

"It'll scare the birds away," she says with a smirk.

It took six months from start to disastrous finish. It didn't look bad, except for the two-inch crack down the face.

I buried some concrete blocks in the garden to set it on and was in the process of looking for help to take it out to the garden when the Mrs. asks, "Where are you going with that thing?"

"Out in the garden where I made that pedestal."

"No, you don't. That's a work of art. You're not putting that Tiki outside. It goes in the family room."

Work of art? Will wonders never cease?

Donna invites the Maui couples to see the Tiki her husband hath created. Everybody agrees it looks like a Tiki—except for that horrible crack. Betty says that Emil occasionally tried to make some dents in his, and John's block is still half-buried in his front lawn. He had heard how hard and heavy the wood was before attempting to move it.

Joe is ready to display his Tiki, so the Maui gang is invited to see it. At his home Joe slowly pulls away a draped sheet to expose his wondrous creation. The place erupts in laughter. The thing is all askew, arms and legs going every which way, one eye lower than the other, the weight so unbalanced Joe had a stick under one corner to hold it up.

When the laughing subsides, Joe scratches his head and, a little embarrassed, asks Donna (now she's the expert), "Don't you think it has a kind of character about it? Donna, what do you really think? Doesn't it kinda have something about it?"

Donna can't stop laughing. She points at the monstrosity. "Oh Joe, I'm sorry. I'd like to say something nice but a Tiki is supposed to be a serious god, a religious icon, and that thing . . ." She's bending over and holding her sides, ". . . that thing is funny—grotesque."

Now everyone in the room is howling, including Joe. Joe's wife, Dedee, who must have expressed her opinion about the monstrosity before we came, was laughing so hard she had tears in her eyes.

The next time we visited their house Donna quietly asked Dedee, "Where is the Tiki?"

Muffling laughter Dedee said, "Well, after putting all of that work into it, Joe thought there must be a place for it, so . . ."

Joe heard the question and pointed at the fireplace, where two large black lumps were sitting at either end of Joe's very large fireplace. "I cut it in half but the damned thing burns like iron. Been trying to burn them for months. I think the Tiki gods are plaguing me."

I wouldn't be a bit surprised. That malformation of a thing was enough to bring tears to the eyes of the gods.

The Seymour Tiki, however, slowly dried out and the crack is barely visible today. Word got around, and our Tiki was borrowed for parties at schools, private homes, and at our club. Donna said we even had offers from people wanting to buy it.

I said, "Why don't you sell that thing?"

"Sell my husband's Tiki? Not on your life."

The Stereo Carnage

At Christmas Greg declares, "All my friends have stereos and I would like one." (All? Hmm. I'll bet—but what do we know?) He picks one out and we give it to him for Christmas. It is probably higher in decibels than anyone else's. We present it to him with the warning that we don't want to be blown out of our house. The night after Christmas Donna and I return home from a cocktail party. Our house is jiggling, as if we are experiencing a minor earthquake. When we open the door the noise is deafening. I rush downstairs and shout at Greg to turn the stereo down.

He puts his hand to his ear and shouts something back like, "I can't hear you."

I go over and pull the plug.

"I thought I told you to keep that thing down."

"I thought you meant when you were not here." That kid's smart. He can really twist things around.

Upon inspection we see that the dining room window is cracked.

Celebrating our twenty-first wedding anniversary at the Hidel House Motel in Green Lake, Wisconsin.

There is a long crack in the living room ceiling and five of Donna's prize wine goblets in the dining room cabinet are in shatters. If that noise had risen two more decibels the house would have collapsed into a pile of rubble.

I said to Donna, "That's it. That uproar box goes."

"Now Don, you can't take the boy's music away."

"Music?" Her precious house is in a shambles! If she had been home when it had happened and then I had come home from work, she would have had her hands on her hips telling me what "my" son had done to "her" house. And somehow I would've been responsible and I would have to go downstairs and get rid of that terrible thing that had invaded our lives.

Occasionally our boys would get into more than average trouble and make Donna and me irritable. A few times this would cause Donna and I to be toe-to-toe hollering at each other about which one of us had given the boys the bad genes and was therefore at fault. Suddenly, though, we would stop in unison and burst out laughing.

Smoking

In 1972 Donna smoked cigarettes and I smoked a pipe. Neither of us were heavy smokers. About this time several acquaintances died from throat and lung cancer and newspapers began to show startling statistics about the harmful effect of smoking tobacco. I quit smoking my pipe and hoped Donna would quit, too. She wanted to quit smoking, and actually stopped twice, but was having a difficult time with women smoking at the club. For a while Donna became a closet smoker, which I knew. I didn't want to embarrass her by confronting her, but neither did I want to lose her. I remember saying to Donna very seriously, "Donna, do you think it's fair for you to jeopardize your health and our marriage by smoking?" She had never thought of it like that, her marriage was very important to her. She never smoked again.

Jeff's Motor Scooter

Jeff finally wheedles a motor scooter out of us, because "everybody has one."

A few nights later I come home, just as Jeff walks in looking like he tangled with a wildcat. His face is bruised, his clothes are torn, his elbow is skinned, and he's limping badly.

Donna is on her knees looking at his wounds. She is murmuring soft soothing words to her fifteen-year-old big hunk of a baby. I am not amused. The kid could have killed himself.

"Okay son, let's hear it."

"Well, Dad, we were riding up the railroad tracks."

"Railroad tracks on a motor scoter?" I holler

"Well, Dad, everybody does it."

"You mean Mr. Gillick at the bike store, old Mrs. Hardy up the block, and Pastor Brandt ride motor scooters down the railroad tracks?"

"Well, almost everybody." he says.

"Where's the scooter?"

"I couldn't drag it all the way home."

Donna intervenes. "Now don't pick on my son. (Now he's her son.) He needs to go to a doctor. His foot is really bad."

The doctor does his best to get the swelling down but the foot is never going to be the same. He's going to suffer for a long time. Surely he learned a lesson this time—the hard way.

A few days later, the scooter is fixed and her baby is running the railroad tracks again.

Greg's Car

After months of wheedling and maneuvering, Greg gets his driver's license and after more wheedling and maneuvering he gets a little blue car. Driving precautions are carefully reviewed, over and over again. Two days later I come home and Greg is sitting at the kitchen table looking very dejected, which is the best way to get sympathy on your side before sharing bad news.

I didn't see the car outside and Greg is looking dejected. Hmm. It doesn't take a fortuneteller to figure this out. "Where's the car?" I inquire.

"It wasn't my fault." *They always start out that way.*

"You had an accident?"

He nods.

"Are you okay?" He looks okay. "And it wasn't your fault?"

He nods.

"Anyone hurt?"

He shakes his head.

"How is the car?"

"Well, Dad, you see, err . . . it . . . um, it doesn't quite look the same."

I'll bet it's totaled.

When Donna comes in, I'm going to talk to her about the genes she gave her son.

We Build A Company

Through a strange set of circumstances, I drifted away from life insurance after twenty years. When I was active in the Jaycees, I had befriended a new Jaycee, Don Kunkel. Don had no family, so he adopted me as his mentor. I encouraged him to go to college to earn a degree, which he did.

Don graduated with a degree in Earth Sciences and became the lone year-round employee of Bernard Domagalla, who had a pond and lake chemical spraying business to control aquatic weed and algae; which was in it's infancy.

It was discovered that green algae did not grow in the water around copper mines, so copper sulfate was dumped in algae-ridden lakes to control algae. The problem was, the algae precipitated out, accumulated in the lake bottom, killed off the fish food chain and resulted in greater algae blooms. Domagalla received a patent by combining the copper with monoethanalamine to keep the copper from precipitating out. Using much less copper it was safer for the fish. He received approval for fish application from the Department of Natural Resources.

Domagalla soon died and his sister was not able to sell the company. The only saleable asset was the patent that would expire in two years. His sister offered the patent and business to Don Kunkel for two thousand dollars.

Having no money or business expertise, Don came to me. I sponsored the two thousand dollars and put my name on a small bank loan to get the business going. We named the business Marine Biochemists, Inc. Don loved the lab work and attempted to create an improved product and patent. But the capital needed to run the business was made by spraying lakes and ponds during the few summer months, when the water was warm enough for the weeds and algae to grow—not by working in the lab. The patent wasn't much good if you didn't sell enough chemical to make it pay and we weren't selling much chemical. With my name on more bank loans I was forced to get involved. I started to fly around the country trying to sell an unknown chemical to chemical distributors.

With Don's chemical background and Domagalla's research papers, a patent attorney, and my credit, we were able to obtain an improved patent. But Don's lack of business skills kept the company in serious financial trouble. The business was close to bankruptcy, so I spent less time in insurance and more time selling chemical.

While I sold, Don uncovered new uses for the algaecide and contributed to the development of a new algaecide and a water-weed control patent.

This is Her Man

When I returned home from a week's travel, Donna and the kids would meet me at the airport. Not normally demonstrative, Donna would put her arms around me and kiss me in front of the whole crowd. Never mind who was watching. I was her man and she was going to let me know right then and there that she missed me and loved me. I looked forward to her greetings—they made up for the lonely hours and days I spent without her.

Greg Goes To College

Upon graduating from Shorewood High School, Greg considered attending The Frank Lloyd Wright School of Architecture. He was, however, concerned that it was too stuffy for him, since formal attire was required each night for dinner.

Greg had been a good football lineman at Shorewood, and was offered a football scholarship from the University of Platteville—Wisconsin. Donna and I expressed our desire that he attend the Wright School of Architecture—but he chose Platteville instead.

Greg spent two semesters at Platteville and then worked in our plant the following summer. He showed excellent dedication and capability and decided the next fall that he did not want to return to Platteville.

Through the patient efforts of Hal Koehn, our plant manager at the time, Greg learned the chemical, electrical and manufacturing engineering from the ground up. Greg soon became a valuable asset to the company.

The Research Continues

The first time Donna and I traveled to Europe was in 1974 with the Wisconsin Golfers Association. We visited Spain and Portugal. On the plane flying over, Donna and I finally had a chance to talk about my research. (It was difficult for us to find quiet time for lengthy discussions when we were at home.) I was reading John W. Gardner's Excellence-Can We Be Equal and Excellent Too.

Donna asked, "Sorry to interrupt, but how is your reading and research coming?"

"It's been hectic building the companies. I haven't had much time to spend on my research, except to read late at night. I guess I'm still reading and absorbing."

"I see you shifted some of your reading to education."

"I just let certain things in one book lead me to others. Incidentally, listen to what Gardner says:

> 'If we are concerned with the shortage of talent in our society, we must inevitably give attention to those who have never really explored their talents fully, and to all those who level off short of their full ceiling. If we ever learn how to salvage a respectable fraction of these, we will have unlocked a great storehouse of talent.' "

I put the book down. "Interesting, huh?"

"Very," responded Donna. "What about what he says on page thirty-five? 'Searching for talent will be among the historic changes of our era, and in the long run prove to be the most profound.' "

"You're reading these books?" I ask.

"Well, not reading them."

"Then what?"

"When you're working I read what you've underlined at night."

"What I underline?"

"Those books are too deep for me to read page by page. You dig deep, where I can't. My mind wanders. But I can focus on what you've highlighted."

"Learn anything?" I ask.

"I see many conformations of your thinking, as I just said. But in addition, I see a number of references to the meaning and purpose of life. This is still an area of interest for you, isn't it?"

"I would think it would be for everyone."

"Yes, but not like it is for you. You think there is a way to find it and you're digging to do so." she said.

"It's that obvious, huh? It's still a lofty objective, but I can't help it. It's there, and it bothers me."

"Maybe it isn't lofty at all. Until we discovered genes, our bodies were considered 'religious lofty'. With genetic research our bodies have become more understandable, more real and practical. Perhaps the meaning and purpose of life is just as understandable and practical."

I was amazed with her. "Donna, that's very good. Did you read that?"

"No. It's just a logical conclusion from the things you underlined," the intelligent lady says.

"And practical?" I say. "That's a good word, and along the lines I have been thinking. In fact, it's an excellent word and takes it out of the area of being lofty."

"Want to tell me what words you are now using in your thinking?" Donna asks.

"It's not all together yet, but human capability, talent, the meaning and purpose of life and humanity seem to be coming together. As you might say, in a practical way."

"Uh, huh. So things are starting to come together for you. Want to talk about it?" she pursues.

"Not right now. I'm not making any headway. It's still all very hazy."

"Sounds to me like you're making more headway than you know. That's okay, I know you will try it on me when you're ready. Remember, I believe in your mission and your ability."

"I know, pretty lady. Your support is very important to me."

Donna And The Snake

Our salespeople in Milwaukee had been in touch with a sheik who lived in Tangier who had bulldozed a lake on his property and was having problems with algae. While in Spain, Donna and I took a side trip via a hovercraft from Gibraltar to Cuete in Morocco, which was near the sheik's home. Arrangements had been made for me to inspect his lake while we were there.

The waves on the Mediterranean Sea were so rough that the captain could not get constant air under the hovercraft without diving into the waves. Those few hours were about the worst beating we ever experienced on water. Many people were sick. This side trip was not starting out well.

After leaving the hovercraft, all of us were bussed to the central city for touring and shopping. As we disembark from the bus a young man who has a yellowish snake around his neck greets the group. The snake must be nine feet long and three inches in diameter.

Celebrating our twenty-fifth wedding anniversary.

"Who would like their picture taken with my pet snake?" he questions.

None of our tour group wants to take him up on the offer, and then, oh no, Donna steps forward and everybody applauds. This woman is always getting me in trouble. Sure enough, when the snake is around Donna's shoulders it starts making agitated motions. Concerned, I press forward without the slightest idea what I will do, but the snake handler beats me to it and removes the snake from Donna's shoulders. He quickly explains that certain hair sprays are offensive to the snake's acute sense of smell.

Later, back on the bus, Donna says, "Sure was a big snake. Strong, too."

I don't respond.

"The snake sure got agitated."

I don't respond.

Looking at me questioningly, "They must have police watching what is going on?"

I don't respond.

"They wouldn't allow anything to hurt the tourists?"

I don't respond.

She puts her arm through mine and rests her head on my shoulder. "Well, okay, I'm sorry. I suppose I shouldn't have done it, but he looked so sad with no one volunteering. I just had to."

I patted her. "That's my girl." Although very self-reliant and confident, I still have to watch out for her. Donna is very precious. I didn't even want to imagine what life would be like without her.

The Sheik Has Eyes For Donna

Donna and I are to be met by the sheik's people at the hotel on the square at a specified time. As we approach the hotel a man dressed as a chauffeur approaches us.

He smiles. "You are Mr. Seymour? Come to see the lake?"

"Yes." How did he know?

"I knew, because your manager wire said to look for a pretty woman."

Donna gave me the "See" look and flutters her eyes at me.

"Please," he says, gesturing to a white Cadillac that looks like it is half a block long. We enter the Cadillac. It is lusciously appointed, with pillows all over the place and a small open bar with a variety of alcohol.

Donna asks, "What are we getting into? Chauffeur? Cadillac? I may be under dressed for this." She has on dark blue shorts, a white halter and sandals. Looks very nice to me. "And all these pillows. Wonder what they are for? Are we supposed to sit or lay down?"

I'm not going to answer that.

Later we enter a palm-lined road that ends at a villa next to a large pond, which is totally green with algae. Someone who appears to be a manager introduces himself. As we approach the pond I can see the problem immediately. Sticking my hand into the water I detect that the planktonic (pea soup) algae has totally covered the pond to a depth of eight inches.

The Research

They obviously had been using copper sulfate to control the algae, which precipitates out to the bottom as copper carbonate and forms a layer. This cuts off the fish food chain. The water wears out its minerals fighting the algae and the pond ceases to function as a water body. Our product "Cutrine" does not harm the water but replaces the lost minerals so the pond can fight back the algae again. In addition, I saw that the pond needed to be deepened, aerated with a few fountains, and required more tree shade to keep the sun from cooking the water. A treed island in the middle would help.

I laid out plans with the gardener as to how he should maintain the pond and told him our distributor would do the follow-up.

As Donna and I walk up to the villa we are met by the sheik. He is a slight man wearing a white suit and a black tie. He apologizes for not meeting us at the pond. It seems to me that his eyes wander over Donna a little long. Donna rolls her eyes back at me as he kisses her hand.

The way he's eyeing Donna, I expect him to offer me twenty camels loaded with forty large chests of gold for her. No way. This sheik isn't going to add my wife to his harem.

The manager and I explain to the sheik what needs to be done to fix his pond. The sheik smiles and nods enthusiastically at every suggestion and invites us up to the villa for lunch.

It isn't large, like a palace, rather it's a nice sized villa with a low wall surrounding lush gardens. The medium-sized sunken living room we are to have lunch in is pillared at two ends and appears to be of a polished stone or marble. There are large pillows around the room. We are seated on white back-less settees. We decline drinks but accept a delicious hot tea.

The sheik is obviously taken with Donna, who glances at me and shrugs. I have to admit that with his dark pencil-thin mustache and pointed goatee he is a charmer.

After a delicious lunch of flaming lamb shish kebab served over seasoned rice, plus exotic dates and figs, the sheik claps his hands and four petite young women appear. They wear pale-blue gauze veils, vests, pantaloons, and skimpy undergarments. Donna rolls her eyes at this.

Three men and a girl appear in a small alcove. They are playing a lute, flute, drum, and cymbal. I can't figure out if this is for real or for show.

One of the dancing girls sets down a tape machine and the music starts. The musicians appear to be more for show, as I can't hear them over the tape player.

These dark skinned girls, all very lovely, start into a graceful dance routine—not the overly sensuous movements one might expect. They look so much alike that they appear to be a professional dance troupe hired out for entertainment.

The music is very nice and Donna is starting to move a little with it. The girls, seeing this, are delighted. One comes forward to bring Donna onto the floor with them. Kicking off her sandals it doesn't take Donna long to follow them. The problem is that Donna, who is nicely proportioned, looks more sensuous in her shorts and halter than the girls do in their skimpy gauze. Donna continues to draw the sheik's attention.

Now, what is my wife getting us into?

Donna is laughing with the girls and really getting into the music. One of the girls whispers to Donna, motions to the sheik and off the girls go with Donna. The tape machine and band follow.

Where they are going with my wife? I'm looking around for big burly cross-armed eunuchs with turbans and broadswords, ready to steal my girl off into the desert. But none are visible.

The sheik asks in good English, "You like young women?"

I respond, "Your girls are very nice."

"I mean your beautiful wife."

He wants my wife for his harem? No way. He can keep his lousy business. Let his pond go to algae. "She's not exactly young," I reply.

"Oh! You been married long?"

"Going on twenty-five years." He wants to know how old she is?

The Research

What the heck? This will discourage him. "Donna is going on fifty." She was really forty-eight but I thought I would age her a little for him.

"Fifty!" he says incredulously. "Like Americans, you are pulling my leg. Fifty?"

"Yup."

He puts his hands up in amazement. "Oh, but she's so youthful and beautiful."

"Yup."

He's not discouraged.

Well, he can keep his forty chests of gold. No one can buy Donna from me. And if he wants to duel, even though I'm not good with a broadsword and am weak at black belt, I have something more macho—Donna. She'd scratch his eyes out.

I change the subject by giving him some ideas about building a waterfall on the other side of the pond and to reduce the aerators. He claps his hands in glee at the idea. He finds a pencil and paper and has me draw an outline of the waterfall for him.

A half-hour later they bring my wife back. She, too, is now wearing skimpy gauze pantaloons, vest and veil, but—thank heavens—over her shorts and halter. They start to dance. Donna, a trim and firm 118 pounds, fits right in and is now dancing like she was always a part of the dance group. The girls dance, turn and gyrate more fluidly than Donna who is in the middle. Donna moves more reservedly and less fluidly but somehow her shorts and halter under the gauze make her look naively feminine. I had to admit that Donna looked gorgeous, and the sheik must've agreed because he clapped at Donna like crazy.

A short time later, I was glad to leave for fear this sheik would find some way to detain Donna. He gave us boxes of dates and figs as a gift.

On our way back in the Cadillac I asked Donna, "Why did you decide to appear like that?"

"Like what?" she asks innocently.

"You know, that outfit was very suggestive."

She was aghast. "My street clothes under that outfit was suggestive?

I was afraid you and the sheik would burst out laughing. That's the thanks I get for dancing for my husband. Didn't I dance beautifully for you? I held back on the gyrations, not like the girls you enjoyed watching."

"Yes, but the sheik was bug-eyed watching you."

"He was, wasn't he?" she giggled.

"It's not funny."

She shrugged. "Well, I was hesitant to do it and I suppose I shouldn't have, but this girl who speaks English said I looked very beautiful dancing in that outfit and it would be a shame for my husband not to see me dance." She shrugged again. "So, I did it."

"I still think you looked very suggestive."

"Didn't you like it?"

"Well, you did okay." *Did I ever?*

The Ancient Gun

Back in Cuete, while we waited for the bus to take us back to the hovercraft, Donna did some shopping. Standing in front of a store, I noticed they had piles of old, rusted flintlock guns in stalls. It looked like an army had surrendered. I picked one up. It appeared to be an early flintlock. I put it back. A boy who was dusting the guns came over to me and shoved one in my hands and says, "One hundred fifty American."

I give it back. I don't need a flintlock.

I'm still waiting for Donna and keeping my eye on the bus outside so that we don't miss it. My eye wanders back to the gun. I don't know why, but it looks different and bulkier. I walk over to look at it again.

The boy gleefully asks, "One twenty-five American?"

It was much heavier and black with age, rather than rusted. What attracted me was that on one corner a slight scratch showed the brightness of the metal. I noticed that people are boarding the bus so I hand the gun back to the boy as Donna comes out with a young salesgirl chasing her with a leather carryall.

"One hundred American," the boy persists. As Donna and I head for the bus the prices for the gun and carryall bag are reduced with every step. We finally shake the kids off by entering the bus.

Dauntless, they shove the bag and gun at us through the window where we are seated. Everyone is laughing. The bus driver starts the motor and starts to move, but has to be careful because these kids have both the gun and bag in our faces. The price of the gun is now down to twenty-five dollars and the bag is only five dollars.

I give up. Halting the driver I give them thirty dollars and everyone applauds. As we move off, a friend in back taps me on the shoulder and suggests that I should arrange to have the gun sent back to the states because guns are not allowed on the plane. I hadn't thought of that.

Donna says. "See, you shop, too. But what do you want with that dirty old gun?"

I have no idea.

Back in the states the gun arrives and I throw it in my closet. Donna was right. Just what I needed—another piece of junk to move around and clean. One cold, snowy day Donna suggests I clean my closet. The gun falls out and again the bright scratch draws my attention. It seems awfully bulky and heavy for the small caliber that it is. I scratch some more. Is it silver? I get out cleaning rags and polish. The black falls away and I discover that the gun is encased, etched and laced in silver. No wonder it was so heavy.

What the heck is this thing? I go to the library and find that the flintlock is a sixteenth-century Swedish make. That's old. But why the silver? Phoning around I find someone who knows early guns. He tells me that in the sixteenth and seventeenth centuries, North African tribal chieftains had their guns encased in silver. When they wanted their men to come to their aide they would flash their guns overhead so that the sun or the moon would glance off of it to draw the men's attention. It's surprising the silver was still on such an early gun, as the silver was usually stripped off old guns and transferred to newer models as they came available. This gun was either stolen or hidden somehow and survived with the silver.

When I told Donna this, she rolled back her eyes and said, "I suppose now you think that makes you a professional shopper?"

Do they have a professional organization? I wonder.

"A novice shopper—you just lucked out," she says.

A guy can't win.

Two years later, I wake up one morning to music like Donna danced to in Tangier. I push myself awake and there is Donna in that pale blue gauze outfit, dancing at the foot of the bed. She must have brought that skimpy harem outfit back in her purse without my knowledge.

She must have been practicing, because she is dancing beautifully. She smiles at me enticingly over her shoulder—with much less reserve than I saw in Africa. She's gorgeous. And then I'm really shocked; she has nothing on under the gauze. Oh well, I've seen my wife with less on and it is a delight to watch her move around the room. She is a lovely, youthful and talented woman. I wonder what I ever did to deserve her.

The tape recorder finally stops and with a mischievous grin Donna comes around the bed, looks me in the eye and says, "You want suggestive? Now you've got suggestive." With that she throws a glass of water in my face, runs out of the room and a minute later is dressed and in her car driving away to do her shopping. I could see her hitting her hand on the steering wheel and her head back laughing as she pulls out of the driveway.

You know, you really got to feel sorry for a guy who is subjected to such excruciating antics by a lovely nymph first thing in the morning.

Are We Out Of Business?

Building the algaecide business seemed more in the realms of my nat-

The Research

ural talent than selling life insurance. Running the company was fun, at least most of the time. The lake spraying did well in the summer months and my chemical sales were improving. I began to drift away from selling life insurance, which bothered Donna.

The business rented an ex-creamery office-lab-garage-warehouse in Waukesha. Donna came out to see the building we had rented. She was horrified at how dirty it looked. What can you expect when the back doors led out to a cinder lot? The next day, when I came down for breakfast, Donna was gone. When I arrived in Waukesha, there was Donna on her hands and knees with a brush and cleanser, scrubbing the office tile floor. During the week she went from room to room. We were surprised at what a nice place we now had.

At this time Don Kunkel was out with the flu, so his crew was spraying on Lake Geneva without him. They had our new barge and equipment that could spray chemicals a swath of a hundred feet. Greg and his football friends worked on the barge during the summer. Don called them the wild bunch.

Donna was washing the windows in my office when Hal Koehn came in and declared, "We have a problem. We have a blue lake." (The color of our chemical.)

"What's the matter with blue lake water?" I asked, confused.

"It's not the water."

"Huh?" I said.

"You know that stretch of white piers and boathouses just beyond the river entrance in Lake Geneva?"

"Yes."

"They're speckled blue now. And a fleet of inboards and outboards, too."

I put my head down on my hands. "Oh boy."

"And that ain't all. The DNR is also out there. Seems there's a lot of dead fish floating ashore."

Hands aside my head "Oh no."

"You want more?" Hal asked.

"More?"

"Seems one of the kids didn't tighten the drain plug on the barge. The plug blew a hundred feet in the air and a stream of water, too. The kids made it to shore, then sat there laughing as the barge sank in twelve feet of water."

"You gotta be kidding. What about our new equipment?"

He pointed thumbs down. "And, they're having a lake association meeting tonight to find out how much to sue us for bluing everything."

Face down on the desk. "Oh lord, were done," I cried

He left me with that.

Donna came over and threw the washing rags down on the desk. With hands on hips, she said scornfully, "You mean to tell me that I worked and slaved for a week to make a decent place out of this dump and now we're out of business?"

Inadvertently Donna could add humor to every situation, sometimes without meaning to.

This was one of the many trials we faced while building the companies. Fortunately, there was a rainstorm that night and it washed away most of the blue. The lake association didn't sue, in fact they were very happy. They could see clear water again. A tow truck pulled our barge out of the lake.

A DNR anti-chemical biologist was still going to recommend the DNR pull our spraying permit and put us out of business. The industry referred to the algaecides and herbicides we used as chemicals. Our Cutrine algaecide replaces the minerals depleted by nutrient fostered algae and weeds, to bring the water quality back to normal. Cutrine was the only algaecide approved for fish culture by the EPA and our swimming pool algaecide Swimtrine was the only algaecide that could be put in a pool and swimmers could then immediately use it.

With EPA and FDA backing, our biologist Don Bezella talked the DNR out of trying to pull our permit. We were still in business.

The Traveling Salesman

Being a traveling salesman was no problem for me because I loved Donna so very much. Donna knew I was faithfully hers. People I knew

The Research

who had been unfaithful had unhappy marriages or were divorced. It took total commitment, trust and true devotion to build a great marriage. Donna and I were totally committed to our marriage.

My career always came first. Donna never pushed me or complained when my work interfered with something that she wanted to do. She was a perfect wife to a company president. There were no airs about Donna, she was well liked and respected by all our employees.

Celebrating our twenty-seventh wedding anniversary at the Hidel House Motel in Green Lake, Wisconsin.

Flying back from Los Angeles one day, I sat next to a newly married man who prevented me from writing down my orders and call reports, by going on and on about his wife. He finally realized he was hogging the conversation and asked me to describe my wife, a question that had never been asked of me before. Considering carefully, I wrote some words that I thought described Donna on a notepaper. Finally, I said, "She is a beautiful lady both inside and out, who somehow combines humility with gentle class. She is wise, intelligent and has a lovely bright confidence that is softly stroked by compassion and friendliness."

He mouthed "Wow!" and said, "That's some lady."

I found my notes in my files several years later. I was amazed how well I had described the lovely woman who cleaned our house, cooked our meals, painted our woodwork and called me husband.

※

As I grew the chemical sales side of the company, our equipment,

Applied Biochemists Inc. officers attending the company's annual meeting and fishing event at Grassy Narrows Camp in Lake of the Woods, Canada. Left to right: Harold Hampton, Secretary-Treasurer; Gary Gigstead, Sales Manager; Don Seymour, C.E.O.; Ray Huntzinger, Employment Manager; and Greg Seymour, President.

machinery and inventory required more capital and loans. It was stressful building a company with bank loans. I worked long hours traveling around the country, selling chemicals to support the spray side of the company through the winter.

Don Kunkel was mainly interested in the lab and spraying weeds and algae. I thought our chemical sales could go worldwide, so I arranged for a loan to start a sales staff. Don Kunkel did not want to sign for the loan, instead he signed a contract with me to pay him a royalty on worldwide sales and I set up a new company, Applied Biochemists Inc. Along with my sales ability, I must have had the right vision and capability, for ultimately I talked the banks into enough capital to build a mid-sized conglomerate of companies.

After Don Kunkel sold out to me I directed two of our new lake spraying biologists, Jim Schmidt and Don Bezella, to experiment in the winter with different chemicals to develop another algaecide patent, which they succeeded in doing. Another of our biologists, David Schulties, later developed a more advanced algae patent.

Ultimately our little company went up against some of the world's largest chemical companies. We usually beat them out in the surface water, swimming pool and wastewater treatment industries. Our sales staff was envied and constantly under attack by sales recruiters.

After one of our company sales meetings in Phoenix, Arizona, with eighty of our salesmen, marketing and executives in attendance, Donna whispered to me, "Not bad for a man Vice President Hack said would never make a salesman."

A Better Career Selection Method

When I interviewed salespeople I used interest, occupational and psychological tests to select the right person for the position. Although these tests are helpful in knowing one's self better, they did not prove efficient in selecting successful salespeople. I decided to devise my own method for selecting salespeople.

I took continued interest in trying to develop a better method of occupational selection. I started with Edward Strong, Jr.'s book, Vocational Interests Of Men And Women. Through the years I waded through every book about tests and testing that existed. I do not want to criticize tests, because they have their uses, but tests alone are not efficient in selecting occupations. Although my system was successful for us, there had to be a way for all people to make better occupation selections. When I had the time, I continued my research to develop a better way.

The Call Girls

Hal Koehn and I had young looking, pretty wives whose mothers' maiden names were similar. Corky's was Kaul and Donna's was Kahl. One Friday, after having a few drinks at the Koehn's, the four of us went to a local restaurant where Hal and I decided to have fun with the girls.

When the waitress came to take our drink order I said seriously, "These are call girls. Give them anything they want."

Hal piped in, "Even doubles, if they want."

The "call" girls with friend Bob Duncan.

This shocked the waitress. With raised eyebrows she tried to look blandly at Corky and Donna for their order. Our wives didn't know whether to go along with the joke or not, but finally they shook their heads at our antics and laughingly ordered a simple cocktail.

Just about then I noticed a table next to us. They had heard what Hal and I had said about call girls. One man, who seemed a little inebriated, grinned and raised his drink in a toast to the call girls. We did not yet have our drinks, so to be polite Corky and Donna toasted their water glasses back.

Two women at the inebriate's table whispered to people at the table next to them and before we knew it the whole room was staring at the pretty call girls. Looking around the room Corky and Donna became aware of what was going on. They tried to smile, even though they were blushing.

When our drinks arrived, the guy at the next table, with a silly grin on his face, bent back in his chair to toast our girls again. The girls politely toasted him back.

The Research

Suddenly Corky put her hand to her mouth and motioned to Donna. Over in a corner booth was a rather staid couple from our church, where Hal was council president, I was a trustee, and Corky and Donna were leaders in the women's group. The couple stared in our direction and talked in hushed tones.

Our girls are now glaring at us. It wasn't funny anymore. Hal and I became very proper. Each time the girls sipped their drinks they held the glasses up high so that their wedding rings could be seen by all.

We ate quickly, because we knew the Corky and Donna would be glad to get out of there. Waiting for our bill, the elderly hostess came to our table and in a sincere motherly way said, "Now, you two men be sure to take these nice young ladies right home."

Hearing that, the drunk next to us let out a "Whoop." His chair slipped away and he flopped onto the floor, spilling liquids all over his table. Evidently not hurt, he lay there holding his sides in laughter.

Hal and I knew we were in real trouble. Not a word was said as we dropped the Koehns off at their house. I received the silent treatment that night, but the next morning Donna was her cheerful self again. Later I heard Donna talking to Corky on the phone and laughing. But that was not the end of it.

Word travels like lightning in our corner of Shorewood, especially in our church. On Sunday the four of us arrived in church at the same time. As we walked down the aisle, a wave of heads turned. A few close friends were pointing at us and muffling laughter. Our girls turned a little red, as they sat in the pew.

On the way out of church, everyone shakes hands with the pastor and the vicar. The pastor tried to smother a laugh, but when he shook Hal's hand, he didn't make it. The Vicar didn't make it either, putting his hand to his mouth he had to turn away.

Oh, were we men in deep trouble. I would list the penance and suffering we were forced to endure in the ensuing days but they are too distressing and heartbreaking to repeat.

We Build A Home

Driving to work from Shorewood to Applied Biochemists, now located in a building we purchased in Mequon, became too far for me to drive each day. Since a very young age, I had wanted to design and build a home of my own. Taking on another mortgage I bought thirty acres of land in River Hills, north of Milwaukee. Our attorney took the liberty of naming it the Seymour Woods subdivision when I was out of town. I eventually sold off twenty-five acres, made a profit, and had the best five-acre parcel for our home paid for.

Donna loved her Shorewood home and did not want to discuss moving. One day when she was looking at a home-decorating magazine, I asked her what style of home she would choose, if we ever happened to build a home. Without bothering to think, she replied. "A one-story, Country French, with step-down living room and family room."

That is what I designed and started to build in 1978. Donna knew I was building a home on the land we had purchased because she helped select the brick, tile, plumbing and lighting fixtures, fireplaces and wallpaper.

She did not, however, accept that we were going to live in the house. Instead she thought we would sell it. When it was near completion, she commented, "It's a lovely Country French home. How much are you going to sell it for?"

"It should be worth much more than we paid for it," I said. "Let's go inside."

"Oh," she commented, "nice entryway and step-down living room. What a nice view on three sides, and a great fireplace."

In the kitchen she said, "Oh, you built it just as I suggested. Wonderful cabinet space and work counters. Some woman is going to really appreciate this kitchen."

Later she said, "Oh, how nicely the master bathroom flows past the built-ins, walk-in closet and vanity. What a beautiful marble fireplace in this large master bedroom. You should get a good price for this place. Some lucky woman is going to love this house. It's just perfect."

The Research

Aerial view of 8665 North River Road.

She's not going to give in.

The next time Donna saw the house, it was nearly finished.

"Don, you did a beautiful job. What a nicely designed front door. Oh, and look how nice that chandelier is inserted up into that half bowl in the ceiling in the entryway. And look, you've recreated that plaster coving over the arches, just like our home on Newton. Some woman is really going to love this place. How much are you going to ask for it?"

"I'll let the realtor suggest a price."

Donna's going to be stubborn to the end.

The next time she saw the home the landscaping was in. Her praises went on and on. "I envy the woman who gets this home," she said.

I could see this was going to go down to the wire. I decided on a full course, win or lose approach. A realtor gave me a listing contract to sell the home. I placed the listing contract with a pen on the dining room table and told her, "Donna on the dining room table is a listing contract to sell the River Hills home. We own the property jointly so you

Front view of 8665 North River Road.

will have to sign it." Normally when I ask Donna to sign something she trusts me and just does it. But the contract lies on the table, unsigned.

I repeat later, "Donna did you hear about signing the contract?"

"Yes dear, I heard." she replies quietly.

The contract is still not signed the next night. I am reading the paper before dinner, when Donna comes in and sits on the arm of my chair. Looking up I see she is wiping tears from her face. "Don, why would you want to sell our beautiful new home?"

Donna is torn between the home she loves, where her life has been so wonderfully lived, and the home she always wanted. I feel ashamed to have put her through such anguish.

Accepting that the beautiful new home is ours, we move in. She tearfully watches as we drive away from the house in Shorewood she loved . . . and I did, too.

Our new home is built on forested land, like a park with birds, ducks, geese, deer, fox, a pond and a swimming pool. Donna loves her new home. It is a lot of work, but we take pride in it and enjoy the exercise it requires.

Neat-nick Donna

Neat-nick Donna required that everything was clean and in its place.

The Research

Donna, checking the water temperature of our new pool, with Mr. and Mrs. Chet Stanley and Shirley Meyer.

Donna would stand around and wait for us to undress, so she could attack the dirty clothes. She loved the smell of wind-blown bedding, so whatever linen could go outside to dry was hung out, and then she would iron up a storm.

Donna always pressed my shirts. When Jeff was born and Donna was still in the hospital I decided to relieve her of this duty and took my shirts to the laundry. She came home the same day I brought the shirts home. Having gone to the grocery store for her, I left the shirts in the laundry box, to put away later. When I returned from the store, I saw that Donna had opened all the shirts and was ironing one.

"Donna, what the heck are you doing to those shirts?"

"Ironing." she answered.

I can tell this is going to be one of those short, clipped, little girl conversations of hers, where she tries to ignore a person. "Donna, the laundry does a good job."

"Sleeves are wrinkled."

"Donna, you do so much around here, and with Jeff it will be more work. We can afford to have my shirts done."

"I do my husband's shirts. I'm good at it," she says primly, holding up and examining a shirt just ironed on a hanger.

"You don't have to stand there doing that. You are on your legs all day," I argue.

"Go away."

"Donna, I really must insist."

That did it. She puts the iron down, comes over, pushes me down on a kitchen chair, sits on my lap and looks me in the eyes. "I like knowing that when you go to work in the morning, that you look nice wearing a shirt I did for you. Don, please," she says sweetly, "may I do your shirts?"

What's a person to do with someone like that? You love her, that's what you do. You love her a lot.

On the other hand, I think when Donna ironed she plotted her next drive to keep her family clean, neat and on the straight and narrow.

Once at a party, I jokingly commented, "Donna is such a neat-nick, that when I get up at two o'clock in the morning to go to the bathroom, I come back and find the bed made."

Donna asked later, "Hon, I'm really not that bad am I? It's just that I want our kids to be clean and neat. I don't want them or you to get sick because of dirt or bacteria accumulating somewhere in the house."

Cleaning For The Cleaning Woman

We had a cleaning woman for a while, but Donna cleaned the house before she came, so the cleaning woman wouldn't find the house untidy. They mostly sat and talked over coffee. Occasionally the cleaning lady felt guilty and did some work, like wash the kitchen floor. But when the cleaning woman left, Donna would scrape the kitchen floor corners with a knife, to be sure they were clean. When the housekeeper decided to retire from cleaning, Donna occasionally mentioned that she should find another housecleaner, but she didn't do anything about it.

The Research

Donna was a bundle of energy. She could not sit for very long before getting up to do some work around the house. She was up bright and early every morning and attended exercise class in Brown Deer, where I understand she was the sunshine of the class. Donna was in excellent physical shape, and to my joyful observance; her shape was very shapely. At times I would observe Donna doing some task, and I'd think that the good Lord really outdid it when he designed this lovely woman. She would sense me looking at her and smiling ask, "Why are you watching me? Something wrong with me?"

"No, I was just thinking."

"And what were you thinking?"

"I was thinking that I'm a very fortunate man to have such a wonderful wife."

Going back to her work she would comment, "Silly, you've had me for years and years. You ought to be used to me by now."

I once had a picture card of Thomas Jefferson that said, "Initiative is doing what should be done, when it should be done, without being told." Greg operates that way and so do I, and of course, Donna. Another saying my stepfather taught me was "Anything worth doing is worth doing well."

Both Greg and Jeff are clean. Greg is neat and organized and puts his things away. Jeff washes his things, then throws them in a pile and hopes they will go away. That bothered Donna. She commented about Jeff, "I'll get even with him. I'll find him a wife who's a worse neat-nick than me."

Where would she find one?

Anniversaries with Warren and Shirley

When Warren Meyer joined the Wisconsin Electric Company as a photographer, he was given an opportunity to become a member of the Milwaukee Junior Chamber of Commerce. At a Jaycee function for

Shirley, Warren, Donna, and Don celebrate their wedding anniversaries.

members and their wives, Warren's wife, Shirley, and Donna met. They became very close friends. Both were Norwegian, their birthday's were two days apart, and we shared the same wedding anniversary. It was the start of a wonderful and lasting friendship for the four of us.

Typically we celebrated our anniversary weekends together at different resorts in the Midwest.

One year at The Wagon Wheel Resort in northern Illinois we were playing golf when two hotshots behind us were dropping golf balls on us on blind holes. At one blind hole they put one ball just past Donna and another rolled between Warren's feet as he was putting. Warren and I looked at each other and nodded in unison. We picked up both their balls and dropped them in the hole alongside the flag. Trying to find their golf balls, which they could not believe were in the cup with the flag must have slowed them down. We did not see them behind us the last two holes.

Warren and I used to get a kick out of remembering that incident. Wondering what kind of luck those hotshots had at trying to convince their friends that they both had a hole in one on the same hole . . . with no witnesses.

When either of us couples was out of the city, Donna or Warren would gleefully send the dumbest cards they could find, without signing them. And the traveling couple always brought back funny and dumb presents for the other.

The Research

The Start of Our Business Travels—The Far East

Paul Loo, our Far East manager, developed new distributors for us. My presence would be required, because most Orientals want to meet the owner face-to-face before any contracts are signed. Meeting the owner's wife was also important.

In 1979, Donna and I left for the Far East. To cut the jet lag, we stopped off a day or so to call on major customers in San Francisco and Hawaii. Landing in Japan's Narita Airport, we were met by Paul Loo's man in Japan, Ito Sigata, who escorted us through customs and on to the Palace Hotel in Tokyo. We were there to eliminate a virulent form of algae that was killing off the decorative fish in the Palace ponds. Our algaecide was the only algaecide approved for fish farming and consumption by the U.S. Food and Drug Administration, therefore it was assumed safe for the Emperor's fish.

Seating us in the spacious lobby of the Palace Hotel, Sigata took care of our registration. Donna noticed several attractive and well-dressed Caucasian women sitting separately around the room. When Sigata came for us, Donna asked him, "Isn't it unusual to have so many women sitting alone in the hotel lobby?" Sigata looked at me as if to ask if he should answer her. I nodded.

He bowed to Donna and said, "I sorry. I have to tell you, they are, well, prostitutes."

Donna said, "Thank you" to him and rolled her eyes at me.

We must have been preferential guests, because we were given a beautiful second floor corner room that overlooked the Emperor's palace grounds.

The Geisha House

After settling us in our room, Sigata told me that he had arranged for us to have dinner in an exclusive Geisha house. He would pick us up at six o'clock. He bowed and left.

Donna looked at me in amazement, "Geisha house?"

"Honey. It isn't what you think. It is like an athletic men's club in the states, where they do business, serve food and drink. In this country, Geisha girls put on a little musical entertainment."

"Well," she said with a slight huff, "I'm not concerned about what they put on, but what they take off." Donna usually fits in well and is open-minded. This wasn't like her. Was she purposely trying to have fun with me again?

"Oh, Donna, that's not right. I'm told the women wear nice floor-length gowns, except perhaps in the massage parlors." Ouch, that was the wrong thing to say.

"Oh, ho. I saw pictures of those gorgeous maidens wearing only little towels around their waists."

"Donna, you know you don't have to worry about me."

"I'm not concerned about what you'll do. It's what they can do to you. They know their business."

Business? "I'm not going into any massage parlor."

"Not without me, you're not."

Is she pulling my leg?

"We'll talk to Sigata when he gets here. He wouldn't dare take someone like you to an unsavory place."

"Wouldn't he now?

"Of course not."

"Well, what do I wear to a Geisha house?"

"A simple cocktail dress will probably be okay."

Half an hour before six she puts on a simple cocktail dress. Wow! What that girl can do to a simple cocktail dress! She's not taking any chances of my attention wandering.

When Sigata arrives he assures us that this is just food, drink, and formal musical entertainment. I don't think Donna believes him because she gives me a "Geisha house is a Geisha house" look.

In the hotel lobby (with a lot of bowing) Sigata introduces us to his nice looking wife (who spoke no English) and his attractive secretary, who is a college graduate and did speak English. Both wear simple cocktail dresses.

The Geisha house neighborhood looks a little unsavory. As we walk

The Research

Donna and Don dine at the Geisha house with Far-East Manager, Paul Loo.

up the wide stairs into a beautiful foyer, Donna's eyes are suspiciously darting around, taking everything in. A gracious hostess bows and smiles. Our shoes were taken and replaced by beautiful soft slippers.

We are led to a small room and seated on cushions at a low table. For foreign guests, there is an indentation under the table for our feet. Hot sake is served in small shallow dishes. Donna declines the sake but accepts plum wine, which she finds delicious.

The secretary starts a conversation with Donna, and soon they are talking like old friends. Sigata's wife must have understood some English as she occasionally nods and smiles. I had not tasted hot sake before. It has a strange taste, but I did like it. The dinner is served in a number of small bowls—and is excellent. It consists of carp soup, mixed seafood porridge, raw fish, mussel, prawn, eel, oyster rolls, and white silver fish. Donna and I have some experience with chopsticks and manage quite well. A bamboo wine accompanies dinner and they serve ice bean cake for dessert

After dessert a curtain parts and two girls playing string instruments and two dancers performing a slow graceful dance enter. They wear traditional long dresses with obi sashes at the back. Donna, now relaxed, takes notice of how and what was served. (Our friends back home will soon be treated to a similar traditional Japanese dinner.)

When we part at the hotel, Donna says good night to the Sigatas and the secretary says to me, "I'm sorry I didn't have a chance to talk to you more. Your wife is so lovely, interesting, and delightful. I would love to have had her here as a friend."

Donna did look unusually beautiful this night.

Back at our room, I said, "See, wasn't that nice, and nothing like you thought."

"Yes, it was a very nice evening. But I wonder what the girls in the back rooms were like?"

Suspicious woman.

One afternoon Sigata has arranged for me to meet with our distributors. After the meetings I arrived back at the hotel in time for a late dinner.

When I open the door, there stands Donna, poised like a model, in a beautiful pink and green flowered kimono, nicely wrapped around her shapely body. Her bright eyes flash above a colorful open fan.

"You like?" she asks from behind the fan.

"I like varieee much."

"I'm so glad you like varieee much, because now you have your very own geisha." She is laughing behind the fan.

"Now Donna, what could possibly give you the idea I wanted a geisha?"

The lovely geisha laughing, "Well, you have one just in case. So now you can stop leering at all the pretty Japanese girls. Let's go to dinner."

I can't remember leering at Japanese girls. She knows that. Ignoring my comment she fans herself and sashays out of the room very pleased with herself . . . leaving me standing there scratching my head. This mischievous little nymph has great fun putting on this kind of scene and leaving her husband off balance and perplexed.

The Research

I think Donna looked for opportunities to space these brief scenes in our marriage, to keep a little mystery, magic and tease about her. Carefully planned, this clever woman put on these scenes with beauty, style and grace. It was great fun for her—and me.

I often muse to myself about how very fortunate I am that this lovely lady is my wife.

When checking out of our room, with Sigata's and a porter's help, I said, "I'll go down to settle our bill and meet you in the lobby."

Sigata replies, "No need. The Emperor is very pleased you come all way here with your fine suggestions. You are guest of the Emperor." He went on. "Emperor said, next time you come here, he wants to meet your wife, who so greatly impressed the young women on his staff."

Fine thing. I come halfway around the world to fix his carp, and all he cares about is meeting my geisha.

On to Singapore

On our flight to Singapore Donna asks, "Don, I see you're reading Kepler, Galileo, and Newton. That's kind of far back. Why these?"

"Remember what Einstein said, 'I have no special talents. I am only passionately curious' and 'I am not any more intelligent than anyone else, just fortunate to have found an area that matches my interests and abilities.'"

"Yes, that was interesting."

"That statement has been haunting me for a long time. There is something there that may be important, but I can't lay my finger on it," I said.

"Or maybe you can, but you're afraid to acknowledge it," Donna challenged.

"Perhaps you're right. I'm reading the writers that Einstein respected most. I'm trying to find the thread of Einstein's thinking."

"Still that talent-humanity concern, huh? Anything happening?" Donna questioned.

"Nothing really," I answer. "But still, I feel like I am slowly building a foundation of answers to build on one day. I hope it isn't just procrastination."

She laughed. "No way, not you. Tell me, are interests, talents, abilities and careers still key words in your search?"

"Yes, I think so. Those words, plus intelligence are somehow linked together. Right careers and solving humanity's problems are still the objective."

"You know, you've been studying and researching this off and on for almost twenty years," she stated.

"I know. And little has come from it. Kind of silly, isn't it?"

"Silly? Not at all. I admire your dedication. I think there's more going on in your mind than you realize. What keeps you going with so little obvious result?"

"Humanity's problems grow worse every day," I reply. "We ignore them and we are not coming up with solutions. I want our kids and other generations to have a future. I feel this urgency that time is running out and that there is something that can and must be done."

"Yes, we see the papers every day. Everyone must realize the danger, but no one seems to be doing anything about it. It's like humanity has always been here and always will. Or that God will protect it some way. Do you still feel the answer to humanity's problems are connected to the meaning and purpose of our lives?"

"It's possible," I say.

"Why do you suppose that you feel this strong urgency, and no one cares about it enough to research it and find some answers?" wonders Donna.

"I honestly don't know," I reply, the frustration evident in my voice.

Our Man in Singapore

From Hong Kong, we boarded a Singapore Airline's jet to Singapore. The petite, attractive Singapore hostesses were dressed in beautiful sarongs and they wore flowers in their hair. They spoke English, Chinese, and Malay.

The Research

Singapore has a vast harbor (jewel of the Pacific), with boats from all over the world. Paul Loo again hurried us through customs, to where his pretty wife, Leng, waited with their car.

In the backseat, Leng and Donna were soon chatting away like magpies, neither Paul nor I could get a word in edgewise. Paul looked at me. I shrugged. He did the same and smiled.

We were deposited at the unbelievably beautiful Shangri-La Hotel, one of the finest in the Far East. The central courtyard is memorable because it looked to me like the hanging gardens of Babylon must have been.

Donna and Leng happily headed off to shop. Paul took me to his office. The door to his office was labeled: Applied Biochemists Inc.—Far East. He introduced me to his assistants, Benny Loh and Chau Meng. Benny attended the University of Winnipeg—Canada and Chau attended the University of Sydney in Australia. Both spoke five languages and in addition to biology, had a string of degrees. Benny and Chau were amazing. I had never seen such energetic and determined sales technicians. To them there was no such thing as failure—anything was possible.

On the afternoon of the following day Paul dropped me off at our hotel. When I opened the door to our room, there stood Donna, gracefully posed in a beautiful flowered sarong. She had a large red flower in her hair and was a vision of loveliness. With a beautiful smile, she puffed her hair around the flower and said, "I hope I have the flower above the correct ear." The darling lady is always dreaming something up.

I hope I'm not giving the impression that Donna is overly (you know), because it isn't so. On the inside of Donna's closet door she had a calendar with slips of paper that had different notes on. Donna could insert a note on each date of the month for me to read in advance. Some of the notes said:

> Is that all you ever think about?
> My back hurts.
> You just want me for my body.
> I'm too sleepy.
> Forget it. I put your birthday present downstairs.
> It's two o'clock in the morning. Are you out of your mind?

She never used the calendar that I know of, and I never looked in her closet for a message. (Husbands get to know the signals.) Donna was a normal American woman. Like Ben Franklin, Donna did everything in moderation; like Emily Post, Donna did everything very proper; and like Donna, most often with love.

I recently found the calendar among her personal items and wondered why she kept it all these years.

Donna and Leng developed such a close relationship that when we left Singapore, Leng (a Chinese artifact specialist) gave Donna an old Chinese painting on a wall hanging scroll. Paul later told me that Leng must have really liked Donna, to give her a painting from her prized collection. Donna hung it on a wall in a nice setting in our home.

Manila, Philippines—Mrs. Marcos

In Manila we stayed at the beautiful Mandarin Hotel as guests of Mrs. Marcos, who was in charge of solving Manila's yearly flood problem. Every year during the rainy season a profuse growth of water Hyacinth accumulates into a logjam that backs up the water in the Pasig and Pampanga Rivers, which empty into Manila Bay. When the logjam bursts, it puts most of Manila under a foot or more of water, for several days or weeks. The water overflowing the sewers is very unsanitary and brings the city to its knees. They tried cutting the Hyacinth but it grew

Dining at the Manila Garden Hotel (left to right): Laurie, a sales biologist; Donna; Kathleen, from the German Tourist Bureau; Don; Edmundo Sarossa, our distributor; and Paul Loo, our Far-East manager.

back faster than they could cut it. Our chemical would deter the growth of the Hyacinth at the tuber level, in the river bottom mud.

At lunch the first day, Donna was impressed with the beauty and intelligence of Mrs. Marcos' daughters, who sat at the table next to us in our hotel restaurant.

Jim Schmidt, our biologist, was there to run the tests. After the tests, we, along with our distributor (the Sarossa Brothers), had an appointment with Mrs. Marcos. Unfortunately we did not meet with Mrs. Marcos, because she suddenly decided to take one of her shopping tours out of the country. Donna was disappointed since she was looking forward to meeting the notorious Mrs. Marcos.

Bangkok—Donna Up The River With A Strange Man?

We were settled in the beautiful Oriental Hotel in Bangkok. Our room overlooked the Choaphya—the River of Kings. That night we dined with the Loos at the fabulous Golden Barge Restaurant in the hotel. It is referred to as the masterpiece, French restaurant of the Far East.

The second day, I was busy with Paul. Donna was scheduled to take a river tour. To Donna the world was a place to see. She had the confi-

The Twentieth-Century Lady

dence to fit in anyplace and the daring to go anywhere and see everything.

I returned to the hotel at six o'clock and my wife was not there. I asked one of the managers if the tour up the river had come back. He told me that the tour had been cancelled because there were not enough people interested, however, one of their tour guides had offered to take Mrs. Seymour upriver.

"You *what*?! You let my wife go up that river by herself, with a lone man she doesn't know?"

"We've never had a problem with our guides. They are very trustworthy," he said.

"But you don't know the kind of crowds that woman draws—and the trouble she can get a guide into."

"You're concerned about our guide?" he asked incredulously.

"Well, my wife, too, of course," I quickly added.

Time passes. I'm now frantically pacing back and forth by the hotel river steps.

Finally, at seven-thirty, Donna nonchalantly strolls up the steps from the river, happily twirling a colorful native parasol.

"Donna, what can you be thinking, going up that river alone in a strange land?"

Unconcerned, she says, "The tour was cancelled and there are so many things I wanted to see. One of their trustworthy guides offered to take me up the river."

"You went up the river for six hours, by yourself, in a little sampan, with a strange man?" I declared, exasperated.

Nonchalantly twirling the parasol, she replied, "It was no problem."

I was ready to tear my hair out in frustration with this woman. Most of the land floods part of the year, so permanent lowland houses are not livable. A large population lives on the Chaophya River. There are desperate river bandits for whom Donna, with only one guide, would be an easy kidnapping target. It was a foolhardy thing to do and I wanted to make it clear to her.

"Donna, that was the wrong th . . ."

"Do you know they wash their food in the river water?" she interrupts.

"Donna, you should never . . ."

"And they brush their teeth in that water," she interrupts.

"Donna, don't you ever . . . "

"And, they go to the toilet in that water." She's ignoring me.

"Donna, they kidnap attractive women and sell them in harems," I blurted.

"Humph, who wants a fifty-year-old woman?"

"Donna, listen to me. You are a very attractive woman. He could have taken advantage of you, or you could have been kidnapped."

She walked over to the elevators in a huff, mumbling what I thought was, "I would have kicked the turkey in the you know what, if he had tried anything."

"Donna!" I exclaimed.

On second thought, she would have. That turkey would have had bodily harm done to him. He would have rued the day he went upriver in a sampan with that woman.

Minburi, Malaysia—A Bowl Of Fish?

In the Malaysian jungle they raise shrimp in large cement tanks. The problem was that the tanks developed a form of algae that tainted the taste of the shrimp. Donna and I were driven half a day into the jungle to look at the tanks. After viewing the shrimp tanks and the algae, a short test showed that our algaecide would take care of the problem.

On the way back, our distributor wanted to treat Donna and me to lunch at a native village that had good food. Donna said she would like to try it. I had been subjected to native food in the jungle several times before and was not excited about the prospect, especially since my stomach had been giving me trouble due to stress. (Our company had recently completed its largest early order shipment. Waiting for me when I returned home from this trip would be a bank note due for three-and-a-half million dollars. If the receivable did not come in as expected I would have to re-do the bank note and possibly lose our

The Twentieth-Century Lady

prime interest rate with the bank. Therefore I was having trouble with my stomach, and anything a little spicy was painful.)

Donna explained that I had a stomach problem and suggested clear soup for me. When the soup was served I was stupefied. It was a large tureen of clear liquid, with a large black, white, and silver carp lying across the bowl. The tail lay on the table on one side of the bowl, the body of the fish draped down in the bowl, and the gills and head lay on the other side. One eye was looking up at me and my stomach rolled over.

At the look on my face and the fish, Donna burst out laughing, as did our guests (without knowing what was funny) to be polite. I whispered to Donna, "What's so funny? Look at that thing. I can't insult them."

Donna could not help but continue to laugh and point at the monstrosity of a fish. She said, "The fish looks okay but you're green around the gills." And everybody laughed again. I managed a painful grin.

To be polite, I sipped a little of the broth but my stomach could not take much. I had them remove the fish. I would be glad to return to the states in a week, and enjoy a glass of milk and a bologna sandwich.

Donna wasn't laughing a few days later when we were taken to lunch at the Chindra Restaurant in the small village of Bangpakoong. We were seated, with our distributors, at a tabletop that turned around. It had about twenty small crocks of green and brown things that looked like they could either crawl under a rock or fly. I explained that I had a stomach problem. But Donna would show them. If they could eat it, she would, too. However, when she put some of the things that looked least offensive on her plate, she looked a little pale, but ate it anyway. An hour later she couldn't wait to get back to our hotel. Donna couldn't eat dinner and had a difficult night.

The next morning Donna still looked pale. I said, "You look like a fish."

The Research

Don inspects a shrimp tank with the local distributors.

"A fish?"

"Green around the gills." And I laughed. But my get-even humor was not very funny. Donna was hurting.

❧

Our Secretary-Treasurer Hal Hampton called. The receivable came in and the bank note was covered. My stomach relaxed,

Her Husband with Native Girls

I had to return to the Far East countries in June 1980. Donna and I had just returned from a Disneyland convention in April. Other things pressing, Donna did not want to go back to the Far East so soon. She gave me that "been there, done that" look and held her stomach. "I've had enough jungle for awhile."

It was less expensive to take Chas Mulcahy, our attorney, along to do the final contracting. Every country has different laws and interpreting and negotiating contract provisions by mail was difficult and time consuming.

The Twentieth-Century Lady

This time Mrs. Marcos promised to be there.

Renting a car in Manila, we were running a little late. Chas was driving a little fast, and a motorcycle policeman stopped us. He threatened to take us in, but when he found we were late going to see Mrs. Marcos, a few minutes later we had an escort of cycles leading us to her.

When we arrived, Mrs. Marcos' advisor informed us that she wanted us to "contribute" the several million dollars of chemical to her country. In my presence our distributor, Edmundo Sarrosa of Trumps Traders Inc., told Mrs. Marcos' advisor, "If that was her non-negotiable position, we weren't interested."

The advisor came back and told us that Mrs. Marcos said, "Think of all the international publicity our product would get."

Edmundo looked to us and said, "Knowing her, she would take all the credit."

We told the advisor that the upriver tests would be expensive to run and if successful the chemical would have to be purchased at the already discounted price. He came back and told us, "Mrs. Marcos would consider it."

Chas had arranged for us to attend a reception at the residence of U.S. Ambassador and Mrs. Richard Murphy. We purchased the Philippine National formal shirt to attend. It was an interesting affair, where we were introduced to local dignitaries and business executives. A few professed interest in our products and gave us their business cards, which we later gave to Edmund.

Trumps Traders Inc., owned by Edmundo and Edgar Sarrosa, is involved in chemicals, sugarcane, and pineapples. They also owned and operated a resort on Sicogon Island, where I interpreted that Edmundo was an island chief.

It was Friday and Edmundo insisted we be his guests at their Sicogon Resort, in the southern Philippines. A limo picked us up at the Mandarin Hotel and delivered us to the Trumps company plane. A few

The Research

hours later, as we approached Sicogon Island, I saw huge, black rounded volcano cones rising up out of the ocean. It looked like the end of the world.

When we deplaned we were greeted with leis and kisses on our cheeks by four scantily clad beautiful young women. The next day the Sarrosa brothers, the four girls, Chas and I, boarded an outrigger to circle the island. The girls laughingly stripped off their skirts to reveal skimpy swimming suits before jumping in the beautiful clear water to snorkel. At noon, we stopped at a large beach with a single thatch-covered cabana sitting in the middle of a deep sandy beach.

Walking in the hot sand to the cabana, we were surprised to see under the cabana a palm-covered table piled with ice. In the ice were shrimp, crab, different kinds of fish, and an assortment of fruit. What surprised us most, was that there were no other footprints on the beach but ours. It was as if "Jeannie" had wrinkled her nose and there it was. They probably swept the beach to add a little mystery. The laughing girls poured champagne and cracked the crab for us.

Wait until Donna hears about this.

It was all very delightful but very innocent. It really was.

Back at the resort, I phoned Donna and told her what I was doing in detail, beautiful girls and all. It didn't phase her a bit. So I asked her what she was doing for fun.

"Golfing with the girls and painting our woodwork."

"The woodwork? We can have that done."

"I like to paint. When I paint I know it's done right," she said.

Fussy woman.

" . . . and it fills the hours while you are gone."

Isn't she nice?

". . . and why spend the money?"

My wife's an awful penny pincher. Am I lucky or what?

It bothered me that Donna did not comment and appeared unconcerned about me gallivanting around a secluded island with scantily covered native girls. So I said, "You don't seem worried that your husband is spending a weekend on an island with gorgeous native girls."

The Twentieth-Century Lady

Donna, at 59.

The Research

Donna's favorite photo of her men, taken in 1984 at the Grassy Narrows Camp in Lake of the Woods, Canada. Donna was glad to send us off to hunt or fish so she could do her fall housecleaning with no one underfoot. Left to right: Greg, Don, Jeff.

"No problem, you know where your heart belongs."
Confident hussy.
"Don't you miss me?"
"No, Goofy. Have fun, g'bye."
She misses me.

159

These were the years that Donna had more time to enjoy what her love had built. Through Donna's unselfish desire to help others, she had become an increasingly warm and friendly person—and people were drawn to her. The freedom of her laugh expressed her joy in life. Her attitude expressed humility, as she continued to develop the quiet style and grace of a lovely woman. These wonderful years were impossible to hold still. They were passing at an alarming pace.

Donna was dedicated to making other people happy. "I want" wasn't in her vocabulary. Her self-interest level, that most humans work hard to keep low, was naturally low and her humanitarian feelings were very high.

Donna had a comfortable home, many nice things and traveled to great places. But she also worked hard all of her life.

Donna was not easily impressed nor did she try to impress other people. She was a great influence in business and gave me support so that I had the best environment to do my work.

She supported my belief that all people are equal in capability and intelligence, as all people are equal in the eyes of God. To Donna, material things can come and go, but the best work is to make life pleasant for others.

Donna had seen her brother, sister and close friends lose their mates. This made her feel a little insecure as her dreams unfolded. There are small disturbing things that happen in most peoples' lives, things that seem big at the time, but overall, Donna was happy and felt so fortunate that she felt guilty.

She began to wonder more about the meaning of her life, its purpose, and how to pay the debt to society for the precious life she had been given.

Take Out the Garbage

After a long hard struggle to make our chemical business grow, I came home one night and proudly announced that we had our first million-dollar sales month. Donna smiled sweetly and said, "That's nice . . . take out the garbage, dear." So much for the glory in that. No guile, puffery or putting on airs with this lady. Our feet must always be firmly on the ground.

Another year the employees presented me with a plaque expressing their appreciation for my vision and success in building the companies. I came home and showed it to her. She said, "That's nice dear. Take out the garbage, please."

But You Have Donna

After Donna's father died, her mother, Edna, came to stay with us for a week or so twice a year. Can you imagine looking forward to having your mother-in-law visit? I enjoyed having her; she was a great lady, like her daughter.

At night I would come home and make myself a martini. Edna would have a small blackberry brandy with me. One time I came home a little beat.

Edna asked me, "You're a little quiet, have a hard day?"

"Yes, one of those." I would tell her the problems with the EPA, FDA, accounts receivable, the bank, the salesmen, the employees, etc.

Edna listened attentively. When I was through unloading my concerns she said, "You do have many problems—but you also have Donna Lou."

"You're so right. I do have Donna Lou." And all my problems suddenly seemed insignificant. How many men with the same or worse problems have a wonderful Donna Lou to come home to?

Donna Entertains and Us Guys Suffer

Donna loves to have guests for dinner. You never know what kind of menu she will come up with next. It could be Japanese, Italian, Russian, Norwegian, Indonesian, Turkish or Creole, and she would make everything from scratch. She loved the challenge of different ethnic foods, but she was so meticulous about the dinner that she would be uptight days before. If Donna couldn't find the right cocktail napkins or candles or was worried about one of the food items, us guys were occasionally barked at.

The Twentieth-Century Lady

Donna's holiday baking.

On holidays, the family gathered at our place. No one would miss it, because Donna always made it special. After the guests left, no matter what time of night, Donna and I would have everything cleaned (her better linens hand washed) and put away before we went to bed.

Although it was usually late and I was tired, I didn't mind helping the lovely lady, because she never failed to put on a great dinner. She worried her way through every dinner, but loved the challenge and accomplishment of it.

There was a list of friends that were privileged to receive Donna's Norwegian and German baked goods during the holidays. At Christmas Donna spent days over the stove, dipping cookie dough on special iron molds and cones to make krumkake, sandbakkelse, faatgmann and rosette cookies; which appeared as cones, rosettes, and butterflies. Sprinkled with powdered sugar, thin and airy, our friends had a hard time not to eating their way through the whole plate at one sitting. I understand several husbands got their fingers slapped by going for one more. It was hard work, but it was Donna's special signature and a work of love, for her friends.

The Sisters Take A Trip

In 1984 I suggested to Donna that she and her sisters, Marlyn and Ramona, should take a trip together, something they had never done.

The Research

(left to right) Ramona, Marlyn and Donna share a laugh.

Donna called her sisters and they thought it was a great idea. They traveled to Germany, where their mother's descendants came from, and Norway, where their father's descendants came from. They also stopped off at the Oberammergau Passion Play in Munich.

Donna Loves Paris—Anytime

In 1985 Donna and I attended a swimming pool show in Frankfort, Germany. We rented a car and drove from Amsterdam to Horsens, Denmark, where I met with Seymour descendants. We then drove through Belgium, Frankfurt, and on to Cologne.

In Cologne, Donna walked all the way up to the top of the Cologne Cathedral; which would be too much for me. When she came down we had a free evening and I asked where she would like to eat. She pointed across the street from the cathedral to a McDonald's. She had had enough ethnic food for a while.

After the pool show we drove to Paris, where we had a reservation at a Napoleon era hotel right on the Tuileries, only a block from the Louvre. We enjoyed the morning coffeehouses with the fresh baked baguettes—and Donna enjoyed shopping the Tuileries. The restaurants and shows were great. Other than being pinched a few times, which Donna returned with blazing looks (when she could locate the Frenchman who did it), Donna loved Paris.

Director Of Career Guidance

In 1986 I am asked to serve on the Building and Planning Committee of Concordia University in Mequon, Wisconsin, a Missouri Synod Lutheran-sponsored college. The university impresses me as I did not expect to meet such dedicated instructors and see such cheerful, polite and well-dressed students on a college campus.

Courtney Meyer, the Concordia football coach, knew of my business background and asked me to share some of my knowledge on how to succeed in business with the football team. In addition to giving each team member a Strong Interest test and counseling them individually, I agreed to present three lectures to the team. It was an interesting working with some of the highest and lowest scholastic students on the campus.

There must have been value in these sessions, because the president of the university, Dr. John Buuck, asked me to take on the responsibility of Director of Vocational Counseling for a year, while the existing director was on a sabbatical. I accepted, because this would help my research by giving me the opportunity to have firsthand experience with college students at various academic levels.

Most students came into the office looking for help in selecting their major and course of study. Other students felt they were in the wrong major but did not know what other subject to pursue. Most of these students did not know that career search tests were available; while others had no confidence in tests.

By this time my research had led me to question the value of career testing leading to career choice. How much does a student know about the positive and negative work involved in the job tasks of the 40,000 (estimated) occupations that exist? How can a person accurately answer questions about occupation activities they know little or nothing about?

At the time (and even as I write this book), interest, psychology and career search tests are all we have available to help people select their study courses and careers. It seemed vital to me—and for every individual—that we design new tools for capability recognition and career selection; especially since a student's study course could be the most influential factor in their life. Individuals need to be able to identify the most healthful occupation for them, an occupation that most efficiently fits their inborn capabilities. So far, the field of education had not discovered a method for doing this. I needed more exposure to different classes and ages of people before I could determine if there was a valid answer.

I had interviewed a large number of potential employees for our companies and conducted Strong Interest tests for most of them. Although many showed interest in some of the test-recommended occupations, it was still difficult for me to accept that any test-suggested occupations could efficiently fit the inborn capabilities of a student. Other students were so naive and unexposed to the world of work that their test results provided little information from which to work.

Some students came to see me right before graduation with tears in their eyes. They felt they had chosen the wrong major, and now it was too late to change. Putting on a joyful front, they could not admit their fears to their parents, friends, or the university. I wondered how high the percentage of students was that graduated in wrong careers every year? This bothered me terribly. Who was responsible for the hopelessness they felt when they looked in the mirror the morning after graduation?

The next year, I consulted with adult students who were attending adult evening classes and working towards a business degree. Most of the adults enrolled in the program so they could eventually earn more money, get promoted or qualify for a better job. Nothing was wrong with these motivations, except I wanted to hear someone say, "I'm here to find a job more suited to my capabilities."

I also counseled a few retired people that were referred to me; and this added another dimension to my research.

I began to regret that I did not have better guidance tools to help students find their best and strongest capabilities. Those who selected to work in the wrong career would be stressed out in twenty years and others would be asking at mid-life, "Is that all there is?"

The conclusion I started to form was that present day education and the natural capability of the student were not compatible. Education has not committed research to finding individual capability, probably because education is not set up to teach according to individual capability. Educators know there are problems with our present system. What we need are acceptable solutions.

The Concordia experience was enlightening, humbling, and at times depressing. I knew that my best efforts were often of little value. All I could do was help the student discover him or herself better. My experiences at the university confirmed my suspicions that more efficient tools for study, career and major selection were badly needed.

After Concordia I had more free time for myself. To escape from business problems, I found enjoyment in writing novels for the fun of it. In writing, I was constantly drawn away from the story line as I wrote page after page of thoughts and ideas on human capability, talent, and choosing the right career. It was as though someone was controlling the direction of my writing.

After reading some of my writings, Donna mused, "The way human capability, talent and careers creeps into your stories, you remind me of someone driving a car with some unseen hands controlling the steering wheel."

The problem of how to help people make an intelligent decision as

The Research

*Enjoying a Concordia golf outing with our close friends
Carol and Gerry Schmidt.*

to their study courses or career selection was constantly on my mind, especially as I continued to interview potential employees for our companies. I would wake up at night thinking about these things. They were in my craw and wouldn't let go. I didn't know then that this need to help people would lead to an unusual discovery and belief that would take over the background of my life and Donna's.

I'm Offered—A Harem?

Doing business in Europe in 1987, I had to make a quick flight to Turkey. I left Donna at the Cavalieri Hilton in Rome because she did not have a Turkish visa.

In Turkey I was to meet Mustafa Sipahi, who wanted to manufacture our chemicals in Turkey. The raw materials cost less in Europe and we could save on shipping costs to European countries. Mustafa led me through customs and took me to the Istanbul Hilton overlooking the Bosporus and the Golden Horn. He apologized that he could not have dinner with me. His daughter was having a baby so he would pick me up in the morning.

167

I was having a drink when the only other man at the bar looked at me and asked in broken English, "Are you an American businessman?" He was robust and had a small mustache. He looked like a used car salesman.

"Yes."

"Would you be interested in a business that produces 100 percent profit a year and provides pleasure too?"

This guy is pulling my leg.

He went on. "I have many Americans who invest in our harems."

"Harems?" Me, with a harem? Donna will do me harm.

"Yes, but hear me out, it isn't what you think." (Well if it isn't I'm a monkey's uncle.)

"We have harems here for a long time, and the daughters born in harems are often not acceptable for marriage. Their best opportunity is to stay in the harem, where they learn to make necklaces, beaded handbags, sequined blouses, and the like. Brokers buy these things and you get the profit. Other girls raise crops, animals and make their own clothes. The harem is self-contained and self-supporting—like some nunneries. Each harem has a spread of women young to old. The old and experienced teach the young and some of the young are very pretty and they are there to do your bidding."

My bidding? I can't believe my ears. Donna will have my head.

"I can tell you're having a hard time believing this," he said. "But there are harems in Istanbul that are owned by Americans. I can show you one that has many pretty girls and is priced for a quick sale."

"Well, thank you, but no. I have more than I can handle right now." *Did I say that right?*

"Here, take my card. If you change your mind, give me a call." The harem broker departs.

I ask the bartender, "Do you know that man I was talking to?"

"Yes, he comes in here often and does business here."

I dropped the card in a waste container. That was the craziest thing I ever heard.

That night I phoned Rome to check on Donna.

The Research

"Hi dear, what's new in Turkey?" she inquires.

"Not much yet, but I had an interesting talk with a promoter who tried to talk me into a new business."

"You want another business!" she exclaimed. I had to hold the phone away from my ear.

"No, dear. I was just trying to tell you that this man wanted me to invest in a harem. So I . . ."

"A harem!" Again I had to hold the phone away from my ear.

"Well, it's run like a nunnery it's . . ."

"Oh God, you want to buy a nunnery too?"

"I didn't say that, we must have a bad connection. The man said . . ."

"My husband wants to do business by connecting a harem to a nunnery. Oh Lord."

"Sweetheart, that's not right. We must have a bad phone connection."

"Donald Seymour, you come back here. I want to talk to you." That sounded pretty clear. She calls me Donald when she is not happy with me.

The connection must have been broken—or she hung up.

The next day Mustafa drove us to Ankara to see his manufacturing plants, which are orderly and adequate. I phone our Mid East manager, Al Karim in Beirut, and Ben Lanza back home to develop the contracts for manufacturing and distribution in the Mid East. (Mustafa confirmed the existence of harems.)

When I return to our hotel in Rome, Donna is her bright self. She says nothing nor do I have to answer for anything. I finally bring up the subject.

"Donna, I really had no interest in a harem or a nunnery."

She bursts out laughing and mischievously says, "I know that Goofy. What more would you ever want than me?"

Conceited woman.

No Cat in My House

My son Scott, who worked for us in telephone sales, deposited a box in my office on my birthday. I open the box and see a cute little ball of fluff. It is a Seal Point Siamese kitten—with papers. All of the employees fall in love with it. Initially the kitten stays in my office, but I have a problem. There is no way the pretty kitten can be let loose in the plant, and it can't live in my office indefinitely.

I put together the best arguments I can think of, and girding my best courage, I approach the powers that be at home. With a deep breath I explain my predicament, "Donna, I have a problem."

"Oh, no. No cat hair in my house and on my furniture."

I open the box and Jeff lifts the gorgeous kitten into his arms. He smiles up at his mother. "Look how beautiful he is, Mother." He hugs the kitten.

I can see she might melt.

"No. No cats in my house."

"He could stay in the summerhouse, Mom," pleads her youngest son.

"What are you going to do with him in the winter?" neat-nick Donna asks.

"By then maybe we can keep him at the plant," I suggest.

Smart Jeff holds the kitten out to Donna. She doesn't want to take it, but she does. She gently holds it, looks in its eyes and realizes she can't hold out against such a precious kitten and quickly shoves it back at Jeff. She's worried that she's melting.

"Oh, Mom, please. I love him and a boy should have a pet." (That was a pretty good argument. I hadn't thought of that.) Donna's melting.

"Oh," she says, throwing up her hands. "All right, but he stays in the summerhouse until winter and then he goes to the plant."

She melted. That cat will never go to the plant.

Jeff names the kitten Freddie.

The next night I come home and look in the summerhouse. No

The Research

Don and Donna enjoy the tulips at the American Club in Kohler, Wisconsin. 1985.

kitten? To my surprise I find Freddie in the living room, laying on a neatly folded towel on Donna's loveseat. He is wearing a leather collar set with pretty colored stones and a metal tag with the name Freddie Seymour, our telephone number, and issued by the Village of Shorewood.

I go into the kitchen. Donna knows I have seen Freddie and ignores me.

"Freddie's on your loveseat."

"He likes it there. He can see us come and go," Donna says.

"He has a tag."

"Can't have him wandering around without a tag."

"He's wearing a very pretty collar," I add.

"Siamese are royal cats to the Siamese Court. Can't have him looking like an ordinary house cat."

She looked up Siamese cats? "I think you kinda like Freddie."

"He's okay."

She loves him.

The Egyptian Debacle

For a year our International Sales Manager, Ben Lanza, had been negotiating with the Egyptian government for truckload purchases of our enzymes to eliminate the accumulation of contaminates in their four fertilizer plants alongside the Nile River. Egypt's agriculture was dependent on the fertilizer plants because ever since the Aswan Dam was built the farms along the Nile no longer received nutrients from the yearly flooding of the Nile. Now in the final contract stage, as president of the company my presence was required.

Upon our arrival in Egypt, I realized the airline had lost my luggage. That evening Donna and I were to be guests at a government reception and on Monday morning I was to meet with Al-Karim, our Mid East representative from Beirut; our distributor El-Nasr Chemicals; and Egyptian government officials

After Al-Karim took Donna and me to the Heliopolis Hotel in Cairo, where we could see the pyramids just beyond, he went from hotel to hotel trying to find my luggage. It was now three o'clock and we were to be picked up at 5:30. I was getting nervous, so I went down to the two clothing stores off the lobby. There was no help. The Egyptians are small people and they had nothing my size.

In our hotel room, Donna twirled around in a gorgeous light green shimmering, sleeveless gown that did beautiful justice to her. Donna asked, "What do you think? Do you think I'll do?"

Do? She looked tightly sensational.

Looking in the full-length mirror she commented, "A little tight, isn't it? I must be gaining a little weight with all the rich food we're consuming." She laughed and shrugged. "Whatever."

Al called and said he had no luck finding my luggage at the other hotels, but was downstairs searching with porters, going through every place the luggage could possibly be.

Both Donna and I are more nervous every minute. I am pacing back and forth. At five o'clock, Al-Karim comes to our room.

"Al, did you find my luggage?"

The Research

He holds up his empty hands but says, "No problem. I just received a call. Several of the reception guests are down with a virus that is going around and the reception is cancelled. And if necessary, I can reschedule Monday's appointment so we can find your luggage, or find a place to buy you some clothes."

The pressure off, I was greatly relieved. Donna looked at me and said, "Now, what am I going to do with this dress?"

I had cruised through the hotel after our arrival and noticed what looked to be an upscale restaurant that would show off her dress. Mind you, I was still wearing the lederhosen I had donned in Vienna. Donna in her beautiful gown and me in my lederhosen would be quite a contrast—but what can a guy do? I hoped the other guests would think my costume was part of some entertainment.

When we arrived at the restaurant we discovered that coats were required. The host, wearing a tuxedo, looked at me and threw his eyes and hands up in despair. He had his assistant seat Donna and motioned for me to follow him. He found a tie and red coat for me to wear. I could not bring the coat together in front, the sleeves were quite short and if I straightened out my shoulders I was sure it would split down the back. Appraising me, he rolled his eyes back again, shrugged and pointed out to where Donna was sitting. I don't think he wanted to be seen with me. I must have looked like Ichabod Crane.

As I approached our table, Donna looked at me and let out a "whoop". This gal is really uninhibited. Everyone in the room looked up at the outburst, and locating the lovely gal, who was laughing herself silly, zeroed in on me. The whole place started to laugh.

A middle-aged woman (probably Egyptian) at a long table next to us came over and lay her hand on my shoulder, "We must apologize for our discourtesy." Looking at me up close, I could see she was pressing her lips together to keep from bursting out in laughter. She saved herself by looking at Donna and asked, "Are you American?"

Donna's eyes lit up in amusement and she nodded.

Then looking back at me, the lady said, "We understand how you came about that coat." *Sure she did. I looked like a bumbling idiot. I do have clothes that fit, you know.*

Then back to Donna. "We were talking at our table about what a beautiful gown you have on. You look so very nice in it."

Nice, she's gorgeous. Donna filled out that cloth like a golf glove.

Then the lady said, "We just came in and are here for a wedding tomorrow. Won't you come and join our table?"

Donna looked at me. I opened my hands with a condescending look.

"We'd love to," said the green-eyed, green dressed maiden, with the green around the gills escort. And, as usual, Donna charmed everyone at the table. Me, the big company president from the United States, received an occasional question out of politeness.

Donna, however, elevated me from Ichabod Crane status, by telling everyone about her wondrous husband. She let them know in no uncertain terms that her husband was great stuff and made exceeding exploits. Eyebrows were raised in appreciation.

The parents of the bride and groom invited us to what turned out to be a traditional high society Egyptian wedding. It was to take place tomorrow in the garden of the hotel. A meeting with local distributors was set up so I couldn't go. But you couldn't keep Donna away.

Donna asked what she should wear. One lady said, "Exactly what you have on. That dress is absolutely beautiful."

Donna enjoyed the pageantry and the ceremony. The bride was beautiful, friendly and enjoyed talking with Donna, who loved the wedding and took loads of pictures.

So there you have it. Donna turns a disaster into another wonderful experience—Ichabod Crane and all.

The Camel Caper

Al-Karim had arranged for a young American archeologist, Jerry Metzer from Chicago, to act as our driver and guide during our stay in Cairo. He showed us a new tomb they were working on and arranged

The Research

for us to visit the home of an Egyptian archeologist friend, whose home the family had occupied for unknown generations. It was a small two-story adobe-like building with a packed clay floor. The friend's parents were small and very friendly.

Under the stairs leading to the second level, the grandfather was making an alabaster vase with iron tools the family had used for generations. Most of the cooking was done on the roof, which had a small covered kitchen and work area. Upstairs, in a room with hand-painted designs on the walls they served us a coke. Donna was entranced by this interesting home.

Donna and Don atop their camels.

We took a camel ride to the pyramids. At the end of the trip I was let down from my camel, but Donna was kept on her camel, which was hissing. It looked like the camel was going to take a bite out of the handler. Donna was frantically motioning the handler to let her down, but he just kept nodding and smiling, making no attempt to let her off.

"Don, I have to get down from here."

I motion for the handler to let Donna down. He nods with a silly grin, but makes no attempt to free her.

"Don, I have to get down, now."

I try again. I receive the same silly grin in response.

The handler's head is close to Donna's foot. "Don, you had better get me down from this stupid monstrosity or I'm going to kick that turkey in the head," seethed Donna.

"Now, Donna, calm yourself."

"I am calm. Get me down from here or I'm going to calmly kick that turkey in the head."

A policeman notices the problem and comes over and instructs the handler (the turkey) to let Donna down. Donna's eyes blaze at the turkey with the big grin as she makes a beeline for the ladies' room.

We had paid in advance, but I found out later that the handler wanted me to tip him before he let Donna down.

When Donna returned, she started to laugh.

"What's so funny?" I asked.

"I wonder if I really would have kicked that turkey in the head."

I believe it. And if he hadn't let her down, I believe Donna would have gone after the camel, too. I wouldn't have wanted to be in his hoofs for anything.

Midnight on the Nile

While sailing on the cruise boat *HS Hotp* on the Nile to Aswan, a strange thing happened to me late one night on the upper deck. In my research, the question as to why some people are talented and others are not has always bothered me. Talent seldom surfaces in high school, yet class reunions often reveal that people who were the least known or voted least likely to succeed are later the outstanding talents and success—often in spite of being poor students in school. How do we account for this? A logical answer would be that everyone inherits a hidden talent that education does not bring out and after graduation occasionally a few people accidentally discover their talents.

Imagine that every human inherited a talent and that there was a method for uncovering talents. Imagine also that our education system was revised so that individuals were instructed according to their talents. The natural talents of teachers would be known, so teachers with comparable inborn talents would instruct students with the same talents. Interested and talented students being taught by interested and talented teachers—wouldn't that be a change?

While I pondered this, the *HS Hotp* moved quietly up the Nile River. I could see how the desert closed in on the narrow band of farmland between the hills of sand and the river. At times the high sand hills looked like a menacing snow avalanche waiting to reclaim its land down to the river. The atmosphere and my thoughts gave me a strange and eerie feeling. There seemed to be a presence that engulfed me, a feeling as though the ancients were everywhere.

In this strange surrounding suddenly the word "talent" crossed my mind again, and a question came to me. Why should talent be limited to a special few? Why should one person have talent capability while someone else does not? Then a very strange series of words invaded my mind: "Everything lapses. Time and years mean nothing. Face the truth of what you believe, no matter how strange it may seem at this fleeting moment in time."

What a strange occurrence and usage of words. What did "fleeting moment in time" refer to? Normally things that come to me make sense, but I couldn't make any sense of this. "Face the truth of what you believe, no matter how strange." That part made some sense. Was it possible the statement referred to what I was starting to believe, that not just some people but every human naturally inherits a talent capability, one that can remain hidden from them until uncovered? That was too unbelievable to accept, and yet as I watched the moon's shadow below the distant sand dunes, I somehow knew it had to be true. Inherited hidden talent exists in all of us; we only need to find a method to uncovering them. But how could we ever do that?

Then a thought came to me. "There is something every human can do better than anything else they can do—and that is their talent." Is this the clue to uncovering each person's talent? Did the ancients give this gift to me or had I instinctively always known this, and now felt strongly compelled to accept it?

When I told Donna at breakfast what I had experienced last night on the deck, she listened carefully and said, "I know you have been questioning this theory, but if all people have an inborn talent, why doesn't it naturally surface? "

"I don't know."

"Does anyone else believe that everyone has inborn talent?" asked Donna.

"I don't . . . wait a minute. Remember on the plane going to Mexico? What did Einstein say about being talented?"

"I remember," Donna said thoughtfully. "He said he had no special talents and was only passionately curious. Isn't that right?"

"That sounds like it," I agreed. "But there was something else about not being intelligent. That we couldn't figure out what he was getting at."

"Yes. Okay, let me work it out," Donna continued. "He was not more intelligent and fortunate to have found interests and abilities. No, wait, I have it. 'I am not any more intelligent than anyone else, just fortunate to have found an area that matches my interests and abilities.' That's it."

I thought for a moment. "Good heavens, Donna, do you know what he was getting at?"

We ended up saying it almost in unison: "Not just some people but all people have some area that matches their interests and abilities, and that is what talent is."

I was speechless. Donna used a tissue to wipe tears from her eyes. "Oh Don, I know why you wanted to remember that. One of the most intelligent minds of all time is backing up what you believe. Everyone is born with talent," she said, sniffing. "Oh Don, I'm so glad. Your belief is right. You're on the right track."

※

That was our first major breakthrough, and because of it, other support surfaced.

In his book, *What Color is your Parachute?* Richard Nelson Boles writes: "Your mission on earth is one which is uniquely yours, to exercise that talent which you came to earth to use—your greatest gift."

The Research

John W. Gardner, in *Excellence*, says, "Generally speaking, individuals whose gifts have been discovered and cultivated have been as chance outcropping of precious rock, while the great reserves of human talent lay undiscovered below."

Robert Sternberg and Janet E. Davidson, in *Conceptions of Giftedness*, state. "Although there are no taxonomy of talents or system of talents classification that is widely accepted, talent is recognized as a set of aptitudes and abilities that predispose an individual to superior performance or achievement."

The reality of all this is that education was not listening to these learned people because education makes no effort to uncover the talents of students. Why not?

There is a lot of work yet to do. I stumbled on the key, now I had to find the door the key fits. I have three concepts to research. Everyone has talent capability, inborn talent and something they can do better than anything else they can do. I wonder. Would it help to take a closer look at the makeup of humans?

Human Activity

Talent research should be of interest to everyone because there is good evidence that each of us inherited a valuable talent that we are probably not aware of and may never know—unless a method is developed to uncover it.

If God gave each of us equality in our physical makeup, why would it be different when it comes to talent? Why would only certain people have a talent capability?

Talent capability may be like a heart or a liver—everyone has one. All humans have the same genetic building blocks; we could not come into being if we did not. If someone has genes that make efficient capability available as talent, then all of us must have those genes. Isn't it therefore possible that we all have talent in some area and having talent is a common human trait? It is logical and makes sense but is it possible . . . everyone in the world is naturally talented?

Although Donna and I believed my theory was logical I was unable to find scientific data that actually stated that everyone has talent capability. Unfortunately being logical and being supported by learned and respected people like Einstein did not prove the theory.

※

The following day I asked Donna if she had any talents.
"Devil's advocate, huh? Okay, I have many talents," she replied.
"Do you?"
"Well, not a talent like a well-known musician or an artist. Maybe I should say I have learned skills."

That was a very intelligent answer. "Can any skill be learned and perfected to talent status?"

Donna thought for a moment. "I don't think so. Real talent is natural. Although it may need training, it is not forced and it's a step above a skill."

"What about all people having a hidden talent?"

"It's kind of far out. How could anyone believe they are highly talented at something and not know it?" the devil's advocate asked.

"But, what if it were true and education has been unintentionally repressing individual talent capability, thus preventing talents from surfacing?"

"You will make a lot of enemies with that statement."

"Hey, now you're playing kind of rough aren't you? Aren't you afraid to discourage your husband?"

She laughs. "No way. My husband is a good hunting dog. Now he has the scent and nothing will stop him now."

"But what if it were true that education as it exists today actually suppressed individual talents—that in reality everyone is talented, even 'poor' students?" I continued.

"Everyone talented? Everyone having unknown talent capability would shake the foundations of education and society. It would set the world on its ear. Wouldn't everyone gravitating to their natural talents create chaos?" Donna asked.

"Talent would have to be educated, and I would presume the change would be gradual," I answered.

"What about the needed labor jobs? Wouldn't laborers be talented, too?

"They could be. Talents would need to be educated and that could accelerate the development of smart robots to do basic labor tasks."

"You already thought about that, huh?"

"They are developing smart robots that can do many tasks," I answered.

"Okay, but as you know, that talent idea is going to be difficult to prove."

"Will it ever. You know, it occurred to me that if all people have hidden talent the uneducated would be included. And, why not? I have seen illiterates show surprising ingenuity. Perhaps education's inability to uncover individual talent is why many people remain uneducated. Once the uneducated know their talents, it could raise their interest, their self-confidence in their ability and stimulate a desire to be educated. With talent, they too, could be productive and make contributions to society. Talent may give them the confidence they have desperately been longing for."

"Wait," she cautioned. "You mean we could take a dropout, someone with apparently low intellect and maybe a learning disability and transform that person into a highly talented individual . . . like Elisa Dolittle in *My Fair Lady*?"

"Good question. If everyone has hidden talent, it appears that may be possible."

"I've learned to respect your ideas—but this is awfully hard for me to accept."

"Perhaps it is, but we cannot overlook the possibility. I have no doubt it will be accomplished. In the future, everyone will have a genetic profile of their most capable and least stressful capabilities, that combination will point to their unique area of talent. People won't work at a career unless it is in tune with their genetic design. Imagine the health benefits of working at job that's suited to your talent."

"Wait a minute, you're getting way ahead of me. What's with this combination of abilities, least stress and genetic design stuff? You're really getting serious about some new ideas and genes now. Yes, I saw the books you have about genetics. That's too deep for me right now. Let's stay with learning disability. You think talent can overcome a disability?" Donna asked incredulously.

"For some children, forced education may be causing some dysfunction. Or a child's genes may be trying to maneuver a child into the arena of their natural abilities," I explained.

"Whoa, that's deep too. But I suppose it could be a possibility." She shook her head. "Back to talent. Question? How many different talents do you suppose there are?"

"I've thought about that," I answered. "There are 40,000 different known occupations and the average occupation has an average of five related job tasks, which equals 200,000 tasks. How many human activities are there in every job task? I do not know. And there may be talents humans have that we do not even know a use for. We may not know how many existing talents there are until we examine all the job tasks and human activities.

"I think talent has to exist in all of us and everyone should have the opportunity to achieve talent status. We only need to find a method of uncovering talent. Why not start researching for it now, when education and humanity need it so badly?" I questioned.

Donna looked me in the eyes for a moment and said, "Those aren't just suppositions. You really believe these things, don't you?"

"Yes, and whether I accomplish it or someone else does, it has to come about in the next decade. People can't go on living such stressful lives due to working at unsuitable careers. What do you believe?"

"From a human capability, health and perhaps genetic viewpoint, it seems logical."

"So, you don't deny talent capability?" I asked.

"To deny talent is to deny that each of us has different interests and capabilities, which obviously we do. Some people have talent and people are capable of being talented. I can't deny that. And that of the

40,000 occupations there is something each one of us can do better than anything else we can do, I can't deny that either. But you have the heavy burden of finding a way to prove it."

"My darling wife, your intelligent answer gives me much support and makes me feel very good. And as for the question, I'm going to try everything to prove it."

The devil's advocate mused at me. "I don't have a doubt in the world. My hunting dog, Goofy, is on the scent."

"Goofy again?"

She nodded mirthfully.

And I mused back at her and smiled. I wonder if this lovely lady could ever know how very much I loved and appreciated her.

Maria Montessori

I became aware of Maria Montessori in 1995. I was pleased to learn that we shared similar beliefs regarding talent and education. She wrote about human personality, personality development, normal development, natural capabilities, natural inclinations, special aptitudes, immeasurable abilities, special characteristics, development of individuality, passion, working the wrong way, fatigue, natural limitations, functioning freely and having a life purpose.

Maria believed that education did not take an individual's personality into account and that forced education went against a child's nature and restricted his/her personality and intelligence. "Education runs counter to human harmony by repressing, rejecting the moral self and erecting obstacles and barriers in the way of natural intelligence development," she said.

Maria believed education should be based on a scientific foundation. She felt that each child had its own personality, consisting of special aptitudes and capabilities, and therefore, each child should be educated and have the freedom to develop according to his/her natural inclinations. "A child's choosing of his own activities stimulates the growth and positive maturing of his intelligence. Science should concentrate on ways a child can develop naturally," stated Maria.

For Maria's objectives to be realized science must find a way to identify each child's special capabilities or natural inclinations. This is where uncovering talent research starts.

As Maria argued, "Man possesses more than he knows" and "Man must be educated to realize his greatness and to become worthy of the powers that are his."

One of Maria's main objectives is to make people aware that children are individually different and if natural capability educated, children would have a positive effect on human harmony once they matured. We must uncover the talents of children early in life and educate them accordingly She predicted that children and adults would have to know themselves better if there was to be peace in the world.

Maria's ideas were often looked upon as abstract or religiously oriented, but history may show that her ideas about children and education were practical and on the mark. The development of a method to uncover talents may be the catalyst to move Maria's objectives forward.

This new area of humanness, human capability and freedom to learn may be a new science and perhaps the most important new science of the 21st century. "The new kind of progress which makes traits and abilities the subject rather than just the source of change will dominate the agenda of the next century, perhaps even the next decade," wrote G. Owen Paepke in the introduction of *The Evolution Of Progress*.

Donna Says We've Hit the Top

At the end of our wonderful cruise along the Nile, we off-board at Aswan and are directed to a boat landing and a small falluca. This is a single sail, Nile boat, so often seen as an Egyptian symbol. Ours was completely carpeted and as comfortable as a Venetian gondola. The boatman pushed us away and motioned to the motor or the sail. I looked to Donna; she pointed to the sail.

The sail filled and, with a slight breeze, our falluca headed across the Nile towards the Aswan Oberoi Hotel on Elephantine Island. The ancient city of Aswan worked its way up the hill to our back. It was a marvelous, sunny day.

Donna lay back in luxury, with her arms spread wide. Casting her head from side to side, taking in the view, she said, "This is really luxury. You know, Don, this has all been so wonderful. I feel like we've really hit the top of our lives. I don't mean it's all downhill, but how much better can it get? I not only have a wonderful life and sons, I have a gentle, loving husband I dearly love."

Jeff's Accident—Greg's Quandary

While we were in Egypt Jeff was in an automobile accident. The doctor told Greg that Jeff might be badly hurt so they were doing x-rays to determine the extent of his injuries. Greg didn't know if he should call us in Egypt or not. The doctor came out with Jeff's x-rays and told Greg that Jeff had a close call, but he would be okay. After Greg saw Jeff and knew Jeff would be okay, Greg heaved a sigh of relief and decided not to call us.

Jeff, not wanting us to see him in the hospital, managed to be released just in time for us to arrive home. We were shaken when we found out what had happened. The deep cut in Jeff's throat had been less than an inch away from being fatal.

Dead Sea With Greg

We promoted Greg out of the plant to the position of vice president and ultimately to president. He earned his promotion the hard way— he earned it. A quick learner, Greg now had the responsibility for production, laboratory, legal and some personnel issues. Greg was an excellent people manager; our employees liked and trusted him.

Although Greg did not go to college he had experience with almost every aspect of the business. Greg, who handled our bromine development project, received a call from Israel about drawing bromine out of the Dead Sea. They wanted our company because other than Great Lakes Chemical, we had the only other bromine registration in the

United States. Bromine is a competition for swimming pool chlorine plus other manufacturing uses.

Greg and I flew to Athens, where we met with a potential distributor and then spent the rest of the day at the Acropolis.

The next day we flew to Tel. Aviv where a driver (provided by the Israeli government) took us to the Daniel Hotel. In the morning we were driven to the Dead Sea to meet with Israeli officials. A day of interesting meetings that could be fruitful.

In appreciation of coming, the Israeli driver was to take us to Bethlehem and Jerusalem. It was a cold night as we approached Bethlehem; the sky was clear and the stars were very bright. To me the experience had a "star of the east" magic about it.

The next morning our guide took us to Christ's sepulchre at a time when no tours were present. A short distance from the tomb, a gold jeweler was hammering out a gold bracelet. We watched him finish and I purchased it for Donna. She treasured it.

The Article

Donna and I took a business-vacation trip to our branches in Dallas, Phoenix and Los Angeles. After relaxing on the plane for a bit, I said, "Donna, I know how busy you are at home, so I brought along the article I've been working on so you can read it at your leisure."

"Oh, you finished it. I've been peeking at some of the material. I have to read it right now." Holding up her hand, she says, "I promise I won't say a thing until I finish." That's an old joke between us, because when Donna reads my writing, she often asks questions before she gets to the end.

I watched Donna as she read the article. I could tell that she re-read some of the passages a few times. She did not say a word, but periodically looked at me rather seriously, sometimes with a frown on her face, and at other times in apparent disbelief.

The Research

The Right Career

Uncovering Talents That Are Mentally, Physically And Healthfully Correct, Lead To the Right Careers

Every human possesses an inborn capability that their unique structure can do more efficiently, successfully and in good health than anything else they can do.

by Donald E. Seymour

All About You

There is not, never has been, nor will there ever be anyone exactly like you. You are a one-of-a-kind combination of invisible life force, with body, looks and personality totally different from any other human. Your core traits, talent and supporting intelligence capability is programmed and fixed in you at birth.

You are capability different because you inherited a unique combination of human activities that you can do better than anything else you can do, and probably better than anyone else can do.

There are a few occupations, in the 40,000 plus occupations or areas of human endeavor, that most efficiently and healthfully fit your unique genetic design. When you find those few occupations, healthful success comes easily. Correct careers promote creativity and enhance intelligence capability.

Because you are born with different and unique capabilities, it is also possible you have a purpose to fulfill or a contribution to make to others and humanity. Uncovering your most talented career must be the important task of your life.

Why Don't You Know Your Talent?

If you were born with unique and different capabilities, why don't you know what they are? And if you did know what they are, how could you find the career you are most efficiently designed for in which to apply those capabilities when there are 40,000 plus known occupations?

A question for the future. Assume you could uncover and develop your natural inborn talents and find a career that matches your talents, will your career compete with the artificial intelligent machines of tomorrow? Surviving human work, not taken over by smart machines, will be highly competitive. If we don't have a good reason to uncover our best talents now, each individual will ultimately be forced to uncover and field the most talented capability to compete with other natural talents.

Many people believe they have talents, but true talent is rare. What most people consider talent is a learnable skill. Talent is naturally inborn and not learnable.

Forcing yourself to compete with skills against naturally talented people creates harmful stress and friction. Drug and alcohol abuse and suicide are attempts to reduce or evade stress and friction. Your genes, knowing you are in the wrong profession for your body and mind, will demand attention and exert pressure to encourage you into the right work for the sake of your purpose and health.

Can You Make Yourself Into Anything You Want To Be?

Albert Einstein said, "The biological nature of man is, for all practical purposes, not subject to change."

An occupation that does not fit, such as one that is practical, idealistic, or "going for the money" can be highly stressful and subtract from a worker's efficiency and well being. By 'fit' we refer to those few of the 40,000 known occupations that you can be most successful at and creative in—with the least effort, because they are in tune with your natural capabilities and health. No one would select a career if they knew in advance there would be a high cost in health, happiness, and longevity of that selection.

Sandra Scarr, a University of Virginia psychologist, says, "We can help direct a human down the path of their natural abilities, but are asking for trouble and friction when trying to mold a human in a direction not in tune with their natural genetic structure."

Old adages say, "Adversity builds character" and "You can make yourself into anything you want to be." The people saying this could not have understood today's stress effect on capability, health and intelligence. If you don't uncover your right career, an enjoyable, healthful and talented success will (except by rare accident) be most difficult to attain and may

The Research

substantially shorten your longevity. Burnout in 20 years and Monday morning heart attacks are examples.

You cannot efficiently or healthfully make yourself a successful doctor, legal secretary or truck salesman if your capabilities are not in tune with the occupation. Poor career selection is difficult to compete against talented competition. Intelligent machines will be formidable competition without an individual utilizing their most efficient capabilities. This competition will increase as more advanced intelligent (wet-brain) machines are developed. If you can't change what you are to succeed, then your only alternative is to uncover whatever you can do best and select your career accordingly.

The full negative effect on the psychological nature and physical health of humans due to selecting wrong occupations is not yet fully understood, however, doctors know that forcing unsuitable occupations on your mind and body creates stress and friction. Drugstore shelves loaded with depressant drugs provide mute evidence that inefficient career selection is taxing our health and capability beyond natural human limits.

Ethics can be and often are sacrificed by wrong career selection in attempting to compete with others who have natural talent. This may be why honesty, integrity and ethics have degenerated.

What You Have To Work With?

Prominent educators believe that very few talents are uncovered. In his book, *Excellence*, John Gardner states, "Generally speaking, individuals whose gifts have been discovered and cultivated have been as chance outcropping of precious rock, while the great reserves of human talent lay uncovered below."

The best natural talent consists of long-term interest, your most efficient talented activities and the healthful application of those activities to a few of the 40,000 known occupations they match best.

Right careers release the highest level of creativeness, inventiveness, problem-solving ability and intelligence. Like a runner's high, the right career is almost effortless, while working in the wrong career is as laborious as running an uphill marathon.

Uncovering natural talents and selecting the right careers has not happened because people don't understand or believe they have inborn talents. Your unique talent does exist and can be uncovered. A talent uncovered at any age is invaluable, even for senior citizens that need a valuable and dedicated interest to look forward to each day during their retirement.

Using Tests to Target Suitable Occupations

Educators, career psychologists and occupation consultants attempt to use psychological and personality tests, interest blanks and surveys to help determine suitable careers and occupations. Tests have value in recognizing occupational interests, identifying psychological and personality types, and are effective tools to help know us better.

There are tests that attempt to target careers by matching an individual's response to the responses of successful people in a particular profession. To respond intelligently and efficiently to occupation-targeting questions an individual needs adequate knowledge and exposure to the 40,000 plus occupations. People know little about a *few* occupations and most of their knowledge is inadequate or wrong. Targeting occupations efficiently with the use of tests may be helpful information but is not an efficient tool for career selection.

The best way to uncover suitable occupations is for an individual to work at each of the 40,000 known occupations until they recognize what suits them naturally. This, of course, is not possible because it would take more than a lifetime to work at each of 40,000 occupations.

Everyone is born with an efficient combination of human activities, referred to as talent, which can be best matched with a few of the 40,000 occupation areas. We need a process to uncover these unique talent combinations and the occupations they fit best. The most efficient way to find occupations that fit your inborn talents is a process that eliminates all of the 40,000 occupations that do *not* fit. Talent is not one activity but a number of mental and physical activities working together. Even the most talented people may not be using their best and most healthful talents; as the high incidence of drug and alcohol abuse and suicide among the talented attests.

How Unique Is Your Talent?

Although there are general categories within the 40,000 occupations this does not mean that you have the same talent in a particular occupation as many other people may have. Human activities or occupations will vary in effect upon each unique individual when used or exposed to different environments, people, places and things. There are millions of artists that paint, but each of them has their own specialty in subject, style and medium. Art critics can identify a prominent painter's work from a distance. Everyone's talent can fit into one of the general occupation areas (painting), but everyone's talent is also specifically different from everyone else. Which is why every individual can do something no one else can do.

The U. S. Department of Labor's *Dictionary of Occupations* has one artist, one musician and one medical doctor in its list of 20,000 occupations. There are many different kinds of artists, musicians and doctors; therefore 40,000 is a more likely figure. As no two of the earth's six billion people look or act alike or have the same fingerprints, there are no two talents exactly alike. Every talent has unique value in some productive area, either alone, in participation with other people or in think tanks.

Qualification Of Talent

Each individual is born with a variety of efficient talent activities, but only a few combinations are highest in interest and capability and lowest in stress. Every human inherits an exclusive talent capability unique to his or her structure. It is what you were designed to do best, is always saleable and no person, machine or artificial intelligence can take it away. It is your exclusive personal capital and your best protection against competition, intelligent computers, restructuring and downsizing.

How Talented Golfers, Musicians and Architects are Uncovered

Great golfers, musicians and architects are uncovered through exposure, education, and working at the activity. We have a better chance of discovering a top golfer than a top brain surgeon because more people are exposed to playing golf than performing brain surgery. Practically anyone can play golf to learn if they are talented at it. And the chances are that if everyone on earth played golf, the current crop of top golfers would probably be replaced by more talented golfers because less than one in ten thousand of the earth's six billion people have played golf.

Human Activities—The Key

As our fingerprints are unique, every human is born with a different combination of human activities. We don't yet know how to locate and take a picture of the exclusive combination of human activities that each of us can do best—like we can fingerprints. It is reasonable and logical to conclude that your talented combination of human activities does exist, even though you don't know what it is.

Work consists of doing a combination of human activities to accomplish a purpose. An accepted method of breaking down work is into the job tasks involved in each occupation. However, humans can respond with greater clarity and sensitivity to individual activities than we can to job tasks that contain a mix of human activities. We need to break down job tasks into a new category that we will name human activities.

What Are Human Activities?

Example: Constructing high-rise buildings is an occupation, erecting building components is a job task, walking on a high girder to attach the components is a human activity. Workers with good balance are comfortable at high altitudes, but others are fearful of heights and this causes job inefficiency and stress.

Chemical Oceanographer is an occupation, obtaining water samples is a job task, taking samples by diving deep into the ocean is a human activity. Some divers enjoy deep diving; others have no interest or are naturally fearful of deep water.

Secretary is an occupation, taking dictation is a job task and shorthand is a human activity. A person may enjoy being a secretary but dislike taking shorthand, which will negatively affect his or her work. Dislike causes friction and friction negatively affects emotions, energy and efficiency. Workers are more creative, productive, efficient and less subject to mistakes and accidents when they are not required to do things that they find frightening, boring or they don't like to do.

In every occupation there are activities that may cause stress and friction, which restricts an individual from full efficiency. The objective is to uncover occupations or careers that are most interesting, capable and least subject to stress and friction.

Interest and Career Selection

An occupation and its job tasks may be interesting but, when reduced to human activities, over time each activity involved may cause some level of boredom, anxiety or stress, resulting in friction. Without knowledge of their natural capability, students select careers that appear most interesting, then discover later that a "dream career" that looked good, now feels terrible. Friction will not only restrict occupation efficiency but also negatively affect an individual's health. An interesting occupation highest in capability and lowest in friction provides the best opportunity for a healthful and successful career.

Mental capability is measured by the amount of curiosity, learning and energy the mind is willing to commit. Motivation consists of energy our bodies and minds allow us to commit to doing, creating and problem solving.

Law Of Probability

Evidence that talents exist may be found in the law of probability. Place an individual in a room with a thousand other people and give each person the same task to do over and over again. In time, some people will quit, be inadequate or lose interest. In those more capable, eventually one person will have the desire and talent to do the task better than anyone else.

If thousands of task rooms were available, eventually you would find the task you do best. It has nothing to do with your appearance, confidence, disability or what you think you are capable of doing. Similar to sports, each individual could graduate to that position they do best. Trial and error can bring natural ability to the surface, if only there was a way to provide trial and error within the 40,000 occupations.

Tomorrow's Work and Careers

If we knew your best careers today, what is the future for your specific career? The direction of technology predicts that in the not too distant future most human work (including mental work) will be done by automation, robotics or knowbots, directed by highly efficient, artificial intelligence. Food chains like McDonald's are investigating the development of food dispensers that would eliminate the need for human workers. General Electric is testing machines (not subject to human error) to replace surgeons that operate on humans.

The current shortage and expense of workers is further incentive for companies to invest in and speed up development of a greater spread of human replacement equipment (robots), which could ultimately eliminate most human work. While companies prefer human workers, when one chain goes robotic the rest will follow to remain competitive.

In *Probable Tomorrows* Marvin Cetron and Owen Davis state, "Most of us will spend our entire working lives bouncing from one career to the next, scrambling to learn the skills of a new profession before some smart computer snatches our current living from beneath us." Peter Drucker calls it the "Age of Discontinuity" where new innovations constantly modify or eliminate jobs. The service and information industries are predicted to provide future jobs, but for how long? Again quoting Cetron and Davis: "Recently, computers have begun to streamline operations in the service industries, which is the last stronghold of human labor, and now machines are being developed with the ability to service themselves." The service and information industry jobs too will fall in the drive to develop more sophisticated machines thereby eliminating human work.

It must be worrisome that no one is predicting where jobs will come from beyond the service and information industries. Is this problem far off or will it come on us with the take-over speed of high technology and the information age? Will this happen during your working life? Michio Kaku, author of *Visions*, says of new machines on the horizon, "True robot automatons that have common sense, can understand human language, manipulate objects in their environment, and can

The Research

learn from their mistakes is a development that will likely alter our relationship with machines forever."

Donna put the page down and looked at me in amazement. "Don, are you trying to say that billions of jobs, all the jobs people do now, will be done by robots? Even medicine, law, and engineering?"

"Not me. Cetron, Davis, Drucker and many others believe so."

"How could that be?" she asks.

"Robots will have immediate access to every library, professional journal and film of every activity available and will be able to assimilate and use that information just as fast. This is something humans cannot do."

"You mean humans will become obsolete?" she challenged.

"Evidently, as far as work is concerned."

"It would take a long time for this too happen, wouldn't it?"

"A few new developments and robots could be rolling off manufacturing lines, like computers."

"Just like that? And in a few years jobs would be gone?" Donna was incredulous.

"I would presume that a few jobs would continue for a short time. Someone would have to manage the robots at first, until that job too would be taken over," I responded.

"People have been saying that robots will take over for years, and it hasn't happened."

"Read on, Donna."

> People have been crying wolf about the machine take-over of human work for a long time. Perhaps it isn't a case of will it happen, but when and how fast. Scrambling to find new and capable work and competing for the surviving occupations may be fruitless without knowing your natural talents and how and where to efficiently apply them. To compete with intelligent machines each individual will be forced to uncover, develop and utilize their best natural talents—perhaps several times during their lives. A person can be prepared for this, if they know their natural talents.

A Process Not Completed

Why present a talent uncovering process that is not as yet designed or available? If people knew the happiness, health, fulfillment and longevity they may be sacrificing, they would demand that education and government develop a way to uncover their natural talent.

You are the best generation to demand that a talent discovery process be developed. It will not come into being without your knowing it exists, is needed and can be done. Knowing I had hidden talents, I would rather spend a lifetime searching and chance uncovering them, than not having searched at all. Searching for your talent is a more hopeful and interesting life. Even without knowing your best talents, in the search, new ideas, values and unexpected interests will show up as you learn more about yourself and your natural capabilities.

Developing The Process

Developing a talent uncovering process may one day result in conforming careers more closely to natural human capabilities. We may even build occupations to suit each individual's capability.

Business, government and education should commit the funds to get this work done. It may take the combined efforts and financial support of business, science and the Departments of Education, Health, Welfare and Labor. It will utilize computer programming, cataloguing, coding, filming of all human activities and possibly virtual reality experiences for human activity exposure.

In the development of the process, other imaginative people will no doubt find ways to make uncovering talents more efficient and effective. A corporation with Microsoft's capability could lead a team of hi-tech companies in the development of the software.

Today's students may become professionally involved in the development of one of the future occupations talent uncovering will spawn that robots may not do.

What Are the Choices?

Will humans hide from the overbearing intelligence machines that mimic every human activity and characteristic, thus depriving people of purpose and meaningful work? We either have to develop a way to compete with intelligent machines, limit the use of intelligent machines or let them take over and make our living by creating a separate talent work world for humans. If talent machines are created, human talent may be isolated from machines to fill in human time.

As no two people are the same, no two talents or talent applications are the same. Talent subjects are subdivided into researching, compiling, teaching, training and writing. The variety of talent applications is greater in number than there are people.

Of the six billion people on earth, there are thousands who have the talent to solve or substantially reduce every problem on earth; whether it is social or environmental (cancer, HIV, war or terrorism). The sad thing is, all people may live their lives without ever knowing they had the ability, joy and satisfaction of creating a better world.

A Talented World

There will be need for crossover talents or the combining of talents to serve a business or subject purpose. The coming century may be "The Talent Century" as a talent industry is born. A talent world where each human will compete with the best talents their unique structure has to offer.

With little training, natural talents can ask unusual questions and make naïve but valuable (out of the mouth of babes) conclusions in talent think tanks. Existing businesses will pay for the problem-solving service of talent think tanks. One person's talent may be valuable in several different think tanks. Using your talent in a talent society may be the only way to earn a living in the future. With thousands of different talent stores and think tank centers, talent may become a vast business—the only business for humans.

Our most difficult people and environmental problems would soon be resolved by uncovering millions of talents that would create a vast flow of patents, inventions and solutions. The first country to develop a talent uncovering process, with a six-month start, would create a river of new patents that would make them the world economic leader far into the future.

Talent Could Solve Problems

Talented people become very involved in their talent, which could fill in the identity vacuum that otherwise drives people to crime, violence, alcohol, drugs, war, terrorism and suicide. In 1998 one in 150 Americans were in prison. A small percentage of the yearly penal cost in the U.S. could easily pay for the talent development process. Uncovering talent would provide a means to keep people out of jail, reduce health, education, and people problem costs. We need to uncover the talents of young people or the prediction that violent crimes will double by 2010 may come true.

Seventy million Americans cannot read adequately. Not because they can't read, but because they don't have a good enough reason—it takes too much effort. All people, including illiterates, need an interesting and impelling talent that is exclusively theirs, to give them confidence, self-esteem and identity. Uncover their talent and they will want to learn with a passion.

You Can Make the Difference

It is fair to conclude that health-qualified talent is the key to maximum success, good health, life-long interest and longevity. If we don't solve education's and society's problems soon indications are that current terrorism is just a prelude of what lies ahead.

A correct career discovery process could come into being in this generation, if we work to bring it to reality. It should be supported and developed as soon as possible. What can you do to help bring correct careers to fruition to benefit you, your family and future generations?

What About You?

Why is it that there never has been nor ever will be another you? Why not 10,000 of you and 10,000 of me, thus saving individual designing? Were you created different and sent here for a purpose—to accomplish something of value and importance no one else can? Will you go though life never knowing if your unknown talent could have helped cure cancer, an environmental problem to save our planet or benefit humanity in some other way? You have the capability to make more of your

The Research

life than you know. Maria Montessori said, "Your mission here on earth is uniquely yours, to exercise that talent which you particularly came to earth to use—your greatest gift."

Talent surfaces when we recognize our most interesting, capable and health qualified human activities into a combination of mental and/or physical activities that can be efficiently, successfully and healthfully applied to specific occupations or other areas of human endeavor.

Let me explain one more time in a different way. When you find the subject in which your interest and capability combination is at the highest level and that combination is lowest in stress; dedicating your time and effort becomes easy. Your talent is your inborn gift, and like fingerprints, no one else in the world has a talent just like yours. You are more talented, intelligent and can make a meaningful contribution with your life by knowing what you were best designed to do and possibly meant to accomplish—no matter your age.

If you find your natural talent and have a way to do something for humanity—you are fortunate. If not, perhaps with the use of your talent you can make your concern known and influence others who can. Perhaps that is all that is required of you.

Saving our world is a very serious business. People die and the world goes on, but the world need only die once and nothing goes on.

Donna finished reading and lay the article in her lap. She put her hands together in prayer fashion, with her thumbs under her chin. She turned and looked at me with tears in her eyes.

Oh Lord, I thought, is it that bad? All the years and time I devoted and it's full of holes and assumptions? "That bad, huh?"

She shook her head, "All your years of research and this is it?"

I nodded. "You're disappointed, aren't you."

"Oh. Don, no. Oh, how far you've come." She sniffed. "Hon it's . . . it's . . . wonderful and I knew you could do it."

"It's still only a theory and not proven," I cautioned.

"Oh, no. Theory, no longer." She held it up. "Don, this is powerful. How can anyone not believe our talent exists?"

"It's good then?"

She laughed. "You silly goof. You just opened the door to the new science of talent discovery. I'm so proud of you," she gushed.

"Well, thank you," I said, slightly embarrassed at her reaction.

"What now? Are you going to submit it to The National Science Foundation?"

"They wouldn't touch something so unproven, especially coming from an uneducated source."

"They are kind of stuffy. I know, you're going to use this to write the book?"

"Do you think there's enough to do it? That's only six pages."

"Don, the way you keep researching, and your mind keeps expanding these things, by the time you're finished, you will have a book and the public will listen."

"I wonder."

I spend most nights working on my computer. Occasionally Donna checks in on me, but stays clear.

One night, I am sitting there, looking at what I have written. Donna approaches the back of my chair, puts her arms around my shoulders and says, "Don't want to bother you, but you look a little frustrated. Problems?"

"You can tell, huh? I'm adding pages and words and citing examples and I've even developed some further ideas. But the more ideas I develop the more holes open up. Like a trail that keeps branching off and I don't know which one to stay on. I feel lost."

"You're trying too hard. Put it down for awhile. It will come together, it did before."

Selling the Companies

Our company was the first member of the Wisconsin World Trade Center. I was one of the founders of the Wisconsin Small Business

Association, a director of a small bank, and managing our eight companies. I was too involved. It was time to turn my full attention to the research.

At the age of sixty-seven I sold the companies. What would I do after years of being the captain of an industry with executives and secretaries to do my bidding? I had tears in my eyes when I signed away the companies, but perhaps now my stomach would finally stop bothering me. I didn't realize what a stressful business burden I had carried all those years. Both of my male forebears died young and I thought it wise to relieve myself of the stress. When I look back on how we built a conglomerate of companies with little capital and numerous bank loans, it seemed like an impossible accomplishment.

When I came home and told Donna how much we were paid for the companies, she changed her response. She said, "That's nice dear," and just pointed at the garbage. Some things never change.

Vocational Guidance Institute

I reflected on the wide variety of jobs and the various responsibilities I had during my career. My business life had given me the opportunity to experience a broad range of activities. From that exposure, I developed areas of interest in highly technical fields, for which I was not qualified. I exhibited some talent in business management and vocational guidance.

Why hadn't my education brought these interests to the surface? If I had capabilities and talents that formal education did not discover, then other people could also have hidden abilities.

Talent is needed to combat competition and to achieve success in business. I started to believe that uncovering natural talent should be the focal point of education. If we could uncover the talents of people, we could educate people according to their talents. This would require a change in how we educate children. Our education system would have to focus on specific talent education.

Too many high school graduates earn good grades and receive scholarships to attend college, and then upon graduation from college they cannot hold a job in their degreed field because they lack interest in the job, find it boring or too difficult.

While I interviewed job applicants for our companies, I met hundreds of people looking for positions outside of their degrees. After working sporadically in their field of study, many graduates gave up, and began to seek work in a different field. After talking and working with many of these people, I realized that far too many individuals have a degree in a profession in which they have no lasting interest, talent, or ability.

One of the worst and most damaging fallacies is that students (and parents) think a person can select a career and then depend on formal education to make them proficient in that career.

Donna watched me struggle with the many other branches of research that my studies opened up. My book idea was not going well and the proof of my theory still evaded me.

We decided to donate a portion of our assets to set up a foundation and hire researchers to organize and develop the ideas I had accumulated throughout the years. The Vocational Guidance Institute, a Wisconsin; non-profit foundation was dedicated to the study and research of finding a way to uncover the hidden talent of every human.

One main objective was to see if any one else was doing similar research and to study the ideas already developed. The initial research subjects were: education; interest; natural learning; talent discovery; career planning; career adjustment; and the effect of wrong careers on life planning, health, intelligence, work, the disabled, family problems, divorce, terrorism, crime, and suicide.

Another purpose of setting up the institute was to develop an Education by Attraction school concept and submit it to the New American Schools Committee.

Greg and I rented an office in north Milwaukee. I interviewed and

The Research

hired the people and Greg managed the office. Connie Amos, our secretary, did great work on life planning cards I was working on, and she used herself for an example. Jory Prosen did special research. Michelle Gagne was our editor.

I also worked on a Riseac School education idea, named after the general headings on Strong's, Strong-Campbell Blank. Michael Puzia developed the proposal and named it "Project Genesis." We submitted Project Genesis to the New American Schools Committee. The idea must have been too foreign for established educational principles, as the committee did not award us a grant to develop the concept.

In 1988 a strong rainstorm passed through the city of Milwaukee leaving in its wake the effects of a "hundred-year flood." A month earlier we had purchased a swimming pool business for Greg and Jeff to manage. The storm destroyed the building and a large inventory. No flood insurance was available at the time.

We lost a lot of money and owed the former owner personal notes on the store. We applied for a United States Small Business Administration (SBA) flood disaster loan for new inventory and to repair the store. No one in the SBA wanted to take responsibility for the loan, so they passed the buck around several city offices for thirty-three weeks. The SBA charter calls for prompt financial help to save jobs and business. A damaged business cannot survive thirty-three weeks without working capital. Ultimately we had to bankrupt the pool business and close the three stores.

The conclusions drawn from the foundation research indicated that some of the concepts I developed were new, had value, and should be pursued. Especially undiscovered talent.

However, I hesitated to voice the idea that many people could have undiscovered talents. I felt my peers would think I was daft. I was afraid

I was wrong because this was a substantial departure from established educational principles.

At the end of two years, I had to close the Vocational Institute office because of the flood loss.

Not everything is roses.

In Retirement

I continued the research on my own. Fortunately my desire to prove my theory did not diminish. I was blessed with having a dedicated purpose during my retirement. I know of others who had good intentions to do contributory things in retirement, but found it difficult to do so.

Donna said we were at the top of life, age-wise it was downhill now, but that did not matter to her. Life was fun; she was happy and grateful. Because of Donna's dedication to help others, fate was kind to her. She retained much of her energy and youthful beauty.

Each day Donna thanked God for her life and wished she could do more in return. She wondered how it was possible to make a meaningful contribution to humanity to show how thankful she was for her life.

SECTION THREE
The Lady

We Lose A Close Friend

Warren Meyer and Donna continued their clown antics through the years. Warren derived great humor and pleasure in upstaging me at every opportunity. I was Warren's special target. He enjoyed placing me in a position where I could not outdo him or get back at him.

Then a cloud came over our foursome. In 1989 Warren had a serious heart operation in Little Rock, Arkansas. Donna and I went to Little Rock to help Shirley bring Warren home after his surgery. When we arrived in Little Rock he was in a coma. Although the three of us witnessed some encouraging signs, Warren did not make it. The following is from the eulogy I gave at Warren's funeral in Milwaukee, Wisconsin on September 20,1989:

"You made it crystal clear to me, that you have a strong unshakable faith in Our Lord. That faith helped shape your personality and the person you became and we learned to love and respect. Our Lord created and sent you here to live, learn and grow in love and faith for some future purpose and you did it very well. Your cheerfulness and helpfulness was well known to all.

Your upstaging me this last one time was marvelous; because you left on my birthday, so I could never forget.

So now, go for The Light old friend and have a good trip. We will see you in some other place and time, where there will be other warm and sunny days . . .when you, we and all of us here will be back together again."

Shirley lost Warren. Donna lost her favorite clown. I lost a true supporter and close friend, who is the other non-relative mentioned in my nightly prayers.

Breakthrough in Jackson Hole

Donna wanted to see Yellowstone National Park. Although I had been there in 1936 with my parents, when I was fourteen, I wanted to see it again and to also visit Jackson Hole, just south of Yellowstone. The name "Jackson Hole" had always intrigued me. It was as if I was being drawn there for a purpose.

We flew to Salt Lake City in August 1990, rented a car, and drove to Jackson Hole. It was as I had visualized it: a remote valley surrounded by mountains and forested wilderness.

Jackson Hole is located in the Grand Teton National Park on the southern border of Yellowstone National Park, which is in the Gros Ventre (pronounced Gro Vaunt) wilderness of the Bridger Teton National Forest, which covers three-and-a-half million acres.

The floor of Jackson Hole, at a 7,000-foot elevation, covers an area some fifty miles long and twenty miles wide at its widest point. Most of Jackson Hole is located in the Grand Teton ("three tits" in French) National Park. The city of Jackson is located a few miles south and east of Jackson Hole. There is no railroad in Jackson Hole, which makes the valley appear even more remote and virginal.

The national Elk Refuge runs from the entrance to the Gros Ventre River down into the city of Jackson Hole, where a fence was built to keep the elk out of the city. But, in winter, when food is scarce, the elk go where they want. They are not bashful or shy like the deer—they don't mind fences at all. They have even been known to break into barns to chase horses out of their stalls and to eat the horse feed.

The Lady

Donna and some of her classmates that attended their 50th high school class reunion in Mt. Horeb, Wisconsin. Donna's ability to maintain her youthful appearance was very striking at this event.

The Twentieth-Century Lady

The Tetons form a high, sharp, striking backdrop along the west side of the Hole, with the Gros Ventre Mountains on the east, the Hoback Mountain Range to the south and the mountains of Yellowstone National Park to the north.

The Gros Ventre Mountains are eroded, rounded volcanic mountains. The Tetons, to the west, are the youngest mountains in North America. They are less than ten million years old and the result of bottom lift rather than volcanic eruption. Rising 11,000 feet into the air, the majestic Tetons look like a great hand in a cavern deep below the earth tore loose huge stalactites and rammed them up and through the crust of the earth.

The area is occasionally subject to minor earthquakes that push the Tetons higher into the air at an estimated rate of one foot every three hundred years. At the same time Jackson Hole continues to sink at a similar rate . . . no one knows why.

On the way north to Yellowstone Park is a chain of seven lakes that was formed when glaciers pushed their way down the Hole. The lakes are clear, cold, and unspoiled. Jackson Lake, with its beautiful Elk Island, is at the foot of Mount Moran and Jenny Lake is at the foot of the Grand Teton.

Most tourists head for Yellowstone National Park or Glacier National Park above Yellowstone, and give the Hole but a passing glance. This is unfortunate because Jackson Hole is one of the most beautiful areas in the world. Every form of recreation is available in the summer, and no finer skiing can be found anywhere in the winter.

This area is known as the Swiss Alps of North America and the wildflower capital of the world. It contains some of the finest virgin camping and trail areas. River rafting through the roaring canyons is sharply adventurous.

We had reserved a room at the Spring Creek Resort, which was located on top of the East Gros Ventre Butte, just south of Jackson

The Lady

Hole. We decided to join the other guests that were enjoying cocktails on the timbered terrace of the resort restaurant before dinner. Donna and I were enchanted by the change in colors as the sun slowly set behind the Tetons.

I was quietly appreciating the view, when the word "talent" again penetrated my mind. The idea that all people could be highly talented at something (they do not know) constantly crossed my mind.

New ideas or solutions often came to me at quiet times in places surrounded by wilderness and scenes of great beauty. On this high butte, my brain decided to invade my thoughts about talent. So go ahead brain, ruin my reverie. Let's see what you have.

Everyone is constantly active; it is built in and automatic. We can't live without doing activities. Everyone is interested in or has a preference for certain activities. We might say every individual has their own activity preference profile, which is a part of their unique personality.

We can describe an activity as being talented when an activity is conducted at a high level of efficiency. Hmm, very interesting—efficient activity. What is talent other than a combination of highly efficient activities working together in some particular occupation or area of human endeavor? Talent could not consist of a scattering of unrelated activities that do not compliment each other. We are all talented when we perform a combination of activities that compliment each other; this results in a high level of occupational efficiency.

Because we are all different, we can't refute that each of us would have a higher level of capability in one of the 40,000 known occupations compared to the other 39,999. But how can we ever know which one it is?

A combination of efficient activities working together results in a talent, or more specifically each person's "Maximum Talent Capability." With those words, I jerked up and almost spilled my drink. "Wow, where did that come from?" I said.

Donna, who was talking to a lady seated next to her, turned to me. "Something wrong?" she asked with concern.

"I've been looking for a way to describe what I have been looking for and suddenly the answer came to me," I whispered.

She smiled. "Oh, great. Tell me later." Donna turned back to her conversation and my mind went back to talent.

My brain continued on. Maximum Talent Capability is an efficient combination of activities sponsored by genes! "Sponsored by Genes?" I exclaimed out loud.

Donna gave me a tap on the arm. There were people on the porch, but other than the woman Donna was talking to, no one paid attention to me. I put my hand over my mouth. No more outbursts like that, people will think I'm a little strange.

In just a few minutes, three things related to talent surfaced. Combinations of efficient activities, Maximum Talent Capability and "gene sponsored".

Maximum Talent Capability (MTC) is a combination of efficient human activities that could be engineered and sponsored by genes. Genes created us and what genes create they also control. Genes create a finger, continuously grow fingernails, and repair cuts in the finger. Therefore genes must be the builders of and control of human activities, that make up and perform the job tasks that make up occupations. It was all so simple and made sense. Everyone could have inherited talent and we have to start at our genes to find it.

At dinner, I explain these new ideas to Donna. At first Donna had trouble grasping the inter-workings. She made me reiterate my thoughts to make it clear to her, and after a number of questions she started to nod.

She said, "What I hear is that each person's most efficient combination of human activities is their unknown Maximum Talent Capability. Genes build and control efficient combinations of human activities that result in talented occupations. Genes are the source of talent. It's logical, simple and makes sense. But how are you going to prove it?"

After dinner we returned to our rustic room, where someone had lit the fireplace to quell the cool night air. Donna, an early riser, kissed me

The Lady

good night and went to bed. My mind is very active. I have more thinking to do.

I put on a warm jacket, opened the sliding glass door, and sat on our private balcony facing the Tetons. The valley and sky are different shades of blue and purple. The Snake River, far below, reflects a silver ribbon of light, and the glacier high in the saddle of the Grand Teton, glows with absorbed light.

So the question is, how do genes create human activity efficiency? At this stage I can't prove that everyone has what the public recognizes as talent, but everyone does possess one or more capabilities in which they could do something better than any other activities they perform.

As an example, in high school football there are some twenty-two offensive and defensive positions on the field. A coach can recognize a particular position that each student can do best or is most talented at by having each player work at each of the twenty-two positions. In comparison, there is no way every human can work at each of the 40,000 known occupations to find the occupation that they can do best or are most talented at. So let's take an occupation apart and analyze the activities involved in it.

▲ Each occupation is performed through a number of job tasks.
▲ Each job task is performed by a number of activities.
▲ Each activity is performed by a number of physical and mental actions, which we assume are controlled by genes.

Actions? That's new, I think. Let's see. Genes create our finger and what genes create, we know they control. So actions are the direct missing link between genes and human activities. But we still have the problem of proving everyone is talented. Back to activities.

Even though some activities occur in the job tasks of many different occupations, there must be thousands of different human activities involved in the 40,000 known occupations. And there appears to be no way to submit each individual to the untold thousands of individual activities and perhaps millions of combinations of activities. This, therefore, precludes using a human activity or occupation trial and error process to find out which occupation an individual is most talented at. There has to be another way.

I refer to Maximum Talent Capability as a combination of highly efficient job tasks, activities, and actions that are somehow accentuated by a specific action or energy to talent status.

Can our genes exert a kind of energy (or mysterious effect) to somehow accomplish that accentuation? I know so little of these things, and the answer (if it exists at all) could not be very simple. How could I possibly solve such a deep scientific riddle? I'm tired. I'll think about this tomorrow. If this answer is required for me to continue with my research, this may be the end of it. I probably have no business in this deep technical stuff anyway.

A cloud settles over me. It is very cool on the balcony, so I go in and gloomily sit by the warm fireplace.

The next day we drove to the beautiful Snake River Canyon where its rough waters entertain whitewater rafters.

Donna notices I am a little somber. Placing her hand on my arm she says, "Don, you look kind of low. Is something wrong?"

"Sorry, I didn't mean to be," I try to reply somewhat cheerily.

"Research bogging you down?"

I nod.

"Tell me about it."

She listens intently as I tell her the ideas that came to me and the barrier I ran into.

When I finish talking, Donna smiles at me and shakes her head in disbelief. "Oh Don, why are you down? Those are wonderful breakthroughs. I'm thrilled. You've made unbelievable headway in one day."

"But, now . . . "

"But now nothing, sweetheart. You've broken through tougher barriers than this. Those breakthroughs came fast, and because you've run into a barrier that has slowed you down, you may be making a mountain out of a molehill." She dabbed her eyes. "Don't you realize what you've done? Maximum Talent Capability is a perfect description of the talent goal, and genes have to be the source of efficient human activities. Oh, Don, these are wonderful and more will come. You'll see."

She's right. They are. Suddenly the day is bright and beautiful. Happily we drive on to Teton Village.

Everyone Has A Maximum Talent Capability

Out on the balcony that night, my mind flings this at me: There is present within each of us a certain efficient combination of human activities that naturally synergize into maximum talent capability. "Synergy." Holy cow. Could synergy be the mysterious energy that elevates efficient combinations of human activities to Maximum Talent Capability status? Could it be that simple? I have to look at this.

In chemistry the right combination of chemicals or elements can release energy. The right combination of human activities brought together may be subject to the same synergy principle.

On this bluff four ideas surface: human activity efficiency, Maximum Talent Capability, genes, and now synergy. We are finding more sources and filling in gaps and may be getting closer to understanding and uncovering every human's inherited talent.

Then this thought occurs to me: Most every human problem is caused by the failure of a person to find something of value within themselves, something that gives their lives permanent and meaningful direction. Natural talent could be that value. I pray that these things are right and will fall into place, so that every human can have the benefit of knowing their inborn talent.

At breakfast I explain synergy to Donna.

"See," she says, "you were making a mountain out of a molehill. I knew you could overcome the barrier."

"Let's not jump to conclusions," I say. "Synergy may be what happens, but what causes it to happen? This is just the opening of a door which could lead the way to the answer."

Nodding and brightly smiling she quips, "But what a door my adorable husband has opened."

Me, adorable? No. Just the pretty lady's play on words.

※

The next day we drive north to the village of Kelly, where the Gros Ventre River comes down and out into the Hole to join the Snake River. Just before the village, the Gros Ventre River is joined by Crystal Creek, which comes down from a high valley referred to as "The Meadows."

(I would one day refer to The Meadows as "McClellan Valley," the name of a novel I have been working on for years. I incorporate the MTC concept in the story. I also wrote a turn-of-the-century novel about a young woman with an unusual insight. I may call it *The Gros Ventre Story*. I have to prepare and polish both of them for publishing someday soon.)

※

On our flight back to Milwaukee Donna acts as devil's advocate and makes me defend every aspect of these new revelations. Impressed because I defend them well, she is enthused.

Depositing her at home, I tell Donna, "I'll be back in a few hours."

"I can guess where you're going."

"You can?"

"To find out how many human activities there are."

I kiss her. "You're pretty smart."

"Gotta be, to keep up with you. Watch the time. Once you get into something new you lose all track of time and I'll be sitting here with a cold dinner again. While you're gone I will be looking up efficiency, synergism, genes and activity-human in the dictionary."

I head for the library at the University of Wisconsin—Milwaukee to find out how many human activities there are and how they are catalogued. I punch activity into the computer and scan through the

The Lady

hundreds of human activity entries. Nothing refers to the cataloguing or coding of human activities. I had hoped that someone would have already catalogued and coded all human activities, but it appears that no one ever questioned human activity before (and we humans perform activities all day long). Nor was there anything on efficiency genes or synergism as related to human activity. I could not believe it.

What have I stumbled into?

I make it home in time for dinner. Donna asks, "What did you find?"

"Nothing. As far as I could find, no one has catalogued human activities or anything pertinent to do with it."

"That's difficult to believe," she says. "You mean I go about washing, ironing, cooking, baking, driving my car, reading the newspaper, and shopping—and no one has listed or catalogued all these things we do?"

"Evidently not."

"I wonder why. Universities are nosy about everything else humans are and do."

"I know. It doesn't make sense," I agree.

"I'll bet I know."

"Oh, great high priestess of Delphi. What great fount of wisdom do you have for me this time?" I tease.

"Goofy. Human activity is just too common. The information was never needed before. You opened up a new can of worms. If your conclusions are right, which I'm convinced they are, you opened the door to a whole new science of how efficient combinations of human activities synergize into talent."

"But I don't think we can prove it without cataloguing all human activities, just like they are now sequencing genes. It would cost millions, maybe more. This further complicates things. People don't even understand talent."

"Don, I think people can understand the difference between a highly talented and a lessor talented violinist."

"That's a good example, but we can't prove what the difference is."

"No, but the difference is obvious enough that someone in science, government, or education should have the imagination and intelligence to want to look into it," argued Donna.

"One would think so."

"I know you will find the difference, because you keep trying so hard." Then she laughed.

"What's funny?"

"I was just thinking. If you succeed in uncovering the talents of all six billion people, the world would be a terrible mess. Everybody trying to learn and use their talents, the necessary work of society would be all a jumble and you would get blamed for it."

"You think that would happen?" I ask incredulously.

"Isn't that where your research is going?"

"Well, I never thought of it like that. I would hope the adjustment would be gradual and that certain uncovered talents would help in the changeover."

"Be interesting to see it happen."

"Donna, you have the darnedest way of seeing things by jumping ahead."

Then with a lovely mischievous smirk she replies, "I'm supposed to. Aren't I the high priestess of Delphi? And by the way, look who's talking. MTC isn't jumping ahead?"

As Barbara Sher writes in her book, *I Could Do Anything If I Only Knew What It Was*, "Each person is a complex mesh of finely woven styles, viewpoints, abilities, tastes and gifts. There's no one in the world that can do what you can do, who can create what you can create."

That nicely describes each individual's Maximum Talent Capability—but how do we uncover it?

The Lady

Caribbean Cruise with Jane Powell

Donna and I took a Caribbean cruise aboard the *Sea Goddess*. On board, Donna drew the attention of and became friends with actress Jane Powell, who was an entertainer on the boat. When ashore, we enjoyed roaming several islands with Jane and her husband.

The ship arranged for a few hotel rooms on the island so the walkers could relax for a while. Sitting in a room talking, Jane Powell sat on one side of the bed and I on the other, while other people sat in chairs about the room. Donna started to giggle. The rest of us wondered what was so funny. Donna burst out laughing. Holding her chest with one hand, Donna pointed at the bed and said, "Who back home is going to believe that Don was in bed with Jane Powell?"

There she goes making fun of me again.

On a cruise the purser assigns the seating for dinner. Passengers are sometimes disappointed with their dinner companions and can request a change, but Donna always managed to make everyone comfortable and have fun.

On one cruise, the purser must have been in hysterics when arranging our seating. Instead of seating us with a compatible couple, we Missouri Synod Lutherans were seated at a table with two retired and ailing Catholic priests. But, Donna soon had us laughing and we found them excellent and interesting people. One of the priests commented to me, "If I had known there were lovely women like your wife, I may not have become a priest."

Sitting by the pool, Donna is applying suntan lotion and I am reading Howard Gardner's *The Unschooled Mind*.

"Interesting?" she asks.

"Listen to what Gardner says. 'Imagine an educational environment in which youngsters at the age of seven or eight have the opportunity to enroll in some kind of discovery school.' "

"Isn't that about the time you think talent discovery ought to start?"

"Yes, I think that is when some students start to lose interest and some start to build resentment that turns into terrorism," I replied.

"Don, I'm sure it must have occurred to you, the impact that individual talents will have on education."

"I don't even want to think about it," I responded.

"You have to, you are getting close to solving the problem."

I put the book down. "I know, and sometimes I dread it," I said gloomily.

"Why? It would be wonderful," she exclaimed.

"The educational establishment will fight changing over to a talent-based structure. I believe we will need individual talent schools. They will have to change and adapt most everything and the education system has always fought change.

"And when teachers accept that they have unknown talents, which probably won't be in teaching (or at least a change to a talented subject), they will want to be re-educated according to their talents and will want to change over in droves. There will be chaos. The establishment will ignore its own talent and accuse, deny, discredit, hate and fight with a passion. It will be aimed at me."

"Oh, no, Don. No," Donna said with deep concern.

"A novice uncovering talent and shaking up their system is going to make them look bad and create resentment," I said.

"Oh Don, they have to care. Think of how the happiness, success, and health of all people will be improved."

"I sent several articles to Education Week. They didn't even respond. Education will drag out the fight. I've worked so hard, so long, and am so deeply involved that I will be overly sensitive. It will be an emotional trauma for me. That and my age, I may not be here to see the acceptance or fruition."

With glassy eyes Donna stared at me in disbelief. "No Don, I can't,

I won't believe any of that. There must be a way. They couldn't do that to you."

I didn't respond.

"And believing this, you are still going ahead?" she asked.

"Since I first inherited this burden, I don't think I've had a choice."

"Oh Don. People have to be smarter and more considerate than that."

"Oh," I sighed. "Maybe I'm wrong and maybe there is a way. But I am fearful. I envision a vicious and deep hurting storm ahead."

(And what I dread most of all, is that you, my dearest one, may be hurt in the storm.)

1991 Our Fortieth Anniversary

The fortieth anniversary card Donna gave to me said, "We built a beautiful marriage together. Love, Donna."

Beautiful marriages are not a gift. They may be blessed, but even then must have a solid foundation and continuously be worked on. A marriage is based on dreams. It must have successes and some dreams must come true. We were fortunate to have many dreams come true. We did have a great marriage, but I don't think we fully realized it. How does one fully appreciate a wonderful marriage?

As I watched Donna at our anniversary reception at the Club, I thought, Being devotedly loved by a lovely person with the qualities, beauty and stature Donna had attained, one cannot help but believe in God.

My family, and most of Donna's larger family, was at the reception. Donna's family had changed and grown through the years.

Ramona and Bill had two lovely daughters, Carrie and Carla, and a son, Brian. When Bill died suddenly, Ramona, Donna and I were a threesome again, just as we started out forty years ago. Ramona has always been very dear to us.

Gracious sister Marlyn Grinde, her husband, Rick, and their daughter Lisa carry on the Arneson and Grinde Norwegian (Sons of Norway) traditions.

The Twentieth-Century Lady

Donna and Don celebrating their fortieth wedding anniversary.

Brother Hilton lost his wife early in life and brought up the kids by himself. He works on the Arneson farm with the help of his loyal partner John.

Brother Dale and his special wife, Eleanor, also carry on the Arneson name with pride. Dale's honesty and ethics are a fine example to his children.

All brothers, sisters, spouses, and many of their children came from Mt. Horeb for our anniversary.

Donna loved music, so I arranged for background music at our anniversary, including Donna's favorite recording of *Chariots of Fire*, violinist Shoji Tabuchi's "In The Garden" and some of Glen Miller's music. Donna and I were Glen Miller fans. One of Glen Miller's songs would help solve one of our talent problems.

Speaking at the reception, I looked at Donna and quipped, "I have still not received my husband certificate of graduation, so I had better watch my step or I'm liable to get tossed out on my ear and there won't be any fiftieth anniversary."

Laughing, Donna shook her head. Her husband's a nut.

The Lady

Vancouver—The Beautiful Lady

Donna had not seen Washington or Oregon and wanted to take a scenic train trip. I wanted to see western Canada, so we tied them together. For our fortieth anniversary we flew to Seattle, rented a car and drove to the Salishan Lodge at Gleneden Beach, Oregon, and then we drove to Vancouver, Canada, where we stayed at the beautiful Pan Pacific Hotel.

After checking in and cleaning up, I went down to the Pan Pacific Hotel Cascades lounge in advance of Donna. We were told to get one of the few cocktail tables overlooking the scenic Burrard Inlet, which I did. I sat half facing the harbor. Occasionally I glanced over to the lobby from where Donna would have to enter the lounge.

As I sat there, I listened to Glen Miller's "String of Pearls" playing softly in the background What a beautiful and original piece of music it is. A thought crossed my mind . . . string of pearls? Something was coming together about human capability and synergism. I had a thought for a brief moment, when something alerted me. I turned and there stood Donna in the hotel lobby looking into the lounge. Seeing me, she gave me a delightful smile. She kept her eyes on me and walked the long distance of the bar to me with her natural model's stride. There was something glorious and slightly breezy about her walk. I often wished I had it on film. I tore my eyes from her for just a second and it looked like every male in the room was watching Donna. Her flared skirt, stride, and brilliant smile were so stunningly beautiful it took my breath away. All the more amazing, because I should not be so overly impressed with a woman who had bore me three children and had lived with me for forty years.

When seated across from me, I told Donna how very beautiful and youthful she looked. She laughed lightly and with a nonchalant wave of her hand said, "Oh, you're just imagining things."

No way. At sixty-five she is still a lovely, youthful woman. How lucky can a guy get?

The Twentieth-Century Lady

That reminds me of an incident that occurred several years later. We were meeting another couple for dinner at the club. Donna was sitting at her vanity putting on her earrings in front of a three-way folded magnifying vanity mirror surrounded by lights. As I passed by she closed it a little hard.

"Darn," she said.

"What's the matter" I asked?

"No matter how hard I try I still look like an old, plain farm woman."

I was flabbergasted. "Donna, you are beautiful."

That made her angry. "Don, I wish you would stop saying that, just to make me feel good, because it doesn't."

"Donna, I am being honest."

"No, you're not." She flung open the two sides of the vanity mirror, turned on the lights and said. "Look."

I bent down behind her and looked at the magnified mirror. She didn't look like my Donna. "Smile," I said. She spread her lips in a smile. It looked put on and plastic. She had been looking at my face and I must have shown disappointment.

Pointing at me. "See. Now tell me I'm beautiful."

"Well, that mirror expands things and doesn't do you justice. You have to look at the overall you. Your hair, the way you dress, your nice body."

"Okay. I work at my hair and dress this body okay, to be a little attractive. At least I try. But I am not beautiful. So stop saying that."

I didn't think it wise to argue further, because I did not know what else to say.

Later at our table at the club, Donna's golfing friend's husband says to Donna, "You look beautiful tonight. Of course, you always do."

Donna said, "Thank you" but gave me an angry look. The other couple looked at each other wondering what was wrong.

So without thinking I blurted, "Donna doesn't think she's beautiful." My big mouth. That didn't help anything.

The other couple started laughing. I had to be joking. Donna turned red and looked at me very somberly. I thought she was either going to crown me, cry or leave the table to gather her wits. The other couple looked at each other and stilled their laugh.

To change the subject I brightened up and asked, "How was your golf game on Sunday?" Donna was able to gather her wits and smiling nicely, joined in on the conversation. In a few minutes her magnetism and charm was obvious. The other couple looked at me, smiled and shrugged their shoulders at each other.

Later Donna's friend motioned me aside.

"Don, don't try to convince her. She looks into the magnifying mirror and looks for little imperfections, like we all do. She's not only beautiful; she's wonderfully precious. If she is ever convinced she's beautiful, she may change, and not be our Donna. No, that's not right. I don't think Donna would ever change." She sighed. "You'll just have to put up with the beautiful Donna thinking she's not." She laughed. "I feel sorry for you."

It occurred to me that it was not Donna's true character and personality reflected in the mirror. She was putting on a bland, straight-faced Donna that did not exist. Without being aware of it, when Donna was with people, Donna blossomed naturally. Mirrors didn't make Donna beautiful, people did.

People who knew Donna, referred to her as "their Donna" or "our Donna" or "my Donna." I presume they did this because they felt possessive of Donna and the friendship they shared.

※

The next afternoon we board the night train to Jasper in Alberta, Canada. We experienced a beautiful mountain and wilderness ride with fine dining in the vintage dining car. Back in our room I was re-thinking Glen Miller's "String of Pearls", trying to re-enact the scene to revive my thoughts from yesterday.

I took a nap mid-afternoon. When I awake, there it is, the fleeting thought. Talent is made up of an efficient and compatible grouping of human activities like a string of perfectly matched pearls—a set of efficient human activities that compliment each other; forming a circle of talent.

In our company, whenever we had a problem, the people who were responsible and showed talent or interest in that particular problem were invited into my office for a roundtable discussion to find ways to solve the problem. This was done in the round because people have the advantage of seeing everyone's nonverbal cues, such as facial expressions, body language, hand gestures and eye contact; which are often a more accurate and truthful expression than mere words.

Sometimes you could almost see the energy, vibration and sparks fly in the air as ideas combined, collided, unfolded and developed. As people discussed and shared ideas, they stimulated each other as they asked questions, explored possibilities, and developed thoughts and solutions.

Synergism probably happens the same way in an individual's mind—when the brain recognizes and has the use of a circle of efficient human activities of common dedication. Efficient mental activities bounce back and forth against each other, opening up more and more neuron circuits and tapping great reserves of innovation, creativity, and problem solving.

With so many different human activities, a matched set of efficient human activities needed to create a person's Maximum Talent Capability (MTC) is not going to be easy to find. That may be why scientists and educators have not been looking for, or are able to uncover, an individual's MTC. If we could uncover or recognize just one individual's combination of efficient human activities, we might uncover the secret to finding every person's talents.

Glen Miller's "String of Pearls" helped clear up a complicated step. Efficient activities that compliment each other synergize and the result

The Lady

is talented creativity and problem solving. Important headway was made. Now, perhaps, I could relax and enjoy the rest of the trip. But I was still bothered by how synergism develops efficient combinations of human activities into a talent and where does intelligence come in?

It appears the application of an untapped reserve of intelligence could be the unknown factor, which modifies and enhances (synergizes) the efficient circle of human activities to talent. This does not change the gene concept, but recognizes the role intelligence plays, and it closes an important gap.

I know more now than I did before, but the problems seem to be growing more difficult. I made headway by establishing how matched efficient and compatible activities become synergistic by drawing on compatible intelligence that results in maximum talent capability; yet other questions remain:

Is there a way to penetrate the genetic structure of the brain to find an individual's most efficient activities? Assuming we find this answer, how do we apply talents to occupations where these talents can be used best?

At the Jasper Park Hotel we have a beautiful room overlooking the lake and glacier. Entering the room, a cherry fireplace welcomes us and when we return from dinner a small orchid lay on each pillow. I tell Donna that if there ever was a place I want to come back to someday with her, this is it.

Sitting in the train lounge on our way out of Jasper, I ask Donna, "I have been trying to figure out how or what the energy is that raises the efficient and compatible combinations of human activities to talent level. Supposedly all people have a high intelligence level when discussing or working activities in which they have a natural interest. Will you accept that?"

"Sure, we are all nosy and therefore more knowledgeable and intelligent about things we are interested in and do well," Donna says.

"Okay. Now, every person's most efficient human activities brought together in one corner of the mind must be the greatest accumulation of intelligence their minds have ever experienced. How about that?"

"But, Don, the knowledge and intelligence of those activities has always been in the mind."

"Sure, but never before was the mind aware of or could the mind bring together the efficient combination of human activities that would automatically unleash compatible intelligence," I argue.

"We haven't uncovered our talent, so that may be why," Donna replies.

"Good conclusion, Donna. So, the application of this cloud of new intelligence is the factor that synergizes the efficient and compatible combination of human activities to talent. Similar to roundtable discussions in my office, those people create a cloud of intelligence by being knowledgeably interested."

"Okay, but why aren't your people in the round super, super talented?" Donna presses.

"Because they are only interested and knowledgeable people and not subject MTC talented."

Donna, her hands in prayer fashion and eyes darting back and forth, is thinking. "Don, let's say you found a way to uncover the Maximum Talent Capability of all six billion people. And you were able to gather the two hundred people highest in cancer talent capability, and after some cancer and lab education, they were put in a room to solve cancer. You think they could do it?"

"What brought that up?" I ask.

"Don't know, just wondering."

Donna got up and started to walk off. "Hey, where are you going?" I ask. "You can't leave me sitting here with this cancer question you just threw at me."

She smiles. "I'm a devil's advocate, dear. I can do anything I want, and besides you're the answer man."

"But how could we quickly winnow down six billion people to discover the world's two hundred most talented cancer problem solvers?"

The Lady

She now looked solemnly and said, "Isn't that what you're trying to do, dear?"

"Well, I think a group like that could. At the very least they could move ahead faster. And not only cancer. Specific talent groups could focus on all health and other problems. Oh Donna," I sighed. "That is the responsibility that scares me. As you know, I have tried to interest the media, education, government, and science to look into this research, but no one will listen. And time is important to so many people."

Our trip is near its end. I am standing on a wooden porch outside the rustic Denali Park Hotel in the Alaskan wilderness. The air is glacial cool as I gaze in the distance at majestic Mt. McKinley, over 20,000 feet high. It is overwhelming and inconceivable that something so massive could be pushed up out of the earth that high.

My mind turns to what is for me a massive and overwhelming undertaking, writing the book that cuts across education, health and scientific professions, making my arguments difficult to defend.

Back home, fall has gone by without a single new thought or idea. My confidence level is very low. It looks like uncovering talent was just a fantasy. It would be so very wonderful for all humans; but now it appears to be an impossible dream.

I lament to Donna, "Sometimes I think I should turn this whole project over to someone more qualified, someone who knows what they are doing."

Donna smiles sympathetically. "Like who?" she asks with a frown.

"Someone more qualified," I reply.

"Oh, I don't know." She considers for a moment. "Your VGI (Vocational Guidance Institute) people found that no one is doing similar research. And this subject is probably one of the most important research projects ever done. It touches on the well being and purpose of every human and the survival of humanity. If there is someone more qualified, why aren't they paying attention to this important issue? Some people must have tried, but didn't have the MTC to break it open, and you did—and are. Don't you realize that you evidently have your own MTC to do it, perhaps in the same way Einstein did, by matching his interests and abilities?"

"Please, Donna. Don't compare me to Einstein. Don't even mention me in the same sentence. Compared to him I'm nothing."

"Not so, in some ways you are better than him." She smirks a little.

"Donna!"

"Well, you are. He couldn't remember his wife's birthday, and you do."

Birthday? Sure. How can one not, with all the little hints Donna has going on around the house that a dinner celebration is coming up.

"Oh, Don, you are so funny," she said in mild reproof. "The both of you are just simple, common human beings who, as Einstein said, 'happen to match your interests and abilities.' That doesn't make either of you super human beings, just fortunate humans. If you don't believe that, you are going against the very foundation of your belief and what you are trying to prove.

"Don't you realize that when you find the proof, and I know you will, that all of us humans will be able to match our interests and abilities, all be equal in purpose, ability and make our own important contributions?"

I made headway by establishing how efficient combinations of activities become synergistic, by drawing on intelligence and resulting in a person's maximum talent capability. But I had jumped ahead and left a gap. How do I find each person's efficient activities in the first place?

More months pass and with all my reading, nothing comes to me. Donna sees my inactivity and suggested I explain the most difficult problem.

The Lady

"There are presently two. Our genes built us, so our genes most know our most efficient activities. Is there a way to penetrate the genetic structure or brain or body to find each individual's most efficient activities?"

"Don, you talked about that before, and I have a question. Our genes built our most efficient activities for a purpose. Why don't we know our maximum talent? Our genes would certainly make that known to us."

"I think because our genes originally created our individual activities for survival there was no need to combine many efficient activities," I answer. "Then we created complicated occupations, and now we want our genes to group efficient combinations of activities to do these occupations. Our genes are confused by this new need, but in time they may so develop."

"Huh!" Donna said. "I'll be darned if that doesn't make sense. Our genes have the knowledge, but don't know it. And you have to find a way to make them give you that information. That's a toughie. What is the other problem?"

"Assuming we find the gene answer to fill that last gap, we must look at the end use of our MTC. How do we find the one occupation out of 40,000 occupations that each person's MTC fits best?"

Putting her fingers in prayer fashion to her lips, "Oh Lord, no one has ever been able to develop even a reasonable occupational selection method, and now you have to do it to make MTC work. Oh Don, I wish I could help."

"Just stay near and be you, that's the best help I could ever have."

On Christmas night as I listen to a church choir on TV, a news announcer comes on and says:

"On this night there are wars going on all over the world. Did you know that in wars there are more civilian casualties, including children, than soldier casualties? All of our prayers have not diminished war. For many people there is no peace on earth."

How can we stop war? Who are these people that make war? Why do they do it? Some people seek freedom through insurrection, but ambition, greed, and a need for personal identity drive most warmongers.

Could any of those people, especially the warmongers and their followers, find a safer and more rewarding way of expending their energies? What if they discovered their hidden talent? Would a talented violinist join an army when he might lose the use of his hand? If followers found their talent, the mongers would not have them to make war. Would talent discovery be of value in bringing peace to earth?

This Christmas night I pray that a way to discover individual talent be found. The remaining problems seem so impossible that I am overwhelmed. Perhaps I am not the person to do this. But who else believes inborn talents exist?

I believe that talent discovery is vital to the future of humanity. Through talent discovery individuals can work in professions that compliment their abilities and health, and all people would have a much greater chance for success, happiness, and fulfilled lives.

Donna again notices my inactivity. "You're still stuck, huh?"

"Am I ever. This gene thing is way beyond me. I don't have the slightest idea how to continue."

"Well, this isn't about genes but it may lift your spirits. You know I like to listen to Charlie Sykes on the radio in the morning. He wrote a new book and I bought it. Listen to what he says. 'The honor roll is a dishonorable institution because it doesn't take into account every child's unique mix of abilities and talents.' Kinda gusty, huh?"

I laugh. "I'll say it is." Then I frowned. "You bought a book?"

She waved my question aside, obviously not wanting to answer it. "And, see Don. He says 'unique mix of abilities and talents,' just like

The Lady

you. Charlie must believe like you do." Then with a superior raising of eyes and weaving of shoulders, she says, "What does that do to you?"

I ignored the superiority put on to improve my spirits and answer, "It certainly raises my spirits. I'll have to read the book and listen to him, too. Strange, you buying a book."

"You're going to pursue that, huh? Oh, well." Donna smiles and shrugs her shoulders. "I bought it for one of your birthday presents, but you needed a lift, so I guess I will give it to you now."

"*One* of my presents?" I question.

"Oh, darn. There I go again. Giving the show away." Then, with her mirthful smirk and fluttering of eyes she adds, "Of course, I mean *besides* me."

I'll bet she never gave me less than one birthday present in all the years we were married. Donna likes lots of packages to open.

"Okay. I'll be serious," Donna says, trying to wipe the smirk off her face.

"*Donna!*"

"Okay. Okay." She's trying hard to keep a straight face. "I see you're reading current science books. I know you feel the answer is in our genes, but do you have a clear description of what you're looking for?"

"I'll try. The object is to penetrate the genetic structure or brain to find each person's most efficient combination of human activities. I don't think the brain has the answer, or we would already know our talents. The most puzzling problem is how to get into our genes to expose our natural capabilities. Our genes must have the answer, because our genes created our abilities and us. But no one has penetrated the intelligence connection with genes as yet. So, how does one communicate with our genes?"

"So, what are you going to do?"

"The closest contact with human activities seems to be our senses. Our senses can stop an activity if they feel we are in danger and encourage us when it is necessary or pleasing. I hope there is some clue in these two books, *A Natural History of the Senses* by Diane Ackerman and *Deciphering the Senses* by Robert Rivilin and Karen Gravelle."

The Twentieth-Century Lady

"That makes sense, never thought of that," she says.

Several weeks later, I put the last book down on the table next to my bed. It is 1:30 A.M. and my eyes are blurry.

The next morning Donna asks, "You're finished with senses, read anything worthwhile?"

"Nothing I can put my finger on, and how did you know I was finished?"

"The books are not on your night table."

I had to laugh. "You know everything that's going on, don't you?"

"I care about my husband."

"I know you do, and I appreciate it."

"So, is your mind blank or is something going on?"

"You sure are nosy."

"Don, get serious. You have been stressing over this thing for some time and I'm worried about you."

"Okay, there is something going on. But I'm not sure what it is or if it has any value."

"All right, let me hear you talk about the senses."

"Senses are safeguards that protect us against activities which can potentially harm us physically and mentally. Our brain may be interested in an activity but if our senses find the activity offensive then before we can continue the activity, our brain must override our senses. So, if the senses turn thumbs down on an activity the senses are not going to cooperate; and to get their point across they will cause friction, stress, and frustration. Our sense personality can have built-in likes, dislikes, or indifference for the most minor things. Our senses may be the most truthful part of us."

A bright smile appears on Donna's face. "My husband is onto something. Go, go, go, let's hear more."

"Don't get so excited."

"Who's excited?" the excited cheerleader asks.

"The brain tells us what it wants to do, the body tells us if we can, and the senses tell us if they will support the function of the activity. Thought patterns, physical motions, and sense interpretations make up

The Lady

what we may refer to as the forces that initiate, control, and qualify human activities."

With wide eyes she says, "Say that again."

I did.

"Oh, I get it," she says. "Our senses can pass truthful judgement on a human activity. That's great. That has to be of value."

"Sure, but there may be hundreds of thousands of human activities, and millions of different combinations of human activities," I reply.

Her smile dims in disappointment. "But, it's a help?" she asks.

"A small one, perhaps," I acquiesce.

"Don, I don't know much about genetics, but you are now able to get into genes through the senses. Aren't you?"

"I think so." I laugh a little. "But what do I do now? Expose hundreds of thousands of human activities to a person's genes for reaction, until I can identify the efficient talent ones? And for what particular talent?"

Sitting up, Donna snaps her fingers and says, "Pshaw, my husband can do that any day."

"Just like that, huh?" I had to laugh. The woman can be so darn cute.

With all-knowing raised eyebrows and a superior look, she says, "There is something you don't know."

"Oh, all-knowing, high priestess of Delphi. I am sure you are going to tell me."

"You, sir, put human activities, genes, and senses together. I'll bet that you could be the first to penetrate gene function through the senses. You, dear sir, may have opened a new door for genetics." Then with an even more superior pose and one eyebrow raised. "They may give my husband a prize." With that she curtsied and gracefully swept out of the room.

I burst out laughing, and call after her, "They won't even listen to me. And besides, I don't need more distractions right now."

Two mornings later I come up behind Donna, turn her around, and kiss her. She sweetly and mischievously asks, "To what do I owe this early morning amour?"

"I know how."

Clapping her hands with joy, "You do? Then with mischievous fluttering eyes asks, "I'm not sure what we're talking about dear." Then she sees I'm serious. "Oh, about talking to genes."

"Yup."

"Sit down and tell me."

"You know how doctors sometimes use sugar pills or a placebo to fool the patient's body into believing the pill is a cure?"

"Yes, I've read about that," she acknowledges.

"I think we can fool the genes into telling us what the best occupation is for a person and that occupation will identify the person's MTC."

Donna frowns. "Sounds to me more like reverse osmosis, what ever that is. Anyway, how are you going to do that? You already said there is no way a person can work at all 40,000 occupations to find their MTC."

"Try this example," I reply. "It's like a mechanic trying to find out what is wrong with a car, but he can't get it started. He uses a battery and jumper cables. Once the car is started the battery and jumper cables are no longer needed. With the engine now running, he can test to find the problem."

"Let me understand this. Instead of going directly for a person's Maximum Talent Capability, which you can't do because you can't get into a person's genes to find out, you're going to use sugar pills and jumper cables to find the occupation that identifies their MTC?" she declares in mirthful amazement.

"C'mon Donna, be serious. I'm looking for a sugar pill, a jumper cable or some kind of crutch to develop a starter preferred activity occupation profile, so that I can get to the person's talented occupation."

"Really!" she says with her naïve little girl look.

The Lady

"Donna!"

"Okay, I'll be serious." She is. "You need a crutch to create a starter what?"

"A preferred activity occupation profile," I answer.

"Okay, you're going to use and discard that profile thing, and that will somehow have helped you uncover a person's MTC?" she says in questioning amazement.

"Very good," I say. "Stay with me. We have the person make a list of ten occupations that appeal to them. We reduce those occupations to job tasks and then to human activities. The person then takes whatever human activities they prefer and places them on a list with the most preferred on top. Discarding all but the top ten human activities we make a human activity computer profile of those ten most preferred human activities."

"Hold it, Don. That's the brain selecting those preferred activities, and you say the brain does not know a person's talented human activities that make up their MTC. It's the genes that built and know our human activities," she challenges.

"That's right, but stay with me. We reduce all 40,000 occupations to human activity profiles with the most used activities in each occupation listed on top. We also make films or CD disks of all occupational human activities so that each human activity can be individually viewed in operation.

"Hold on," she says. "Forty thousand films and profiles? That will cost a fortune."

"Every activity must be vividly viewed, so that the senses can retain those found most preferable. And if we can use virtual reality simulations, which are more vivid, the senses can judge even better. Labs where people could actually do the activity hands-on would be the ultimate."

"Don, you said there could be several hundred thousand human activities used in occupations. Virtual reality and labs with 200,000 different activities going on could cost millions and millions," she exclaimed.

237

"I can't visualize such a lab, but as far as cost is concerned, they are spending three billion to sequence genes, which will be important to medicine, science and some people. MTC will help everyone and save untold millions in crime, terrorism, and health care costs. It would eliminate the need for much of corrective medicine."

Donna nodded. "Okay, I accept that."

I continue, "We then run the person's human activity profile across the 40,000 human activity occupation profiles and the computer throws out ten occupations the profile fits best."

"Don, you said the starter profile was worthless. You feed junk into a computer and you get junk out."

"Ah, true. But there's gold in that junk."

"How so?"

"We take the preferable human activities from those ten new occupations the computer threw out, and add them to the original list of preferable activities. The person re-aligns the list according to their preference top down, and keeping all but the top ten we have an improved profile."

Her eyes light up. "Ah ha and . . ."

She puts her hand over my mouth to silence me, and then with her hands against her chin and her eyes darting around, she interrupts, "I got it. You do that again and again until no new occupations come out of the computer and you have the occupation that best fits a person's MTC profile." Her hands still against her chin she continues, "Oh Don, you found the way! The last occupation is our best occupational Maximum Talent Capability." She throws her arms around me. "Oh Don, you got it! Hon, you did it." Sniff. "I knew you could do it."

"Maybe you did it," I suggest.

"Me! I didn't do it," she protests.

"The love, devotion, support, and belief of a lovely, wonderful woman can do wonders for a man," I say

With Donna's help all the pieces of the puzzle ultimately fit and now the book can be written. Book? Oh Lord, it is easy to talk about writing a book, but now the reality of writing a book is here. Me, the English genius, write a book? Well, maybe I can get help.

Talent discovery is unknown territory. When people finally pay attention, it will be highly controversial, shockingly revealing, and completely foreign to our way of thinking and what people have been taught to accept.

This search for MTC is doable, and future generations will find new and better ways of uncovering talent even more efficiently. Everyone's best-fit careers can be identified and maximum talent capability will be available for the benefit of everyone.

We know there is a long hard road ahead, but if education, government and business will join together to develop it, MTC will no longer be a fantasy.

This was a happy time for us.

The Marching Boards

Donna worked at keeping our life interesting. You never knew what she would do next—or what stunts she would pull on me. I thought I would pull one on her. For Valentine's Day I made a front and back sandwich board. It said in big letters, "I Love Donna." Wearing it, I marched back and forth on our patio, so I could be seen from our kitchen window.

Donna came out and stood with her hands on her hips, and a half grin on her face. "What on earth are you doing?"

"Too cheap to buy a card," I reply. (Still marching.)

"I can see that, but what are you doing marching up and down?"

"Want to tell the whole world I love my wife." (Still marching.)

"But there's no one here but us."

"Well, maybe they'll come." (Still marching.)

"You're nuttier than a fruitcake." Shaking her head, she goes back into the house.

(Still marching.)

Donna must have thought about it more, because she comes back out, lifts the board off my shoulders and throws it down on the patio. Then, holding me tightly, she gives me a nice wiggle, a very sweet kiss, and laughingly runs back into the house.

Brazen hussy.

The Writer and The Book

Several months go by, and I have not done more than shovel some pages about when Donna asks, "How's the book coming, Don?"

"Oh, I'm reading about writing a book and developing chapters here and there."

"You don't sound very enthused," she deduces.

"Writing a book is a big project. Imagine someone like me, who disliked English, and seldom passed it in school, now writing a book? I feel like a cab driver trying to fly a 747."

She laughed. "That's funny." And then more serious. "Don I wish you wouldn't belittle yourself because you had some bad marks in school. I am very proud of you and what you accomplished. I'll bet none of the students you went to school with could hold a candle to you today. Education failed you, and the other high mark kids you went to school with too, but somehow, that something special about you surfaced."

Shaking my head, "I have an outline—but writing a book? I don't know."

"Considering the things you have done, and knowing your subject so well, writing a book will be child's play."

"Sure, easy for you to say," I comment.

"Don!"

"Okay, I'll get going—somehow."

It was time to publish what our human capability research had led us to believe. With the help of my staff, which consisted of a devil's advocate, a Delphi priestess, my house staff sergeant, and Freddie the cat stepping on my computer keys, I started rolling out chapters. I was also fortunate in finding a staff-sergeant editor in Traverse City, Michigan, who ran out of ink crossing out the superfluous words I had written

The theme of *The Key To Your Unknown Talent-A New Discovery About You* is: "In the 40,000 known occupations, there is a talented vocation every individual can do better and in good health than anything else they can do. And there is a way to find it."

The Maximum Talent Capability method of individualized education will no doubt cause commotion in education. My purpose now is to help educators understand that, "You can lead a child to school but you can't make them learn anything not in tune with their genetic design."

Donna said that statement should be used often, until education accepts the truth of it. It will be difficult for some people to believe the genetics of it, but read what Sandra Scarr, University of Virginia psychologist, says about genetics: "We can help direct a human down the path of their natural abilities, but we are asking for trouble and friction when trying to mold a human in a direction not in tune with their natural genetic structure." So education is going to have to try and debase her, too, to defend forced education against natural talent gene-based education.

There is a long hard fight ahead, but if enough people believe, we can change forced education to education by attraction that will lead to right careers.

Her Husband Has Excellent Taste

In the fall of 1996, I come home and find Donna crying. She has been worried for days about telling me that her engagement ring has been lost. She went through everything over and over, moved everything, tore the garbage apart, but to no avail. She thought she put her ring on the kitchen counter to do some washing. She felt undressed without her ring. It hurt her terribly to be without it.

That Christmas Donna opens a big box, a smaller within, another smaller box, boxes all over the place. Finally, a ring box. Her mouth opens and tears stream down her face. She had the diamond ring I always wanted to give her. I agonized over hundreds of rings in a dozen stores—this one seemed to me to be Donna's ring.

I told her it could be taken back and she could have any style she wanted. "Oh, no, the diamond is perfect," she says.

I said, "I insist you look. You must have been looking at ring settings and you know what you want. You will not hurt my feelings. Above all I want you to be happy. It must be right." Of course, I've now sold a shopper on shopping, and to Donna this was a challenge! And the next day, off she happily goes.

A week later the searching must have stopped, so I ask," Did you find the right setting for your ring?"

She pulls me away from my desk, sits in my lap, kisses me, holds out and flashes her ring. "I found the right husband who found the right ring. My husband has excellent taste," she says with confidence.

Husband Still In Training

Wonderful person that Donna is, it was sometimes a little strenuous living with a staff sergeant neat-nick. When we agreed to get married, I didn't know that I automatically signed up for a life-long husband-training course. I must still be in training to be a husband, because I still have not received my husband certificate of graduation.

Years ago, I did receive an anniversary card that said: "Certificate of Merit—This is to certify that Don Seymour is a Husband Par Excellence. He is Master Zipper-upper, Foot Warmer, Checkbook Balancer, Chauffeur, Electrician, Plumber, Escort, Playboy, and Lover.

Certified by "Donna" His ever-loving Wife.

Notice it isn't a certificate of graduation, just of "Merit." Now that I'm retired and going downhill, I don't think I will ever graduate. And if I do, I'm sure I'll have to go for a "Masters!"

Donna, The Wife

Donna heard about husbands being underfoot in retirement and was apprehensive about having me at home full-time. It was no problem for us; we liked having each other around. We joked a lot, I often brought her flowers and candy, and she shook her head and laughed a lot—at me.

Even in my retirement, Donna's life did not change much. Her home, church, golf, modeling for Goodwill, and helping people continued to consume her time.

Donna had so many fine qualities that I never ceased to wonder what she saw in me. This lovely lady who decided to marry me, is smart, loving, capable, intelligent, responsible, frugal, a wonderful homemaker, and a gourmet cook. What a treasure Donna is, so neat and the scent of her under any circumstances was fresh and youthful. She took great care of herself, going to exercise class most mornings and constantly whirling around our home.

Because Donna so loved her sons and me, it took courage for her to force the issue when she felt we needed to get back on the right track. She mostly drank wine but occasionally had a vodka and tonic, of which her limit was two. In company you would never know she had two drinks, but when the family was together for supper and comeuppance time was overdue, a second drink gave her the courage to tackle us. When we saw her hands on her hips we looked for someplace to hide, but to no avail. We were going to have to account for our sins and omissions then and there.

It was a great feeling to have a home we had once dreamed about. Every morning I woke up and saw a different scene from every window, in any type of weather. I never got used to it; it was beautiful and Donna was there.

The Meaning and Purpose of Life

One evening Donna came and sat by me while I was typing on the computer. She never interrupted because she knew I could lose my thought. I finished typing and sat back and looked up at my lovely wife. "Problem?"

"Don, got a minute to talk?"

"What man could resist talking to such a lovely woman?"

"Silly. I'm serious."

"Sorry, at your service, ma'am."

"Well, how should I say it? There are times when God, the soul, genes, and human capability don't form an understandable meaning and purpose life pattern. They don't fit clearly together. I believe in my soul, God, and holding tight onto my faith, but with so many people Godless, and religion and prayer under such a cloud today, one wonders if one's belief is ninety-nine percent the truth. That one- percent of not knowing for sure is scary. It takes so very much faith to hold at bay.

"Sometimes I feel your MTC is important to our soul and humanity. And when your MTC is developed it will help people lead more purposeful lives and reduce that one-percent of doubt to a fraction. But I can't put this together in my mind."

"That's very observant," I said. "And you feel there could be a connection?"

"Don, although we have never talked about MTC in those terms, I often felt you were evading the religious aspect, even though you probably had thoughts about it. Just for me, I would like to know what your thoughts are."

"So, you understand my reluctance to tread in this area?" I asked.

"I sensed it," she admitted.

"What you are asking me to do is to lay a trail for life using God, the soul, genes, humanity, and MTC as checkpoints to make sense of life. Oh sweetheart, that's a tough one. I am not a theologian or philosopher. I'm just a practical person. It's bad enough I dab around in areas I have no business in, so what I say will come from a rather practical viewpoint and may only make sense to me," I cautioned.

She put her hand on my arm. "Don, now you're hedging. You, being the most original thinker I know, and having uncovered the human capability ideas and developed MTC, must have some idea about how to make sense of these things."

"Okay, I will tell you how I think these things go together, but you help by acting as devil's advocate as we go along, okay?"

"Sure, it'll be fun."

"I thought this was serious."

"God must laugh at us all the time," Donna stated matter-of-factly.

"He'll probably laugh at me."

"I don't think so. He needs what you are doing for his people."

"I hope so, because if I thought He didn't, I would lose the dedication and motivation to continue."

"So, don't be bashful. Be a practical theologian and philosopher for me," she encouraged.

"Well, first of all, unless you believe in the soul and a Supreme Being, I can't visualize how life could have any meaning or purpose."

"How do I know there is a soul?" she asks.

"The soul is very practical. It makes itself very obvious."

"How so?"

"It goes in and out of our bodies quickly, like a swinging door."

"Example, please?"

"A baby is, except for muscular contractions, an inanimate fetus until it is born, when suddenly the soul pops into it and it is a live human. If the baby stops breathing, the body cannot support the soul; the soul pops back out and returns from where it came. The same thing happens when we die, the moment of death is a quick departure. The soul doesn't linger while the body deteriorates."

"That's interesting. I believe the baby has a soul, but it's hard to believe in life after death." she says.

"Which do you find more difficult to believe, that a fetus in a woman's body continues to grow and when it's born somehow the fetus is inserted with a soul and it then becomes a living human? Or is it easier to believe that the soul leaves the baby's grown body at death and returns to whence it came?"

"Looking at it that way, death is easier for me to believe. Tell me more about the soul," she requests.

"There is no question the soul exists and is somehow directed to come here or some other humanity in the universe, to experience, learn and improve. Life here is not a complete process or a completed story, just a preparation, a step, a learning process for our souls to use in other times and places," I explain.

"Other humanities?" she asks.

"If you believe in a higher deity, you must believe it is intelligent enough to have more than one humanity, in case this one is made extinct by carelessness, destroyed by an object from outer space, or ultimately the sun burns out and our planet becomes lifeless."

"Makes sense." Donna thinks for a moment, then asks, "What if we live worthless lives here and our soul does not learn or improve?" Then a thought dawns on her. "Oh, I think I get it. If the soul doesn't mature it's given a second chance, has to come back and do it all over again until it improves enough to go on. Is that right?"

"It's an interesting supposition, but of course we have no way of knowing."

"Okay, but, how do we know the soul goes on?" she asks.

"It obviously came from someplace when we were born and when we die it has to go someplace. To improve is a forward movement, everything in the universe moves forward."

"That's an interesting observation." Her brow furls in question. "Isn't it hard to believe that we go on?"

"Isn't it even more difficult to believe we came here in the first place?"

"Yes, I suppose it is," Donna admits. "Let's set that aside for a minute. Do animals have souls?"

"The soul appears to be made up of a life force and a consciousness. Both man and animals have a life force, but man also is life conscious. As I remember from somewhere, the difference between man and animal is that man can take two things and make a useful third out of them. This is referred to as human intelligence."

"Any other way man and animals are different?" she asks.

"Look up at the heavens. Only man can go out there, explore and make use of it. Animals don't have the means, desire or reason to go out there. Nor do they care to develop the means to record their history," I say.

The Lady

"That makes sense. Do each of us have our own meaning and purpose?"

"Ah, now you're getting down to where you started," I state.

"I guess I am."

"Well, I would say that humans have a common meaning and purpose, but individually we have our own unique built-in capability to accomplish it."

"Built in?" she questions.

"The method of accomplishing our individual meaning and purpose must be in the genes that built us, along with our unique individual capability and talent to accomplish it."

"But as yet, you can't prove we have uniquely different capability and talent," Donna argues. (She's taking her devil's advocate role seriously.)

"It is obvious we all have different talent capabilities for a purpose."

"Then why don't we know it?"

"I can only conclude that education, in its common-knowledge process, ignores the individual capability built into our genetic design. Our education system makes no effort to uncover or to develop a means to uncover each individual's natural talent so students can be educated accordingly. I often wonder if there are other humanities in the universe whose education is more accommodating to individual needs, and therefore, their civilization is more advanced and in far less danger of extinction," I reply.

"Now, there's a new idea. That could explain why our humanity is in so much trouble. It makes sense, too. I recall you saying that if humanity on earth becomes extinct it would be education's fault for not uncovering the needed talents to solve humanity's problems." She thought for a moment. "Don, how does our soul relate to humanity?"

"I look upon our humanity as a part of a universal humanity, that is a ribbon of invisible electrons traveling through the universe, picking up our souls when we die and transporting them to the next place and time we have earned. That is how it occurs to me."

"Ah, I see," she says. "Our souls come here to experience and learn and if we uncover our maximum talents and learn to use those talents to live well, serve others and benefit humanity here on earth, we earn our next destination. If we don't uncover our maximum talents and therefore cannot live efficient, fulfilling and contributory lives, then our lives here are wasted and our souls have failed to mature. Hmm." She thinks for a moment and asks, "What about genes? Aren't they kind of anti-soul or anti-irreligious?"

"The human body was once considered a religious mystery—now it is but a practical genetic organism that can be studied and repaired. So it is, I believe, with our souls. The soul is a practical force that one day will be understood and worked with. Together our genes, life and soul have a common purpose. Other than faith, genes are as close to God as we can get. How could God create our bodies to house our souls without genes to build our bodies?"

"Hmm," she pondered. "Never thought of it like that."

"That's only as I see it," I said.

"Could there be a different meaning and purpose other than the way you see it?" she asks.

"I often wonder. There appear to be no other important factors to build on. We are built by genes with independent natural capabilities that when efficiently put to use, create useful lives, preserve humanity and build strong souls for a higher being's purpose. What else is there?"

Thinking a moment she responds, "Yes, what else is there?" After another pause, "Why doesn't God just make us perfect talents to begin with?"

"I can only believe that with a problem-ridden earth threatened with extinction, God needs a world of free-will humans to solve the problems. Evidently, for all of us to be uniquely different in thinking and to solve those difficult problems we have to be independently responsible for our thoughts and actions to develop the many different ideas needed to solve the problems. For his free-will purpose, people have to grow independently, without control or interference, or we are but robots or puppets."

"Oh," she said, "that is why He doesn't step in to stop war, pesti-

The Lady

lence, and starvation because we would become controlled robots without free will. Our personalities would be diminished because we would run to Him for every little thing, rather than being independent and responsible human beings. So it's control or free will and it can't be both ways." Then putting her hands prayer-like with her fingers against her chin. "Thus, to improve our souls through uncovering our MTC is the objective and purpose of our lives and God's need of us is the meaning in life."

"Donna, you said that very well. It reminds me of what Pope Paul II said, 'The people of hope are those who believe that God created them for a purpose and that he will provide for their needs as they seek to fulfill his purpose in their lives.' And I like what former actress Eleanor Powell, who turned to the ministry, said, 'What we are is God's gift to us. What we become is our gift to God.' Donna do these thoughts help provide some answers towards the meaning and purpose life pattern you asked for?"

"I think it does, but it's hard to believe something so reverent or Godly could be so practical and simple," Donna replied.

"These are but suppositions. That's why I am so reticent to talk about MTC in that context."

"Don, will I ever know my MTC, to improve my soul and contribute to the meaning and purpose of my life?" Donna is serious.

"Your beautiful soul must already be at a high level, but without support for MTC development, I don't know that MTC uncovering will happen in our time," I apologetically reply.

"My beautiful soul?"

"Yes, your soul must be beautiful and very well developed," I confirm.

"How can you say that?" she asks.

"Because you are such a beautiful person in so many ways."

"Don, you're prejudiced," she declares.

"No I'm not. I'm observant. And my love, that is one argument you will never win with me," I firmly state.

"Hmm. One last question. If your idea is right, about humans needing their MTC to improve their souls, what about all the past generations that didn't know their MTC to improve their souls? Doesn't seem fair."

"I am not the one to answer that. But it does appear fortunate that in our time MTC has come along when humanity is most seriously threatened and needs it so badly. Soul improvement may be different in each stage of human development. Each stage of humanity may have its own soul improvement qualification."

"Don, this is what's bothering me. If my Maximum Talent is not available, how will I be able to make a contribution to humanity and pay the debt I owe for my wonderful life?"

"Donna, you do so much to help other people," I stated.

"I try, but that should be expected of all humans. I need to do something special to preserve humanity, to know my debt to humanity is paid," Donna insisted. "That's what I've been thinking about. Sure I have helped people as much as I can, but what good have I done if there is no humanity?"

"Oh, I didn't think of that," I said.

"The only way my life can have meaning and purpose is if humanity goes on. Promise me it will." She puts her hand over my mouth. "No, don't answer. You can't promise, can you? Carl Sagan was humanity's champion and now there's only you and you know how to save it and no one will listen. So there it is. The only way my life can have meaning and purpose is if there is humanity."

"Donna, I can tell this is important to you, but why all of a sudden is it so important?"

Donna looks off in the distance and says quietly, "I don't know. It's just a feeling I have, that I must be a responsible person for the wonderful life I was given, especially when so many others have not."

She was somber for a minute, then forces a smile. "Don, sorry to put this on you on such a nice day. I know you will do your best for humanity."

The Lady

It was quiet around the house for a few days, so I knew some mischief must be afoot.

Here she comes.

Standing with her hands down in front of her and a mischievous eyebrow raised. "I suppose you are wondering why I didn't say something about your soul, when you said nice things about mine," she says.

"Well I . . ."

She cuts me off. "You would just get a big head."

"Well . . ."

She cuts me off again. "I like you the way you are."

So why . . ."

She cuts me off—again. "So, I'm not going to tell you." And, with that she laughs, bows and sashays out of the room.

I knew it was too quiet.

Formal night on the MS Nieuw Amsterdam, the day we passed around Cape Horn of the Magellan Straits

A Wonderful Marriage

In the fall of 1998 we flew to Buenos Aires for Mardi Gras, then cruised to the Falkland Islands, around the Cape of Magellan, and up to Valpariso, Chile. It was a beautiful trip. Usually Donna is anxious to return home after a few weeks of travelling, but this time, Donna said the trip was so wonderful she didn't want to get off the boat.

I remember looking at her several times during the voyage, wondering what her secret was for looking so young, beautiful and vibrant at the age of seventy.

251

The Twentieth-Century Lady

Holland America Line
A TRADITION OF EXCELLENCE

ROUNDING CAPE HORN CERTIFICATE

A Proclamation

To all ye who have traveled the same path discovered
by brave Dutch explorers Isaac LeMaire and the Schouten brothers.
This daring trio organized the daring expedition that consisted of two ships
that searched for a sea route to the Pacific, south of the Magellan Straits.

On the evening of January 29, 1615, the trio sighted land in
"the shape of a crouching lion" and it was
unanimously proclaimed "Cape Horn."

Know ye that

Donna Seymour

has kept with a "Tradition of Excellence"
by successfully navigating Cape Horn
at a latitude of 56 degrees 00 minutes south,
longitude 67 degrees 22 minutes west
on this, the 02 day of March 1998,
aboard Holland America Line's
ms Nieuw Amsterdam.

Master
Captain Edward G. van Laane

Certificate verifying our cruise around Cape Horn.

The Lady

As I look back, I never seemed to appreciate how wonderful our lives were at the time. Whenever we argued there was always an "I love you" tone in the background of Donna's voice. Like most people, we had difficult financial times and other disappointments—but the trials and tribulations were but building blocks for a wonderful marriage. As the years went by, we retained a high level of love and respect for each other—we enjoyed a life-long love affair. I read somewhere that the best relationship is one in which your love for each other exceeds your need for each other. Love by itself is wonderful, but deep love, loyalty, and unending respect are magical. I was never disappointed or ashamed of Donna, even in a small way. She was vivacious and lovely, her conversation was entertaining and her laugh a joy.

I remember the near tragedy we had on our honeymoon when we missed the ferry, which turned out to be a wonderful memory. And looking back at the pain of my first marriage, I now understand that if the divorce hadn't happened, I would never have had Donna for my wife. That would have been the worst tragedy of my life. Strange, how things happen and people come together, almost as though they were supposed to—for a purpose.

Her 1998 anniversary card to me said. "You promised me the moon and the stars, and you delivered."

A Lady Of Few Words

Donna came into my den to sharpen a pencil.

"Donna, what if Maximum Talent Capability was available before we were born? It may have diverted our lives and perhaps we would have never met. I wouldn't like that."

"Silly, exactly what does that serve? We did meet. We are here." Kissing me on top of the head she laughs. "Forget it dear. Concentrate on positive things."

I said, "Hon. Sit down a minute."

"My husband has a problem?" she asks as she sits on the davenport.

"A little discouraged. I know the MTC research and conclusions are right, but no one with authority will listen. Talent discovery is needed so badly and there is no way to prove it without an expenditure of millions of dollars."

Donna said, "We all need it, humanity needs it and our country needs it. As you said, 'The first country to develop MTC with a six-month lead will come up with such a rash of new ideas, patents, and intelligent solutions that they will be tomorrow's world leader in all ways.' Your course and direction are now set. It's only figuring out how to get it done that evades you. I don't know if you will find it. If you don't, someone else will. But your book and research establishes that you are the father of human capability genetics and I am very proud my husband did it."

"Thank you, that's profound coming from you. Let's see what else you're withholding? Summarize for me how you perceive where all this was going."

"Profound? Me?" She laughs. "Well, let's see how I can best describe it." Donna pauses for a moment, giving her answer careful consideration. "We live our lives like a pool ball on a pool table; being accidentally or purposely hit around the table of life, either by forces unseen or fate, over which we have no control. When maximum talent capability is known and used, humans will no longer lead out-of-control, helter-skelter lives with little meaning and serving no apparent purpose. When we uncover and learn our inherited talent we will lead more controlled, directed, successful, and healthful lives. We will know the meaning of our lives and accomplish the purpose for which our one-of-a-kind genetic structure was designed; and in doing so, each of us will find a way to use our talents to make a direct or indirect contribution to the preservation and forward movement of humanity."

I was astounded. "Donna, that's beautiful. You understand so clearly and said the whole thing so well and with so few words."

"I don't know what's so great about it. They're mostly your ideas, dear."

"No, not mine alone. You put those words together in a very con-

The Lady

cise way and tied it so neatly to humanity's needs." The lady is amazing.

She said, "I heard what Carl Sagan said on television, that humanity is in our hands and our growing, unsolvable problems have humanity close to extinction. With Carl Sagan gone, no one seems to care about humanity. It worries me that no one is or can do anything to protect us from unknown terrorists—except your understanding of the problem and the MTC answer you've developed."

"It troubles me, too," I said.

"Don, I don't know how or when MTC is going to come about. I wish I could help. There must be people somewhere who can recognize the value to humanity of uncovering our hidden talents."

"I know. The problem is how to find them and reach them, so they will understand. Until we find some responsible and recognized supporters, we will have to keep writing and sending out news releases—and that's expensive. If you want to help why don't you accumulate information about humanity's problems on your own and incorporate what I have laying all around the place and organize them?"

"Okay, I can do that," she says.

After Donna collected news of terrorism from TV, newspapers, and magazines she became very concerned about the terrorist threat to humanity.

She Takes No Prisoners—In Golf

We belonged to the Tripoli Golf Club for forty years. Donna had only one enemy on the golf course . . . the golf ball. In her class, Donna was a strong competitor, as her many trophies attest. In addition to golfing with the women on Wednesdays, Donna and I golfed as a couple with our friends on the weekends.

On the golf course I received no special status or treatment. I was just another golfer. And if Donna had a bad day at golf, I was sometimes subjected to indignities.

Donna swings at the ball and it does not travel far. She glares at me. "What did I do?"

Some of our Tripoli golf friends gathering at the home of Jim and Betty King. Front row (l to r): Janet Hayes, Lois Malkasian, Betty Rivard. Second row (l to r): Al Malkasian, Don, Donna. Third row (l to r): Paul Erickson, Gerry Schmidt, Arlene Erickson. Back row (l to r): John Hayes, Carol Schmidt, Clete Rivard.

Why is she glaring at me? "You restricted your back swing," I reply.

"I did?" Another swing. The ball goes to the left. She glares at me again and demands, "What did I do now?"

"You moved forward with the swing."

"How do you know?" Donna demands.

"I was watching."

"No, you weren't. When I looked up you were following my ball."

Isn't that what I'm supposed to do?

We're at the top of the hill, looking down on hole No.5. Donna asks, "What club should I use?"

"Your four wood."

256

The Lady

"I don't like my four wood."

So she takes her three wood and knocks it past the flag and over the green. She gets in the cart and won't talk to me. She's funny and I start to laugh. She glares at me and then starts laughing, too.

"Don," she asks on a slanted green, "where should I putt the ball?"

I look it over. "You're going to have to hit it to the top edge of the green and let it roll down."

She hits it only halfway to the top and it rolls ten feet past the hole. She glares at me. "A lot you know."

In a sand trap Donna looks up, tops the ball and it rolls back to where it was. Looking fiercely at me, "Now what did I do now?"

"You looked up."

She uses a vile farm word she would never otherwise speak.

"Donna?"

"Well, so what," and then mumbles, "what makes you an expert?"

Her great shape makes her look sexy in shorts and a T-shirt. That's nice, so I smile to myself and let the terrible indignities roll over my head.

Back at the clubhouse, Donna is all smiles and laughter again, like nothing happened. The golf course is the one place her husband commands little respect.

The Book

I published the results of my preliminary research in my book *The Key To Your Unknown Talent: A New Discovery About You*. As the Genome sequencing project nears completion, the importance of human capability genetics may find its place. I believe that every human is born with equal ability and intelligence, but does not have the best use of their inborn assets because education is not dedicated to uncovering individual talent. Albert Einstein said, "I am not any more intelligent than anyone else, just fortunate to have found an area that matched my interests and abilities." All people have an area that matches their interests and abilities, which is their unknown talent.

The Key To Your Unknown Talent is a pioneer or cutting-edge book that helps people understand, believe, and search for their unknown talents so they can live more interesting, meaningful, and fulfilling lives. Like Donna once believed, people wrongly think if they have special talents the talents would naturally be known. This is usually not the case because education forces people to conform to standardized learning. Education often represses individuality and prevents natural talent from surfacing. By selecting study courses and work that ignores natural gene capability, natural inherited talent is forever buried.

When Donna first saw the printed copy of *The Key To Your Unknown Talent* and to whom the book was dedicated, she was surprised and pleased.

"Oh. It's dedicated to me."

Who else?

When Donna read the Vancouver Inlet lounge scene in the book (which she had wanted me to remove), where to me she appeared so beautiful, she looked up at me and growled.

The night she finished reading the book, she came into my den, put her hand on my shoulder, and said, "Don, that's a wonderful book. It's not only an enlightening and interesting research story, but also a book that everyone can understand and should read. Not only for themselves but to help people they care about, especially those having trouble finding their way. It gives people hope. Let's them know they are special, have a special talent and have a meaningful place in the world. I was also thinking that if prisoners could find their talent, we would need fewer prisons. MTC is still not proven, but it opens doors never opened before to help all people." She lay her cheek on the top of my head. "I'm so very proud of you."

Donna Believes

Donna has always been a great help to me in question and answer sessions. I asked Donna, "Have you ever had the feeling you could be very talented at something?"

She answered, "You want me to play the devil's advocate again, huh?

Okay. You say that everyone is different and there is something everyone can do better than anything else they can do. But you also say there are 40,000 occupations a person can be talented in, but how could I ever find my maximum talent capability without trying them all?"

I answered, "If you could find a series of compatible activities that you like, are good at and are least stressful, you could be talented."

"Whoa, that's a pretty big jump. What I hear you say is that if I like an activity, am good at it, and it is least stressful to my genes, and if several of these efficient activities can be brought together and used in a particular occupation, that would identify my Maximum Talent Capability?"

"That's very good, keep going," I encourage.

"You're saying a violinist that likes music, has good tone ability and feel in his fingers, and these activities are the least stressful compared to anything else he or she does—that is what being a talented violinist is."

"Keep going."

"I know you also said that each of us has a certain combination of efficient activity genes that when they come together they synergize into talent. And . . ." she stopped and put her hand to her head. "I'm sorry. I'm lost. I think I know where I wanted to go but suddenly the thoughts seemed to have shorted each other out."

I said, "You seem to be trying to bring a practical and gene approach together to substantiate that everyone could be talented."

"I'm sorry I couldn't help. I didn't make it."

"But you did help. I saw how your thinking went and where you got in trouble and it's making me think. Try summarizing what you know about talent, meaning, and purpose." I said.

"Okay. We have identified four of the factors involved in the meaning and purpose of life: God, humanity, our souls, and us genetic beings. The key to the meaning and purpose of life and humanity's terminal problems may be the same, because unless we uncover the needed problem-solving talents to solve humanity's growing problems, humanity on earth will die and then whatever factors or ideas there could otherwise be are meaningless.

"God has an imperfect world of humans that challenges us to uncover and use our maximum talent capability to independently and without interference solve our imperfect world problems," she continued.

"Hey, that's new and very good," I say.

She goes on. "Needing a world of different, free-willed, independent thinking people He created a blueprint of a human that is mostly the same but different in the way we look, think, act, and what we are capable of doing. He then created genes to build our bodies to accommodate our souls that expedite our independent thinking, free will, and talent."

"Expedite? That's an interesting word."

Tapping me on the head. "Please stop interfering with my train of thought," she said. "If we don't uncover and use our God-given maximum talent capability to solve the problems overwhelming humanity, then humanity on earth will die, and then nothing else makes any difference.

"If we do uncover and use our inborn maximum talent capability to solve these problems, then we are the free-willed humanity God set out to create and we are worthy of survival. We can't go on forever defending ourselves from an unknown, unseen terrorist enemy without them breaking through time and again. We can only hope that we have the time through MTC to change the character and ethics of humanity, and can successfully defend humanity until that change takes hold."

"Change the character and ethics of humanity?" I repeat. "That, too, is very good."

She ignores the compliment and goes on. "The meaning of our lives is to uncover and develop our maximum talent capability so we can live fulfilled lives and improve our souls while on earth. The purpose of our lives is to use our maximum talent capability to save and preserve humanity for future generations. Along with God, humanity, our souls, and us genetic beings, maximum talent capability is the missing but needed factor to find the meaning and purpose of our lives.

The Lady

"Other than divine interference, which is free-will improbable, I can see no other openings to the solution of both human and humanity's problems. There, do I have it now?" she asks.

"Yes, dear one, that is how I see it and very well said," I say.

"But, Don. How can something be so simple and practical as the maximum talent capability you developed, be the key to something so unbelievably important to humanity and the meaning and purpose of all our lives?"

"Donna, I didn't originate our genes that create our individual maximum talent capability, God did. I was looking for the answer to our growing personal, education, and humanity problems, and realized the only way the problems could be solved was through a higher level of human problem solving capability. I just stumbled onto maximum talent capability as the answer and gave it a name."

"No you didn't just stumble on it." She stamped her foot down. "You have to give yourself more credit than that. You believed a solution existed and dedicated time and money on years of research," she argued.

"Whatever. Still, I question MTC because I can't prove it and no one else seems to think it has any value."

"Don, MTC is too simple an answer. Everyone is thinking, 'Me, a major talent at something, if so why don't I know it?' Even though we can't prove it, I know that if you had the backing you could uncover my maximum talent capability."

"And if we did, what would you do with it?" I question.

"I've thought about that. At my age, the education and use of it would add great interest and challenge to my life, and it'd be fun. And if not my first talent, perhaps my second or third level talent could somehow help humanity with its problems, and give my life meaning and purpose," Donna answered.

"So, you thought about second and third level talents. That's excellent, keep going, think some more," I encouraged.

She put her hands to her head. "I can't. Please not now. I feel like someone just pulled all the wires loose in my head. Don't know what else there is to think except that this is what God wants us and needs us to do."

That almost brought tears to my eyes. "I remember what John Wheeler said. 'Why should the universe exist at all? The explanation must be so simple and so beautiful that when we see it, we will all say, "How could it have been otherwise?"' Perhaps in the proper time He will let us know the wonder and beauty of it all and it will be simple and make sense. But if we don't uncover and use the MTC He gave us to save our humanity we may never know."

"Oh Don. We must make people understand that humanity is in the path of extinction and needs an MTC solution."

"I know, and if it ever comes into being, your help has been invaluable in making it happen."

"How am I so valuable?"

"You listen, read, and absorb—and in doing so you add new words and simplicity to the direction of my research. Your questions often make me look at the total concept in a new light. To my knowledge, you are the only human that fully understands and believes in the Maximum Talent concept. If you could not believe it, I may have discarded the whole idea as unworkable and a figment of my imagination. Your intelligence, wisdom, and belief made the difference as to whether I continued human capability research. Donna, we are an excellent team."

"Thank you, I like that. So, I have been of help."

Much more than you know lovely lady.

Donna Models For Goodwill

At this period of her life, Donna donated her time as a model for Goodwill Vintage Fashion Shows. At the Little Black Dress show I attended, Donna came out in her little black dress. She had a slight sashay about her walk, which expressed her self-confidence and love for life. A woman sitting in front of me in the audience leaned toward her neighbor and said, "Isn't she cute? I wonder how old she is."

Donna modeling for Goodwill industries in the fall of 1999.

The other replied. "I would guess forty-something, but the other models are older so she could be a very young fifty." Donna was seventy-one.

At the other "Fashions Through The Decades" show I attended, each of the models dedicated their dress to a glamorous male of that period. I don't remember the names chosen, but when it came time for Donna (who was last) she announced, "This dress is dedicated to my husband, Don Seymour." Her love and loyalty were unshakable.

Donna became skillful at every homemaking activity required of her and she could do most crafts (especially Norwegian) well. When she saw something that would compliment a setting in our home, she examined it carefully and if it were possible to make, she made it.

Donna helped whenever she found people in our church or her exercise class that needed assistance or to be taken to time-consuming radiation or chemotherapy treatments. In the past few years Donna assisted her friend Ruth Duncan in caring for Ruth's husband, Bob, when he was wasting away with cancer, and later when Ruth herself had cancer.

A respected friend, Marion Byrnes, who worked with Donna at the Red Cross, once startled me by saying, "You two really deserve each other." In my view, Donna had so risen in stature that I felt complimented to be considered in the same class as Donna.

It always amazed me that this lovely lady freely gave her continuing love, devotion, and loyalty to me. She never demanded anything for herself. Donna was worthy of all the love and devotion a man could give.

I came home and found Donna sitting at the dining room table with papers spread out.

"You look pretty busy. What are you working on?" I asked.

She looked at me very sorrowfully, as though she was going to cry. "What's wrong?" I asked.

"I'm working on that project you gave me to organize articles about humanity and terrorism," she said.

"Oh." Now I understand.

"Don, I found some things I don't want to accept. I know I've read about some of these things in the paper and seen them on the news, but never all together like this. This frightens me. I don't want to know these things. How could all these things be happening? Did you know all this before you gave me the assignment?"

The Lady

Concerned I say, "As you know I knew we were in trouble and needed solutions."

She is almost angry as she responds. "I knew we were in trouble too, but nothing like this. We are losing our forests, fisheries, coral reefs, clean water, farming land, and climate stability. Our land, sea and air is being transformed from a life support system to waste heaps. We are introducing thousands of new chemicals into our air, water and land, without knowing what the effects may be. Our oceans are over fished, we are fouling the water and poisoning our fish, and depleting our clean water supplies.

"We have lost one half of all the species of plants and animals. Natural oil will run out in this next century. The average temperature has risen five degrees in the last hundred years because of global warming. The oceans have risen two feet, forcing some people off the islands their forefather's have inhabited since beyond memory. Advancing oceans are salting millions of acres that used to produce food. And one in six, or one billion people, are undernourished or staving. Don, did you know this?" she demanded.

"Well, Donna, I told you that . . ."

"Oh, never mind," she says exasperatingly and goes on. "And did you know that if every human on earth adopted the lifestyle of a poverty level American, we would need at least four earth's to sustain that level of consumption? Our planet does not have the resources for six billion people to live that way. Did you know that?"

"Well, I . . ."

"And it took 130 years for the earth's population to increase from one billion to two billion people in 1930, three billion in 1960, four billion in 1975, five billion in 1988 and now six billion. And did you know that with continued global warming and salting and poisoning our land and water, we continue to lose millions of food acreage and fisheries every year?

"And did you know that scientists say that in another fifty years the earth's population could double to twelve billion? And if one billion people are starving and undernourished, how can we possibly feed twelve billion? Don, how can earth absorb those kinds of conditions and survive?"

"Hon, don't get angry at me," I plead.

"I'm going to get angry at someone, and all you talk about is terrorism and education. Did you know that outbreaks of E.coli, salmonella, Listeria and other pathogenic bacteria carried by farm animals could destroy humanity? That some new virus or mutation could spread across the world via air travel before we knew it existed? And people at the Center for Disease Control, say that it isn't a case of if such a disaster could occur but when, how far, how fast and if they can control it. God this is awful.

"And, they say that we live in a time in which every living system on earth is in decline, and that the rate of decline is accelerating and our health, marriages and ethics are declining too. People think it's normal for suicide to be the second leading cause of death in children. This is crazy. The earth is going and we are powerless to do anything about it."

"Yes, I know," I sighed.

"Oh you do, huh? Did you know that a group of scientists risked their careers by secretly circulating an unauthorized report that the earth was dying? And the corporate press denounces them as fanatic alarmists, whose wild claims lack scientific proof and whose recommendations would bankrupt the economy.

"And did you know that in 1992 sixteen hundred world scientists and 140 Nobel scientists signed a document to warn the world about these things and hardly anyone knew about it? Good lord, Don. How can our lives have any meaning if we diminish those of our descendants? What's going on? Why are they hiding these things? Why don't they blaze it across the headlines, make people sit up and notice and demand something be done?"

I respond, "They can't alarm and scare the public when they have no answers. A wave of desperate people could start more end-of-the-world incidents and damage. People would lose hope, stop planning, and change their lifestyles. People would give their savings away and do all kinds of strange things, and others would take advantage of them."

"But Carl Sagan told us what had to be done and you developed the only way to find the problem solvers we need. This is our only hope. What's the matter with the media, are they stupid?"

"No not stupid. And as far as the media is concerned, it's like we are trying to tell them there is a miracle cure. There are few miracles and the media has been burned so many times by miracle things that they need proof—and I can't provide it. I am talking about unknown talent, human activity, maximum talent capability, and senses and genes. That sounds like an awful and unrelated mix of things and hardly worth a writer's time to investigate."

"Oh, lord Don. What are we to do? You have the only solution and no one will listen."

"Just keep trying and hope for a break."

"While Rome burns." Donna sighs. "Don, you have the only hope for our planet and humanity. There must be a way. Please, you have to find a way to make people listen."

"Donna, I'm writing all kinds of papers, sending out news releases at $200 each and copies of my book, talking to people, writing to those in authority, even to the President, Vice President, Secretary of Education, and our senators and representatives. I'm trying to reach someone who will try to understand."

"So, what is happening?" Donna asks.

"Not much. Seems most people in authority have unimaginative clerks intercepting the information. But, they send nice thank-you letters for the book and the information. The problem is people can't comprehend what I am talking about. It's too foreign to them. I'm doing everything I can."

"I know you are," she said," "You'll keep trying, I know." She gathered all the papers together, then said, "Don, this stuff is horrible, scary stuff. Soon it will be out of control."

Still A Lovely Woman

As the years passed, Donna quietly grew in warmth and countenance. We seemed to reflect on each other and grow together. We could not help but change through the years. Me, from a young man with a wife and child and out of a job; to a C.E.O and owner of a mid-sized conglomerate of companies. Donna from a young woman whose confidence was shattered by disappointments; to a warm, beautiful, and respected woman.

Donna was a wonderful combination of body, heart, mind, and faith. Very down to earth, Donna would never accept that she was wonderful. She became a natural charmer, not because she wanted to charm but because she wanted to bring joy and laughter to everyone she met. Through the years that wonderfulness shined through more and more and enhanced her loveliness.

Our dedication to helping others and our belief that all people are equally talented and intelligent kept us from thinking we were better than anyone else. No matter what the occasion, Donna fit in beautifully, not just fit in—she enhanced it. The beauty of her inner-self seemed to glow from within to help her retain a beautiful and youthful appearance.

I had attended a publishing convention for several days to promote my book. Donna was busy and could not come. Now retired, I seldom went anyplace overnight without her.

On my way home from the airport, I stopped at the mall near our home to pick up a sports-coat. In the mall, I noticed a woman walking a short distance ahead of me. I couldn't help but notice the nicely styled hair, the youthful shape, and lovely legs. She walked with such casual style and grace that wondered what she looked like. Fortunately she stopped to look in a window. Perhaps sensing my presence, she looked my way . . . and brightly smiled at me . . . her husband. Twirling around she said, "Hi, dear. How do you like my new fall outfit?" And puffing her lovely hair with the back of her hand, "And how I reshaped my hair?"

The Lady

Donna was seventy at the time. Strange that I didn't recognize my wife's walk, the different hair-do must have thrown me off. No, I never told her. And no, I don't make a habit of following beautiful women around.

Someday They Will Understand

I remember what Donna said to me when at times I was discouraged, "Don, Maximum Talent Capability came to you in a series of flashes. It took me years to fully understand and believe it. Think how hard it is going to be for others to understand it. Look how hard it is for people to understand Einstein's theory of relativity. I sure don't, and as the theory of relativity is important to science, Maximum Talent Capability will one day be important to all humans and the meaning and purpose of their lives. When they understand, I'm sure they will invest in the equipment to do so. They must, they have to."

I needed her to say things like that.

I Am Your Sunshine

When Donna attempted to learn computers (which she never felt comfortable using) her instructor told the class to type and print one simple statement. When I came home it was sitting on my desk.

> "Dear Don; I am your sunshine."
> Donna

Is she ever.
A week later another appeared.

> "Dear Don, you light up my life."
> From your sunshine. Donna

Does she ever.

The Twentieth-Century Lady

The World Tumbles

June 6, 1999. Donna is not feeling quite right and goes to her doctor. She comes home and tells me they want to admit Donna in the hospital for some tests. In the hall outside her hospital room two solemn doctors tell me that Donna's lungs have substantial emphysema and one lung has a half golf ball sized malignant tumor. Donna's condition is terminal. At the most Donna has eighteen months to live.

I am in shock and cannot talk. Nor can I accept this news. I decide not to tell anyone. After all, Donna is a confident and strong fighter. She can change any odds. Others have; Donna can, too. Donna had great confidence in her four doctors, all were highly experienced and prominent in their field. Nevertheless, I lived with this awful reality from that day forward and worst of all, Donna would live with the threat of cancer from now on.

My lovely wife was terribly threatened. Our wonderful world had tumbled. The reality of cancer is very difficult to accept, it's like entering a different world. I don't know how many times I shook my head in disbelief.

The doctors outlined a program for treatments.

Scouring the libraries, medical journals, and the Web for new medical advancements or areas of hope, I learned that malignant tumors could sometimes shrink and even disappear, but that cancer and emphysema together was a very bad combination. Emphysema continues to expand and destroy the lungs' capability. The surviving lung oxygen nodules must work harder, and in doing so increase the chance of carrying cancer to all the organs of the body. As a person fights, many end up in a wheelchair and ultimately waste away.

Reading about lung diseases, I then recalled that Jean Ann our baby, died of fibrosis of the lungs an hour after she was born.

I used to take Donna's good-night kiss for granted, but now I value her kisses more and more. They were always soft and sweet, the sweetness of her lingered like the scent of garden flowers.

A Difficult Year

An appointment is scheduled to discuss the possibility of operating on the cancer. While discussing the surgery, the doctors tell Donna that after the operation she might not be able to golf and could be in a wheelchair. She thinks for a minute then says, "I've had a wonderful life. I loved it and I have no regrets. If it will help to operate, then let's do it. What must be must be."

After further tests it was decided that surgery with advanced emphysema would not be wise. The operation door was now closed. Donna would have to fight on her own.

Continuously operating oxygen units were installed in our home. I occasionally followed Donna around, untangling a hundred fifty feet of oxygen hose. Told to exercise, Donna was never still anyway. When outside our home, Donna would not carry an oxygen unit, nor did she seem to need to, although I had one in the trunk of my car. Doctors said her great physical shape allowed her to go without oxygen, even while playing golf. This was encouraging.

Donna typed and carried this card in her wallet the last year of her life. It expresses her wonderful attitude towards life.

People who did not know

> I have no yesterdays, time took them away, tomorrow may not be...but I have today.
>
> ---
>
> To err is human, but to think of someone to blame it on is genius.
>
> ---
>
> Those who bring sunshine to the lives of others—cannot keep it for themselves.
>
> ---
>
> Don't walk ahead of me, I may not follow.
> Don't walk behind me, I may not lead.
> Walk beside me... and just be my friend.

had no indication that Donna had cancer and emphysema. Nor did Donna show symptoms to those who did know. In public Donna was her cheerful self, laughing, smiling, and never gave a hint of what she felt inside.

At home Donna was sometimes withdrawn. No one can be cheerful all of the time. I knew the despair she must feel. Both of us kept our relationship as positive as possible. She knew I was there for her.

Every morning after my breakfast was neatly laid out, Donna would quietly read the Lutheran Portals of Prayer. Her faith was important to her.

I called Ramona and suggested she spend some time with Donna, which fortunately she did. Marlyn wanted to be there too, but her concern had to be for her husband, Rick, who could not be left alone because of a physical problem.

Ramona told me later that Donna said while driving one day, " I guess I should be planning my funeral." Ramona told her she had plenty of time.

One day I accidentally came upon something Donna had typed:

"Lord God, sometimes I feel so frightened by all the challenges and uncertainties of this life. By the power of the Holy Spirit, fill me with courage each day in your strength."

This was the time of life when negative events threatened Donna's life. Now vulnerable, it was the time of life when her faith must be strong. She was now fighting for her wonderful life with all her courage and faith.

New Year's Eve Party 2000

At our club's New Year's Eve party, Donna was given and wore a year 2000 party hat. My heart sank when I saw it on her. The last month of the year 2000 would mark the eighteen months. At the stroke of midnight I held Donna very close and long, so she couldn't see my eyes.

We talked about the positives on the way to fourteen chest radiation and twenty chemotherapy treatments. How ironic, that the treatments

The Lady

she had taken so many people to, were now for her. Her beautiful hair came out by the handful after the radiation treatments.

We received cards indicating prayers were being said for her in many places and religions. I tried not to show my worry or concern; everything was going to work out well. Suddenly the tests showed the lung cancer was shrinking. In six months Donna's hair grew back and she looked wonderful. We were so thankful.

A few months later the cancer was growing again and the cells showed up in Donna's brain. Our hopes were dashed. Twelve more radiation treatments and her hair was gone again, now permanently. Whip-lashed back and forth, Donna tried not to let me know her despair. I tried not to let her know mine. How could this be happening to such a cheerful, bright eyed, lovely woman?

Thank You

A week after the bad news, I came home and Donna said, "Please sit down, Don. I want you to listen to what I have to say." She started reading from notes she had made. I didn't like the sound of this at all.

"I have been going over our life together and making a list of things you accomplished and those things we have done together. Other than being wonderful and us having fine sons, the first few years were formative years. Then you, a poor student without a college degree, became successful in life insurance and earned a degree.

"You bought the house in Shorewood, which at the time I thought we couldn't afford, but you worked hard to pay for it—and I loved it. After taking on a large mortgage, you joined a golf club and bought me golf clubs, even though I had never golfed. I could have crowned you with one of those clubs, but it was the right move for us, and me, as I learned to love golf and we developed many wonderful friends there.

"Then you left your successful insurance work to take on a small, ailing company. I was very concerned. Often I bit my tongue, because I wanted to object to what you were doing, but because I believed in you, I held back. I'm glad I did. You made the business successful and

The Twentieth-Century Lady

we traveled the world. We golfed at Harbor Town, Rancho Bernardo, Pebble Beach, Innsbruck, La Quinta and other major golf clubs all over America. We met and were in the homes of wonderful and interesting people from all over the world. Those were wonderful business and vacation trips.

"And, in building the companies you helped many people find their careers. Without ever taking science or chemistry, your ideas resulted in several patents and you were responsible for a weed and algae handbook."

I tried to interrupt. "But . . ."

"Please dear, I have to finish this. You spent a lot of money setting up the Vocational Guidance Institute and hired people to research human capability, the problems of education, and right and healthy careers. You have no education in this area, but you and your people developed Education By Attraction and submitted it to President Bush's New Education Committee.

"You found that forced education represses individuality and builds up resentment that can lead to terrorism and then you developed a terrorist solution. You studied work and careers, and found that by uncovering our Maximum Talent Capability all people are equally talented, intelligent, and can find their most talented and healthy careers, so they can plan successful and meaningful lives. Because of your work and research in occupational testing you were asked to be Director of Career Guidance at a university."

I tried to interrupt again, but she held up her hand.

"Please sweetheart, let me finish. I must do this. Concerned with humanity's problems, you established that we must uncover and educate the talents of all people, because new and higher talents are needed to solve humanity's problems, or there may not be a future for humanity. I would like to believe that God would save humanity on earth, but sometimes seeing all the terrible things going on, I don't know. I was impressed by what Carl Sagan said, 'We are the first species to have taken our evolution into our hands.' And you said, 'Humanity's one hope is to uncover and educate the talented experts needed to solve

The Lady

humanity and terrorist problems, because it's obvious we do not have them now.' With Carl Sagan gone I believe you are now humanity's only champion; because you don't just talk, you develop real solutions for humanity's problems.

"I confess, I did not always understand your theories, they were so far out and so different from what I was educated to believe. But in time, going over and editing your work again and again, the ideas started to make sense, and now I understand how original and right your research is. It's too bad people are not ready to accept these solutions, because they are so badly needed. People aren't picking up these ideas because you are way ahead of your time. Neither science, education, nor government is ready to accept the practical truth of inborn talent and human capability genetics. Like me, it's going to take people time to understand.

"Don't deny other men and women the opportunity to help you. Your work is needed. You are the author of human capability genetics and when gene sequencing is completed and they turn their attention to practical gene applications they will find you are already there, and perhaps, then understand.

"I especially like what you said, 'Every person owes a debt to humanity for giving them life'. It should be a dedication of everyone, so they understand the need to uncover their talents to pay that debt to humanity. People think humanity has always been here and always will be. I thought so, too, but watching and accumulating news and news articles about terrorism, I came to understand we are wrong. They did not listen when Carl Sagan said that humanity is close to the edge of extinction. You must continue to press your ideas to preserve humanity until they listen. Let's hope it's not too late.

"Remember coming back from Iowa, before we were married? I told you that I believed in you and your vision of helping people. I never dreamed you would come so far. Remember that falluca on the Nile, when I said I thought we hit the top? Then you wrote a book that opened the door to talent. There is no top with you. Your book, *The Key To your Unknown Talent,* will one day be considered a major accomplishment. I love it. It is the meaningful story of your humanitarian research. I am in it. It is dedicated to me and that means so very much to me."

She was biting her lip to hold back tears, so I was finally able to interrupt. "Sweetheart, you can't give me all the credit. The love and devotion of a very wonderful woman gave me the confidence and dedication to do this research. You edited, asked questions, and made comments that made me think things through again and again, which helped me continue to find solutions I may not otherwise have found. Those were invaluable contributions. We are a team.

"Whenever business associates, here and in foreign countries, met you, it added respect to me. Your presence often opened the door when needed. Our overseas people remember me as the husband of the warm and friendly Donna.

"Your love gave me the motivation to make you proud of me, and to earn and keep your love and respect. I don't know if I could have accomplished anything without you. Please believe that, because it is true."

Donna responded, "Thank you for saying that. I'm glad if I helped, because I wanted so very much to be the wife you needed. But I believe you would have done these things anyway. It's what you are and I sometimes think it's what you were meant to do.

"Oh, Don. Isn't this kind of silly of us? I am trying to give you credit for all the things you have done and you are saying you could not have done them without me. In reality, the most important thing is that we loved each other deeply and wonderfully, as God would have wanted us to. And in doing so, we used the talents He gave us to help His people find their best capability to live more meaningful and contributory lives and use their talents to preserve humanity for future generations.

"Remember our conversation after the pageant, coming back from Gloria's? You asked where my life was going? I said, there's so much negativity, disappointment and grief in the world that I wanted to help people be cheerful, happy and feel good about themselves. And I'd like my life to have a purpose and make a difference. I believe part of my purpose was to help you uncover the hidden talents of people and through it their purpose in life. And when you accomplish it, as I know you will, then my small part will have helped make a difference."

She folded her notes, and with a tissue to her eyes said, "Whenever I lacked understanding, was out of sorts or angry with you, sometimes you were angry with me, too, but you always ended up gentle and loving. It was always wonderful to come back into your arms. There was a time before we were married that I questioned marrying you. Just to think I almost married another and would have missed this wonderful, loving, and fulfilling life I have had with you."

I tried to interrupt, but she put her hand gently across my mouth.

"And if I am not here, you must go on with the work that is so badly needed. I know you love me, turn that love to our work. Don't shut yourself off from people who may be needed to bring your research to reality.

"And now I want to say this well, so you will always remember." She started to cry and put her hand to her mouth to get control. Starting out with a half-restricted voice, "You are a gentle, loving, and understanding husband. More than I ever hoped for. So happy to have you love me. So fortunate and proud to be your wife. Thank you, my dear husband, for a wonderful life, way beyond anything I could have ever dreamed. I am grateful you are working to give my life meaning and purpose. I am content and I love you so very much. Please always remember that." She kissed me, then with her hand over her eyes, hurried out of the room.

A flood of tears burst from my eyes. Oh Lord, she's closing her life. I didn't know what to think or say. A world without Donna—I can't even imagine. I don't want to imagine.

Please dear Lord, don't take her from me.

A Difficult Month

Donna never cried in front of me, although a few times did I see her sitting quietly, holding her hands tightly together, perhaps in anguish.

Every morning I placed a flower, a verse, or a loving card where she was sure to find it. It became a game. Where was the next card? In her jewelry box? Next to her toothbrush? Mixed in with her nightgowns or under-things?

※

One evening Donna sat on the arm of my chair and looked off in the distance. "Don," she said quietly, "if education had paid attention to John Dewey, Albert Einstein, and Carl Sagan, and we had discovered a way to uncover individual talents by now, would highly talented cancer researchers have discovered a cure?"

Tears came to my eyes. I could not answer.

She put her head against mine and said, "The reason I ask is, I don't want you ever to blame yourself, you did so much more than anyone else and everything you could."

But it wasn't only cancer. The emphysema continued to spread. Through it all, Donna was courageous.

To Make A Contribution

I had thought Donna's health would preclude any further attention to what I considered our research. She kept *The Key To Your Unknown Talent* on a table in reach of her chair and occasionally I saw her reading or holding it and thinking.

One evening, she said, "Don, I don't know if I'm right in this, but can't education's problems of dropouts, wrong, failed, uncreative and unhealthful careers be happening because education concentrates on the job tasks of occupations rather than the human activities involved in each individual's natural talent?

"If we are to solve education's and humanity's problems by uncovering the talented experts needed to solve the problems, we need a simple explanation and comparison between wrong education and right education. I don't know if this is right, but this is how I understand it: Education is based on what educators assume we should learn

The Lady

rather than on what we genetically are and therefore need to learn. Education's problem of dropouts and wrong and unhealthful careers happen because education concentrates on the job tasks of occupations and not on each individual's gene-sponsored human activities.

"Drawing a simple comparison like that makes sense to me and perhaps will be more understandable to others. Let's see if this is it. We use assumptions, emotions and market conditions to select wrong careers rather than what naturally fits our genetic design. Education then attempts to force a student's mind and body to fit into a wrongly selected career. Thus our genes rebel by causing stress, which uses up our energy and limits our intelligence, creativity, and problem solving ability, as compared to the Maximum Talent Capability approach that uncovers our natural capability, to enhance our intelligence and synergize our creative and problem solving ability. And in doing so, identifies our best low stress occupations because our natural talent fits our genetic design.

"What do you think?"

I looked at her. With her concerns, Donna is still remarkable, intelligent and caring.

She went on, "I'm sorry. It just kind of came to me."

"Sorry?" I said. "It's a clear and simple approach, and you covered all the bases beautifully. It's just that I'm astounded. You just reduced the problem of education to a simple comparison. You cut through everything. It's a great deduction."

She asked, "We can use it, huh?"

"There is no question we can use it. What I was thinking is, if you can so deduce, why can't education?"

"Don, maybe it's because they don't want to, unless it's fully proven. And they don't understand that humanity's future may depend on it."

"We should use your simple description to challenge education to understand it," I said.

"So, it's good then?"

"Yes, sweetheart, it is very good." With her desperate problems, how is she so concerned? "But what suddenly brought this up?"

279

"I wanted to contribute something. I'm just sorry that MTC has not been developed so I could uncover my highest talents and find a way to use them to make a meaningful contribution to people and to preserve humanity."

※

For Donna, this is the time to pay her debt to humanity, so she wasn't found wanting. Donna believed there was a genetic conscious or life credo built into humans, that when we take on the responsibility to repay the debt for our life we become more worthy of having our dreams come true. She had done her best. She had loved deeply, faithfully, and as she said to the doctors, "I have no regrets. I've had a wonderful life."

※

I dreaded Christmas 2000, for that would be the doctor's estimate of eighteen months. We spent St. Patrick's Day at our club and those who knew, commented to me on Donna's cheerful attitude and how wonderful she looked, even in a wig. During that time I wrote a new terrorism article which Donna read:

We Can't Preserve Humanity By Being Defensive

"If humanity's growing problems continue, they will overwhelm humanity and it may cease to exist," says human capability researcher Donald Seymour.

Fifty years ago, no person had the capability or weapons to destroy humanity. Today thousands of unknown terrorists have the knowledge and capability to use biological and chemical weapons and bombs that can cripple or destroy humanity.

Carl Sagan said, "Nearly all our problems are made by humans and can be solved by humans. We are the first species to have taken our evolution into our hands. It is up to us to save humanity, now teetering on the edge of self-destruction."

"If the solutions to humanity's problems are not forthcoming we can only conclude that humanity is lost. If we aren't intel-

The Lady

ligent enough to see and believe it, we are sticking our heads in the sand," says Seymour.

Obviously we do not now have the highly talented problem solving people in the areas of humanity's problems. In Seymour's book, *The Key To Your Unknown Talent — A new Discovery About You*, he states, that the needed talented problem solvers exist in the populations of earth.

Educator John Gardner partially supports Seymour in his book *Excellence*, which says, "Individual's whose gifts have been discovered and cultivated have been as chance outcropping of precious rock, while the great reserves of human talent lay uncovered below."

If all people have hidden talent, why don't they know it? Seymour thinks forced education represses natural talent so it seldom surfaces. He says we can develop a talent discovery process that can uncover and identify each person's inborn Maximum Talent Capability (MTC) and educate by wrapping the three Rs around their talent.

Albert Einstein may have backed up Seymour's claim when he said, "I am not any more intelligent than anyone else, just fortunate to have found an area that matched my interests and abilities."

Seymour says, "Einstein is saying that all people are equally intelligent and everyone inherits an area (talent) that matches their interests and abilities."

Humanity's one hope is to uncover and educate the talents of all people and accelerate the education of those needed to solve humanity's problems. Seymour explains, "There is only one humanity and no second chance to save it. We must demand loud and long of education and government representatives to develop and support a talent uncovering process to find the problem solvers needed to preserve humanity and so our children have a future.

"Don, it's an excellent article. Pray to God they will listen. I am so fearful of a diminishing joy of living, especially for the children and the future of humanity itself. Don, one day one of us will not be here and if you survive me, promise you will do something special just for me, to preserve humanity."

Don and Donna, two weeks before she succumbed to pneumonia and died. (June 2000)

I Lose My Sunshine

I know Donna purposely kept her distance from me because she feared that her problems might be contagious to me. Accepting this, perhaps, was a mistake on my part, because there were so many times I didn't console her in my arms, so many things I didn't do or say. We could not admit to each other that she may be gone. She was doing well without oxygen, we both thought we had more time.

After the last radiation treatment Donna did not feel well and wanted to go to the hospital. The doctors thought she was just weak and decided to admit her in the hospital a for few days to get her strength back. Her immune system was weakened and pneumonia set in. The doctors now said her time was a matter of hours, at the most a few days. Donna wanted no tubes to keep her artificially alive.

Donna had been in a coma for hours. As I sat there holding her

The Lady

hand, she suddenly forced her eyes half-open. Flecked with gray, they seemed to be questioning me. I strongly sensed Donna was worried about me. I whispered, "I'll always love you. I'll be all right if you have to leave. Your mother, father, and grandparents will be there to welcome you, just as they were here when you were born. I love you." She seemed to understand and strained to keep her eyes on me as long as possible, but they slowly closed.

Nurse Claire Meisenheimer, a friend from our club, came and helped with the vigil. A short time later Donna's breathing quietly stopped.

I sat there through the night, holding Donna's lifeless hand. I know the nurses and doctor kept approaching the door to Donna's room. They wanted to make a final determination of death and take her body down below. I reluctantly had to let go of her hand; Donna wasn't there anymore.

My sunshine was gone.

I left the hospital in a daze. The world seemed to go on as before. Weren't bells going to ring, choirs sing, or something? Wasn't the world going to show some sign of the passing of such a wonderful and valuable human? But all was quiet.

Driving home I thought, Where am I coming from? What day is this? July 8, 2000. A hospital. Why was I there? To see Donna? She died? No, that's not possible. Not, laughing, bright-eyed, full of life Donna. No that could not happen. She's gone.

I didn't cry. I don't remember anything, until the next morning. I went out to get the paper and walking back down our driveway I suddenly realized Donna would not be here anymore. It started with a deep moan, a sound I never heard come from me before. Great sobs overtook me and shook me so I could hardly walk. I sat down on the cement, held myself, and cried. The words from her song, "You Are My Sunshine, rang in my ear: "I'll always love you and make you happy, please don't take my sunshine away."

My sunshine had been taken away.

My Promise to Donna

Let's see if I can keep my promise to Donna by convincing you and the world that there is a way to save our planet. As Donna once said, "Promise me there will always be future generations of laughing children to enjoy Easters, Christmases and birthdays."

This is to keep my promise to Donna, to do something for her . . . and to help solve the problems of our declining world and humanity.

We have polluted and unbalanced the air, land and water of our planet by overpopulation and overuse and we are helpless to do anything about its continuing decline. We do not know what the synergy of all these problems will result in or do to our planet. Not having been faced with this problem in the past, we do not know how or when a total collapse of our planet could occur. But we do know that our planet continues at an increasing rate of decline. As Carl Sagan said, "Our planet is teetering on the edge of extinction." We have made some gains but continuing overpopulation and pollution accelerates the decline and unless reversed our time may run out any day.

As our population multiplies, fresh water, agricultural land and ocean fisheries are being poisoned and shrinking. In the last century earth's population went from one billion to six billion and one in six of the earth's inhabitants (or one billion) are undernourished, starving and attempt to live without fresh water. Scientists are concerned that if the population continues at its current pace and our planet is still habitable (in not too many years from now) people may begin killing each other off for food and fresh water.

A Supreme Being has not interfered to stop or retard the decline of our planet, and other than making small gains against a few problems, neither science nor government knows what to do about the array of problems that continues to accelerate earth's decline.

Who must attempt to do this?

Carl Sagan summed it up for us when he said, "We are the first species to have taken our evolution into our hands."

It must be up to us.

Author Fred Branfman wrote, "Humanity has reached a critical mass in material consumption. . . .You and I are alive in the first moment in history when one generation's material comfort threatened the well-being of later generations. . . .If we continue this misuse of power, we will be cursed."

What can we do?

Carl Sagan also said, "Earth's people created the problems and only people can solve the problems. . . .We are unlikely to survive if we do not make full and creative use of our human intelligence."

Whatever is done must be done by people making the full creative use of their human intelligence. It is not being done now, so whatever is to be done must change the character and dedication of the earth's six billion people to want to uncover and use their creative intelligence to save our planet.

But people can't and won't be forced to change, so whatever is done must be something people will want to do and urgently need. It must uncover the wealth of creative human intelligence that results in the problem-solving talents needed to solve our problems.

And to be effective whatever is done can only be accomplished by reaching all people on earth in a short span of time.

What is it that every human wants and needs that can reach and release the creative human intelligence of six billion people, quickly change our character, and unleash the problem-solving talents in time to stop and reverse the damage being done to our world?

Something new and different must be found or uncovered.

Donna and I believe that Albert Einstein may have given us a clue when he said, "I am not any more intelligent or talented than anyone else. Just fortunate to have found an area that matched my interests and abilities."

By matching his interests and abilities Einstein released his creative intelligence and became one of the world's most talented problem solvers.

Can we find a way to uncover everyone's unique interests and abilities and make creative and intelligent problem solvers out of all of us, in different areas? Is that what talent is? Certainly every normal human would quickly want to know if they have an unknown talent and higher creative intelligence. Could these talents possibly exist in all us, without our knowledge, and inspire the least appearing intelligent of us?

Educator John W. Gardner may have answered this for us when he wrote in his book, Excellence, "Generally speaking, individuals whose gifts have been discovered and cultivated have been as chance outcropping of precious rock, while great reserves of human talent lay undiscovered below."

There are people who believe great reserves of unknown creative talent may exist.

Being talented at an activity, object or subject is what people naturally crave to have, learn and enjoy because it provides what human's most desperately need—self-esteem, identity, recognition, respect and purpose in life. If we can find a way to match the interests and abilities of all people, which also releases their creative intelligence, then most, if not all, normal people would have a strong interest in uncovering their talents as soon as possible. And in the billions of talents, there cannot help but be a wealth of the talents we need to solve earth's many problems.

Donna and I agreed with Sagan, Einstein and Gardner. We believed that in the 40,000 known occupations, every person has something they can do better than anything else they can do, but don't know what it is. That something is each of our best capability or talent. I refer to this as each human's Maximum Talent Capability (MTC), which is every human's unique genetic area of capability that can release unused areas of creative intelligence.

If we haven't uncovered these talents in the past, how do we do it now?

Computer, visual and virtual reality industries are capable of designing software visuals and simulations needed to support the development of the MTC process. Our government sponsored gene sequencing to help many of us; our government should also sponsor MTC development to help all of us and our planet.

I believe education can use the Maximum Talent Capability process to uncover each student's (and adult's) most interesting and capable MTC and can educate those MTCS by wrapping the 3-Rs around the student's MTC.

People who are able to use their inborn talents are less likely to get in trouble. Uncovered talents would reduce the costs associated with crime, violence and health care. These savings would more than pay for the development of the MTC uncovering process.

Every human's talent could contribute in some way to solving humanity's problems and at the same time give meaning and purpose to their lives. Carl Sagan said of the need to solve humanity's problems, "No social convention, no political system, no economic hypothesis, no religious dogma is more important."

Most, if not all, people are currently working at untalented and stressful jobs that restrict their natural intelligence and creative problem-solving capability. Psychologist Sandra Scarr wrote, "We are asking for trouble and friction when trying to mould a human in a direction not in tune with their natural genetic structure."

Our planet *is* in trouble.

After my extensive research, I believe it logical that in not too many years, no one will enter an occupation or profession that is not in tune with his or her genetic structure.

No matter what your belief, if there is a Supreme Being and that Supreme Being has not stopped the decline of earth then perhaps that Supreme Being built in us the ability to do so. The answer could only be a talent capability we have always had but we have not yet uncovered. God created us and working through the abilities he gave us may be the way he intended for us to preserve humanity on earth.

Some people argue that because MTC is unproven the MTC process is too far of a stretch. If developing MTC is not possible, then humanity on earth may not survive. What else do we possess that can quickly uncover human creative intelligence?

MTC is unproven, but our only choice is to try to make it work. Fujitsu, the Japanese firm, has a motto: "Whatever man can dream, man can do."

We must believe that it is God who is doing the stretching . . . through us . . . and we can do it

Pray that we have the time to pursue this.

※

To the reader: Write to me (c/o Talent Discovery Press, 3900 West Brown Deer Road, Suite AA110, Milwaukee, WI 53209) and let me know if you are or are not convinced that we need to take this action. Let me know what you think. If you are convinced, for the sake of future generations, please write to your local newspaper editor your congressman and the President and tell them so.

Do everything you can so that "There will always be laughing children and Easters, Christmases and birthdays for them."

We need your help and as quickly as possible.

Reflections

I had nightmares of losing Donna many times during the last year, and each time I reached over I was relieved to find her sleeping. I was not prepared for when I reached over and felt a cold and empty bed.

※

Forty-nine years ago, the good Lord saw Donna in Madison and me in Milwaukee. He must have decided we would make an excellent combination and make a meaningful contribution, so he brought us together. The barriers to our coming together were far too difficult to not have been engineered by Someone.

※

The words used most often to describe Donna in the sympathy cards I received were energy, smile, bright, joyful, delightful, pretty, lovely, bubbly, laughing, warm, friend, friendly, caring, great lady, vivacious, and beautiful inside and out.

The Lady

Letters from several members of Donna's family to me said, "We know how much Donna loved you. We too care for you and love you. Don't stray from us. Your are family."

Donna's passing left a deep hole in many lives.

※

At the funeral in Milwaukee, one smoker friend asked if there was anything they could do. I said, "Donna mentioned she was concerned about your smoking. Perhaps in her memory, you could quit smoking." And they did.

The friend told others and I heard the same happened at two other funerals. So, Donna's caring continued on in ever expanding circles.

※

We took Donna to the church in Mt. Horeb, where we were married and another service was held. After the service the funeral director motioned to me that they were going to close the casket for the last time. He took off the engagement ring Donna so loved, then looked at me. I motioned, no. I wanted the wedding ring left on. I bent over and kissed cold lips, the lips that had always been so lovingly warm and soft. I couldn't watch the cover come down.

I thought at my mature age that I would be more stoic. I never knew I was capable of shedding so many tears—so very often.

※

Now I look for Donna in every room, but she is not there. At night I reach for her but her side of the bed is vacant. I talk to her, but there is no answer. I miss the sweetness of her good-night kiss.

One day I must face the hard reality that my precious wife is gone.

※

The Twentieth-Century Lady

A cocktail party for Greg's thirtieth Shorewood High School reunion had been scheduled at our home. Even though it was only three days after Donna's funeral, I knew Donna would have wanted it to go on. Everyone in attendance knew Donna's bright smile. The men, who had known Donna when they were only boys, found her death a milestone in their lives.

I remember what Donna said. "Don, if education had listened to John Dewey, Albert Einstein and John Gardner years ago, we may have already uncovered the people with the talents to solve cancer, and those now dying of cancer could have lived. This is a horrible condemnation of education."

My failure to make people in authority understand the need for MTC may have cost my beloved's life. I have to live with that.

Some people and religions believe we live over and over again; that we select and plan our lives and death. I would be relieved to know that Donna so planned it and spared herself a lingering death. Donna knew it would destroy me to watch her waste away and she knew I had work for us yet to do.

I am so fortunate to have work to do that I care about, especially at my age and at this trying time in my life. I would like to help every elderly person have a strong and interesting work dedication. Uncovered talent would do that so I continue to work towards that end.

The Lady

Donna's beautiful soul is out there someplace, reappearing on some new planet in the estimated 50 billion galaxies. Her soul that created her consciousness, mind and body still retains the blueprint of her lovely self and will recreate it again and again, improving a little each time. Our souls could bring us together again.

I have this recurring dream. The years pass. My work is done and my eyes close here for the last time. But my eyes close for just a few moments and then they are open in another place and time. I am on a path, coming out of a dark forest. I feel different. I feel as though I can run like I did when I was very young. My hands, why they are clear of age spots. Something has changed me. Now, out in the open, the colors are vivid and the flowers are so beautiful. I don't know this place. I am alone. What am I doing here? There are weathered rail fences on both sides of the path so I suppose I must go on. Oh, up ahead is someone sitting on a bench, reading a book. Maybe they will know what I am to do. It's a woman. As I get closer to her I can see she is very nice looking, more than that, she is a beautiful young woman. I walk up to her. She senses my presence and looks up at me with a brilliant smile . . . a smile I know so well. And my Donna Lou says to me, "Hi, dear."

I believe He is just starting with Donna and me, and that He will not break up such a valuable combination. We have lives yet to love, learn and grow to contribute to His plans.

Working at her faith and believing in the Bible, Donna was concerned by the biblical reference about humans not knowing each other after leaving this life. Donna brought up the question several times and must have made a decision about it. For our forty-ninth anniversary on May 26, 2000, she found an anniversary card for me that said, "We were meant to be together forever. Love Donna."

Please Lord, may it be so.

The Twentieth-Century Lady

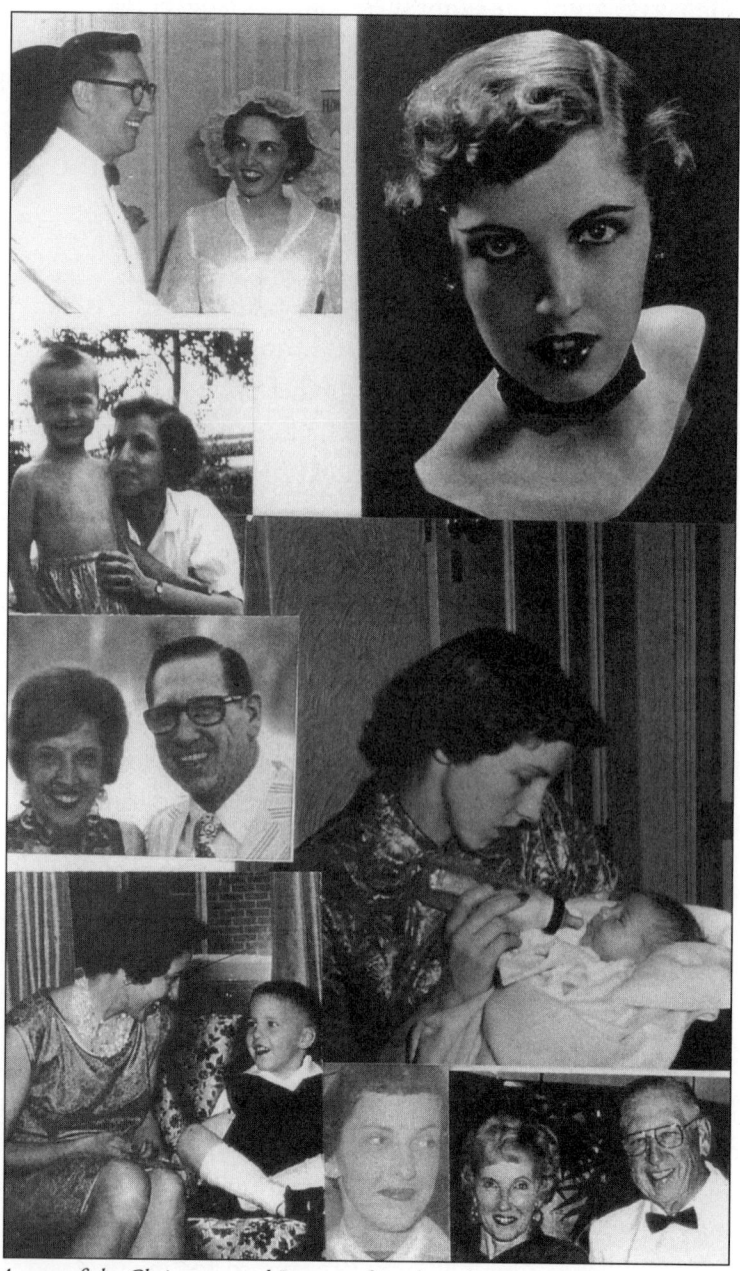

A copy of the Christmas card I sent to friends and relatives in December 2000.

Afterword

It may not be long before I join Donna—I had better finish the account of her life.

One friend at Donna's funeral said, "You two made a handsome couple. You were so full of the energy of life, one could see the brightness and feel the flow of energy between you."

Another said, "It was so interesting watching you two plough your way through life, building companies, uncovering talents of people, challenging forced education and developing terrorism solutions. Too bad people aren't ready to listen, but that's because you two were ahead of your time. It's such a disappointment to see your duo come to an end. Your dedication to help people and humanity must be that from which legends are made."

In the introduction I asked, "What would one of the best of the twentieth century's ladies be like and what would be her dedication to life?" What is so different about Donna and the quality of Donna's character as to make her worthy of being representative of the twentieth-century lady?

She would come from humble means, a plain girl who would develop into a beautiful and charming woman. Because of her unselfish nature she maintained a beautiful and youthful appearance—even into her seventies. She was lovely, loving, wonderful and precious.

She would have developed areas of natural beauty, style and grace. She would be intelligent, wise, honest, interesting, fun, laugh a lot and be warm and friendly.

She would have a high level of morality, love deeply and be totally and unselfishly dedicated to her marriage, husband and family.

Afterword

At this point there are probably many wonderful women in the twentieth century that fit this mold, but Donna went further.

Donna was so dedicated to making other people happy and feel good about themselves that she put together and carried a card in her purse to constantly remind her of this goal.

Donna, unusually intelligent, assumed a responsibility and indebtedness to God and humanity for her life. To pay that debt she worked with me to develop ways to preserve humanity for future generations.

She believed and shared my goal of uncovering the hidden talent every human inherits at birth, to maintain the health and happiness of every person. In doing so every human will find the meaning and purpose of their lives, fulfill their destiny and have the means to help save humanity.

Donna was not a famous writer, politician or entertainer. Nor was she one of the famous beautiful women who influenced the twentieth century, like Jackie Kennedy, Grace Kelly and Oprah Winfrey (who straddles two centuries). Donna was a little known everyday wife, mother and friend who made an art of being a woman.

Adding all these qualities together we have a woman about whose life legends can be made.

This is the first "Century Lady" book and perhaps someone will write a book about the twenty-first century lady. It may go on for centuries, and in doing so people will want to go back, read and compare these wonderful women to theirs. . . and Donna Lou's memory will go on.

It's the year 2001 and a lovely twentieth-century lady now belongs to a century gone by. Unless another Donna is recreated, I doubt future centuries will develop a more wondrous lady.

Future centuries are challenged to do so and future writers are challenged to find one.

Bibliography

Ackerman, Diane. *A Natural History of the Senses* (New York: Vintage Books), 1990.
Bolles, Richard Nelson. *What Color Is Your Parachute* (Berkeley, CA: Ten Speed Press), 1988.
Citron, Marvin and Owen Davis. *Probable Tomorrows* (New York: St. Martin Press), 1997.
Einstein, Albert. *Ideas and Opinions* (New York: Random House), 1994.
--------. *The Quotable Einstein* (Princeton University Press), 1996.
Gardner, Howard. *The Unschooled Mind* (New York: Basic Books), 1991.
Gardner, John W. *Excellence* (New York: Harper Row).
Kaku, Michio. *Visions* (New York: Doubleday).
Montessori, Maria. *Education and Peace* (USA: Henry Regnery Co.), 1972.
Papke, G. Owen. *Evolution of Progress* (New York: Random House Press), 1993.
Rivilin, Robert. *Deciphering the Senses* (New York: Simon & Schuster).
Sagan, Carl. *Billions & Billions* (New York: Random House), 1997.
Scarr, Sandra. *Life Magazine*. April 1998, p. 191, 241, 287.
Seymour, Donald E. *The Key to Your Unknown Talent* (Milwaukee, WI: Talent Discovery Press), 1996.
Sher, Barbara. *I Could Do Anything If I Knew What it Was* (New York: Dell), 1994.
Sternberg, Robert and Janet Davidson. *Conceptions of Giftedness* (Cambridge University Press), 1986.
Sykes, Charles J. *Dumbing Down Our Kids* (New York: St. Martin's Press), 1995.
Wheeler, John A. *Readers Digest*, September 1986, p. 261.

Index

A
abilities, 148
  Einstein and, 70
Ackerman, Diane, 233
actions
  definition of, 212
  Maximum Talent Capability and, 212
  physical and mental, gene controlled, 212
activity – human
  circle of efficient and compatible, 225
  combinations of, how many, 212
  code-cataloguing, 197
  dislike causes, 193
  dummy, preferred activity list, 235
  efficient, talented, 190, 210
    efficient combination of, 193
  gene sensitivity to, 193
  and Maximum Talent Capability, 210
  library of visuals or virtual reality library of, 235
  mental, 191
  physical, 191
  preference list, 235-237
  profile, 235-6
  and senses, 232
  synergistic, 214
  what are, 193
"adversity builds character," 189
Alaska
  Denali Park Hotel, 229
  Mt. McKinley, 229
alcoholism, 188, 191, 198
algae, 124
  Cutrine, 131
Allen, Bradley Corp, clock, 47
Amos, Connie, 204
animals and man, 246

Applied Biochemists Inc., 133
  Far East, 150
artificial intelligence, 190, 196
  human work, takeover, 197
  intelligent machines, 190
  mimic human, 190
  wet-brain, 190
Athens, Acropolis, 186
audiovisuals (videos), 236-7

B
Baird, Robert W., 48, 56
Bangkok
  Oriental Hotel, 154
"be anything you want to be," 190
Bethlehem, 187
biological nature of man not subject to change, 190
blueprint, human, 260
Bolles, Richard Nelson, 295, 297
brain
  human activities, and, 237
  Maximum Talent Capability and, 237
Branfman, Fred, 285
Buenos Aires
  Mardi Gras, 251
business – talent uncovering, 198
  MTC talent needed to succeed, 203
Bush, George
  New American Schools Development Corporation, 203, 297
Buuck, John Ph.D., 165

C
call girls, 133-135
Campbell, David, 203
cancer, 198, 200, 228, 270, 285
capability, human, 167-169
  natural, 19, 197
  unique, 189

Index

career
  adjustment, 205
  chemical oceanographer, 195
  competition, 194
  correct, 189
  counseling, Concordia University, 166
  (dream career) looks good but feels terrible, 194
  creativeness, and, 189, 191, 226, 278
  Guidance, director of, 165
  health, 167, 191-192
  interests and career selection, 195
  learn new, scrambling to, 197-198
  life expectancy - longevity, and, 191, 201
  mentally, physically and healthfully correct, 188
  planning, 204
  problems, people with, 69
  restructuring - down-sizing, 193
  Right, Career Article 187-199
    right effortless, wrong laborious, 190
  secretary, 193
  selection methods, 71, 135, 167-169, 232
  successful, 189-190
  tests, 166
  tomorrows, 194
  wrong, 72, 190, 277
Cave of the Mounds, Little Norway, 51
children, 230, 240
Christmas, 13, 25, 30, 55, 82, 90, 97, 106, 113, 162, 231-232, 241, 280, 292
Chrysler Corp., 38, 48
Citron, Marvin - Davis, Owen, 195
C.L.U., Chartered Life Underwriter, 70
combination of human activities
  intelligence synergizes, 227
  interesting, efficient, least stressful, 20, 199
competition
  career, 196
  for work from robotics, 196
  McDonalds and General Electric robotics, 194
  talented, 189

computer
  ability to service themselves, 195
  capability more than humans, 195
  eliminate jobs, 195
  intelligent, 192
  snatches our jobs, 195
  software, 199
Concordia University, 164
confidence, 198
cookies, 162
counseling
  Director of Student, 164
  for the retired, 166
creativity
  correct careers promote, 188
  bodies and minds allow, 194
  intelligence, 277, 283
  Maximum Talent Capability, and, 225
  synergism and, 225
crime, Americans behind bars, 188
  double by 2010 prediction, 197-199
  saving cost of, 236
cystic fibrosis, 92, 97

D
Davidson, Janet E., 179
Dead Sea – Israel, 186
degrees, failed, 202
Denali Park Hotel, Alaska, 229
Denmark, Horsens, 164
Dewey, John, educator, 70, 276
disabled, 182
  disability, learning, 184
dropouts, 184, 278-279
  have talent, 182
Drucker, Peter, 195
drugs, 188, 191, 198
dysfunction, 182

E
earth
  on decline, 264
  problems, 197, 265-266
    forests, fisheries, reefs, 264
    salmonella, listeria bacteria and animals, 266
    sea, fresh water and farmable land, 265
    chemicals and waste material, 265

Index

global warming, 265
world population growing, undernourished and starving, 266
education
  careers and, 279
    wrong, 279
  Donna summarizes on education, 278
  dropouts, 182
  education by attraction, 203
  everyone has one, 180
  and genetic design-our, 245
  learning, 194
  learning disability, 182
  Maximum Talent Capability, and majors, college, 167
  New American Schools Committee, Pres. Bush, 202-203
  problems, 215
  Project Genesis, 203
  repressing talent, 180
  school – discovery, 220
  talent, 177
  teaching according to natural talents, 177
  uneducated, 181
Egypt, 172, 185
  Aswan Oberoi Hotel, 184
  camel caper, 171
  Heliopolis Hotel, 172
  Nile River, 172, 177
Einstein, Albert, 70, 147, 178, 180, 230, 257, 269, 278, 281, 285-286, 290
  intelligence, 178
  matching interests and abilities, 179
  talent, 178
Eisenhauer, Dwight, Pres., 74
emphysema, 270-272, 278
environment, 199
  solving problems, 197-198
ethics sacrificed by wrong careers, 190

F

Falkland Islands, 251
fingerprints, 191-192, 199
football, selecting best players for positions, 213
40,000 occupations, 212

how much does a student know about, 165
law of probability of finding right, 194
matching talent with, 191
no way to submit an individual to, 212, 256
our best capability in one of, 210, 230
reduce to human activity profiles, 235
Dictionary of Occupations and, 191
4-H club, 5, 15
Franklin, Ben, 150

G

Gagne, Michelle, 203
Gardner, Howard, 220
Gardner, John W., 120, 179, 189, 257, 281
gene/genetic
  actions and, 21
  building blocks, everyone has the same, 180, 211
  controllers, 211
  communicating with, 231
  could be the answer to MTC, 230-232
  design, unique, 182, 192
  fingers and nails, 211
  God and, 246, 261
  Maximum Talent Capability, and, 230, 234
  not in tune with our natural structure, Scarr, Sandra, 239
  penetrate – communicate to expose MTC, 231
  profile, 182
  senses, penetrate through, 233, 255
  sequencing, 217, 236, 253
  source of talent, 211
  synergism, 216-217, 223, 226-227
General Electric developing robots, 194
Genome Project, 253
Germany, Oberammergau
  Passion Play, 163
  Cologne Cathedral, 163
God, soul and religion, 242

Index

golf competition exposure, 192
Goodwill Industries, 262
   fashion shows, 262-263
Government
   Depts., Education, Health, Welfare and Labor, 197
Grassy Narrows Camp, Lake of the Woods, Canada, 132, 160
Gravelle, Karen, 232
Green Lake, Wisconsin, 44, 114, 121, 131
Gros Ventre Story, The, 216

H

Harper method beauty salon, 3, 18-19, 21
Hawaii, Maui, 109
   Tiki, the, 111-115
health
   anxiety, 11, 193
   cancer, 165
   career, 187
   depression, 25
   frustration, 148, 234
   heart attacks, Monday morning, 189
   life expectancy, 200
   immune system, 282
   negative effect on not understood, 189
   occupation effect, 198
   saving cost of, 236
   stress, 182, 188-189, 191-193, 199, 201234, 279
Holland America Line, 251
human activity
   activities, efficient combination of, 192
   cataloguing and coding, 197
   circle of efficient and compatible, 227
   combination of, 193
   computer program, catalogue, code and film, 197, 216
   efficient combination of, everyone born, 191
   exposure, 197
   compatible combination of, 191, 200
   genes source of, 214
   humans respond with clarity and sensitivity, 193
   individual profile, 236
   Maximum Talent Capability, and, 211
   profile, preferred list, 236
   preferred list, re-align, 236
   senses interpretations initiate, control and qualify human activities, 233
   synergy, 214
   what is, 193
humanities-other, 246
humanity, 200, 228
   contribute to, 73
   defensive, can't preserve being, 278
   God our soul and, 246
   other humanities, 246
   preserve, 246, 248
   problems, 148, 257
   will God protect, 148
human's free will, 249, 260
   become work obsolete,195
hyacinth, water, 150-151

I

identity, human, 198
Illinois,
   Wagon Wheel Resort, 142
illiteracy, 181
intelligence
   barriers to natural development, 184
   capability, 188
   creative, 285-287
   Einstein and, 70
   synergism, 216-217, 223, 226-227
   unknown factor, could be, 148, 225
interest, 149 190
   Einstein and, 70
   stress and friction, 194
   talent with, 200
inventions, 197
Italian cooking, 88
Italy, Rome
   Cavalieri, Hilton Hotel, 167

J

Jackson Hole, Wyoming, 209
   Spring Creek Resort, 210
Japan
   Emperor's Fish, 143
   geisha house, 143-145
   Palace Hotel, 143

Index

Jasper, Alberta, Canada
  train to, 225-226
Jaycees(also see Junior Chamber of Commerce), 3, 6-8, 14, 27, 29, 31, 69, 116
Jefferson, Thomas, Pres., 141
job tasks, 165, 182, 192-193, 212-214, 237, 278-279
  definition of, 194
  how many are there, 183
  human activities into, 194
  occupations - breaking down into, 194
  performed by activities, 213-214
  without jobs it will be an all-talent world, 198
jobs
  chemical oceanographer, 194
  efficiency, 194
  high rise construction, 194
  secretary, 194

K
Kaku Michio, 196
Key to Your Unknown Talent, The, 240, 256, 279

L
lab, human activity exposure, 237
Lake Geneva, Wisconsin, 130
law of probability
  of finding talent, 195
  trial and error using sports elimination method, 195
learning
  Riseac Interest, 203
life, efficient, fulfilling and contributory, 246
  purpose of, 247
  purposeless and unfulfilled, 72
  out of control, 254
  longevity (life expectancy), 190, 200

M
Mackinaw Island, 44
Madison, Wisconsin, 18-19, 48, 288
Magellan-Horn, Cape of, 251, 252
majors, college, 166-168
Malaysia
  Minburi, 154

Chindra Restaurant, Bangpakoong, 155
Marcos, Imelda, Mrs. 150-151, 156
marriage, a beautiful, 96, 221
Maximum Talent Capability (MTC), vi, 211-212, 214-216, 218, 226-228, 230-231, 236-239, 241, 244, 249-250, 253-255, 258-262, 267, 269, 274, 279-281, 286-287, 290, 297
  business and, 198
  is, combination of human activities, 211
  country, first to develop, 252
  creativity, 225
  crime, 199
  development, 285-286
  difficult for people to understand – accept, 268
  definition of, 211
  developing, 197, 200
  Donna's, 259, 261
  financing development, 198
  find, not easy, 225
  genes, sponsored by, 210, 214
  God, soul and religion, 242
  health, 199
  library of visuals or virtual reality
    library of, 236
  meaning and purpose of life, and, 242, 258
  process not completed, 196
  profile, 236
  sponsored by genes, 211
  start of, 199
  synergism, 216-217, 223, 226-227
  think tanks, 191, 197
  uncover, 227
McClellan Valley, 215
McDonalds, all robotic, 163, 194
McGivern, Ben, 59, 63
meaningful purpose in life and MTC, 72, 120-121, 242
  God, humanity, our souls and us genetic beings, 257
  supreme being and, 243
MTC and, 242-245
mental capability
  curiosity, learning and energy of, 194

301

Index

Mexico, Mexico City, 70
  Acapulco, Bahia Hotel, 74
Meyer, Courtney, 165
Microsoft, MTC development, 198
mid-life work crisis, 166
Miller Glen, 221-226
  "String of Pearls", 223, 226
Million Dollar Round Table, Life Insurance, 67
Milwaukee, 21, 27
  West Division High School, 24
Milwaukee Junior Chamber of Commerce, 3, 6, 13-14, 26, 29, 31, 67-68, 143
Milwaukee Vocational and Adult School, 87
mind
  and efficient and compatible activities, 226
  allows creativity, 194
Miss Milwaukee Pageant, 3-10, 34
  Miss Congeniality, 11, 14, 28, 34
Momsen, Willard (Bill), 56-59, 62
  The Composite Award, 61-64, 85, 87
Montessori, Maria, 70, 183, 199
  your greatest gift, 199
Morocco, 120
motivation our bodies allow, 194
MTC *see Maximum Talent Capability*
Mt. Horeb, Wisconsin, 15, 21, 35, 41, 46
Mundie, Paul Dr., 57-8
My Fair Lady, 182

N

National Science Foundation, 201
natural learning, 204
Neiman Marcus, modeling, 19
neuron circuits, tapping reserves of creativity, problem solving, 225
New American Schools Committee, Pres. Bush, 202-203
Newton, Isaac, 69
Nile River, 172, 177
Northwestern Mutual Life Insurance Co., 55-56
not on our planet, 215

O

occupations
  20,000 to 40,000 occupations, 166, 190
  exposure to, 191
    to find right MTC fit, 230
  genes and, 190
    in tune with genetic structure, 190
  health effecting, 194
  broken down into human activities, 193
  health, 190
  reduce to job tasks and human activities-profile, 235
  list to create human activity profile, 235
  selection method, 230
  success, 190
  that do not fit, 191

P

Pan Pacific Hotel, Vancouver, Canada, 222
Papke, Owen G., 186
Paris, France
  Louvre –Tuileries, 165
patents, 197, 254, 274
Philippines, Manila, 152-157
  Marcos, Imelda, 150-151, 156
  Mandarin Hotel, 152
  Manila Garden Hotel, 153
  Sicogon Island Resort, 157
planet earth's unsolvable problems, 263
Pope Paul II, 248
Portugal, 119
Post, Emily, 150
Powell, Jane, actress, 219
preferred activity profile, 237
prison, adults in, 198
problem solving
  creativity of, 194
  creative intelligence, 285-287
  humanity needs, 257
  tapping reserves of, 195, 225
profile
  human activity, 236
  preferred activity list, 236
  using dummy to eliminate, 236
Project Genesis, 203

Index

promise, the, x, 284
Prosen, Jory, 205
Puerto Rico, 102
Puzia, Michael, 203

R
read
  70 million Americans can't, 198
recreation
  Red Cross, 263
retirement, 190, 204, 242-243
reunions
  new successes, 178
  Shorewood High School, 118, 290
Riseac School, 203
River Hills, Wisconsin, 136
Rivilin, Robert, 233
robots – knowbots, 181, 194
  artificial intelligence, 189-194
  competitive, 189-194
  crying wolf about job take-over, 197
  replace humans, 189-184, 196-197
  replace surgeons, 195
  and tomorrow's careers, 195
  what humans can't do, 196
royal family, the Seymours, 89
Russell, Bertram, x

S
San Antonio, Texas, 19
Sagan, Carl, 250, 255, 267, 274-275, 278, 280, 284-287, 295
Scarr, Sandra, 188, 241
schools
  dropouts, 278-279
  suicide, 188, 190, 198, 202, 266
self-esteem, 198
Senior Service League of America, 60
seniors need interests, 191
senses
  Ackerman, Diane, 233
  truthful, are, 233
  brain must override, 233
  cause friction, stress and frustration, 233
  judgment in, 234
  interpretations initiate, control and qualify human activities, 233
  likes, dislikes, indifference, 233

Rivilin, Robert – Gravelle, Karen, 233
Seymour, Gregory, 52-55, 59, 63-66, 68, 78, 81-86, 94, 97, 99-101, 104-106, 110, 113-118, 129, 132, 141, 159, 185, 202-203, 290
Seymour, Jean Ann, 93, 96, 270
Seymour, Jeffrey, 68, 78, 94, 97-98, 101, 106, 115, 139-141, 159, 170, 185, 203
Shangri-La Hotel, 150
sheik, the, 121-127
Sher, Barbara, 219
Shorewood High School, 118, 290
Singapore, 148-150
software, 285 (see computer)
Sons of Norway, 221
soul, 243-244, 249
Spain, 118, 120
Sternberg, Robert, 179
stress and friction, 190, 194
  capabilities – stressful, 183-184
  drugs and alcohol, 189
    heart attacks – Monday morning, 190
  occupation, career burnout, 190
Strong Campbell Interest Inventory, 57, 164-165
Strong, Edward Jr., 133
students, 164-166, 176-177, 179-180, 193, 196, 202, 220, 240, 247
success
  career, 200
  sugar pill, 235-236
suicide, 71, 188, 190, 198, 202, 266
surgeons, robots replacing, 195
synergism, 216-217, 223, 226-227
  genes and, 216
  human activity, 226
  MTC, and, 216
  "String of Pearls," 223, 226

T
talent, 149
  activity efficiency, 226
  people inherited unknown, 178, 179-180
  capability, 181, 184
  century, is born, 198

Index

creativity expressed as, 226
same varies in each human, 191
educated according to, 178, 220
education represses, 181
Einstein and, 70, 179
skill and, 180
gene sponsored source, 211
health, 188
highest in interest-capability, lowest in stress, 192
human activity, 225
matching with 40,000 occupations, 191
natural, 188, 191, 197
learnable, not, 189
probability, law of finding, 195
reserves of lay hidden, 191
second and third level, 261
solves problems, 200
uncovering, 183, 192, 197
   they will learn with a passion, 199
unique, 191
why you don't know your, 178, 188
talent discovery, 200
   think tanks and stores, 199
   talent century, the, 199
(our) surfaces, 200
will you never know your, 200
world, 198, 200
Tangier, Morocco, 120
teachers
   re-educating according to natural talents, 178
   teaching students according to natural talents, 178
terrorism, 197-198, 202, 220, 238, 255, 264, 266, 274-275, 280, 293
terrorists, 255, 260, 274-275, 280
tests-career, interest, psychology, 69, 166-168, 191
   not efficient for career/occupation selection, 191
think tanks, 191, 197, 304
3Rs, 285
Tiki, the, 111-115
Tripoli Golf Club, 81, 255
Trumps Traders Inc., 156
   Saroosa brothers, 151, 157-158

tumors, malignant, 270
Turkey
   Ankara, 171
   harems, 169-171
   Istanbul Hilton overlooking The Golden Horn (Bosporus), 167-168

U

U.S. Dept of Labor
   Dictionary of Occupations, 191
   Job task code system, 192-193
U. S. Small Business Administration, 204

V

Vancouver, British Columbia, Canada
   the beautiful lady, 221-223
violence, 198
virtual reality, 196, 237, 286, 297
   laboratory, 236
   library of human activities simulations for exposure, 237
Vocational Guidance Institute
   Project Genesis, 203
   Education by attraction, 203
   New America Schools Committee, 202-203

W

war, 197-198, 231-232, 248
winnow, 228
Wisconsin Small Business Association, 200
Wisconsin World Trade Center, 200
Wheeler, John A., 262
world
   creating a better, 197
   an all-talent, 198
   saving our, 201